A text and study concerning the science of numerology, complete with charts including personality, habits, soul urge, expressions in life, problems, past, present and future.

A deep and thorough study in plain language into the hidden mysteries of numerology especially concerning forecasting.

The Numbers
of Life

Kevin Quinn Avery, D.Ms.

The Numbers
of Life

Revised and Enlarged

Interior Illustrations: Carl Methfessel

Dolphin Books
Doubleday & Company, Inc.
Garden City, New York

First published in paperback by Freeway Press, Inc., 1974
Reprinted in the French language under the title LA VIE SECRETE
DES CHIFFRES by La Jeune Parque, Paris, France, 1975

ISBN: 0-385-12629-8
Library of Congress Catalog Card Number: 76-45969
Dolphin Books edition copyright © 1977 by Kevin Quinn Avery
Copyright © 1974 by Freeway Press, Inc.
Printed in the United States of America

DEDICATION

To Mary Dickell Smythe (Boorman) of New York, with whom I will break the circle.

INTRODUCTION TO THE NEW REVISED AND ENLARGED EDITION

It is not often an author has the opportunity to change or enlarge his original work once it has been published. In this respect I am fortunate. With this new edition being published by Doubleday I have been able to include an advanced study of cycles in Chapter 39. I have also been able to correct the few misprints in the original edition published by Freeway.

Over a quarter of a century ago, at the age of sixteen, via a meeting with a numerologist/kabalist, I became interested in the subjects of astrology and numerology. This "chance" meeting was a definite point of destiny in my life. The first decade of this time span was spent, as much as possible, in an intensive search for knowledge and understanding concerning these subjects. Having originated from an earth-oriented, materialistic heritage, the tendency to doubt all aspects presented was strong until the component elements were proved accurate. During my twenties, I considered the occult sciences a hobby, perhaps an interesting parlor game. During my thirties, having been convinced that very little is left to chance and that control is maintained by pre-set influences which to a large degree are almost unalterable, I employed my knowledge of self-seeking in the world of form. In the past few years I have come to the realization that while employment of occult knowledge is correct for positive self-advancement, it is not an individually owned phenomenon, and must be shared.

During my formative years I traveled all over the world, seeking out teachers to further my knowledge of astrology and numerology. It was in the natural sequence of events that I also became exposed to metaphysical knowledge. Working in the professional world of numerology, with all its attendant spheres of influence, I am involved in many metaphysical seminars, in which I find a surprising lack of knowledge concerning inner awareness and power, as well as an indiscriminate blend of diverse beliefs and half-truths. This text is an attempt to present knowledge in a true light.

The science of numerology must now be freed from the chicanery that has surrounded it for centuries. Likewise, it must be divorced from charlatanism. The term "occultism" denotes secrecy, and the cosmic time has come for this veil to be lifted. But the sacred science must remain attached to the occult world, for at the present time it is in this world alone that man has had the courage to delve into the meaning of life unhampered by restrictive dogmas. There are those who wish to treat occult studies as pure sciences, separating them from their spiritual message, but real truth can only be found by those who are willing to open the books of inspiration and revelation that contain the cosmic truth of the God-Force, as well as the textbooks of science.

There exists a law that governs the universe. Order and direction are maintained upon this earth. Very little is left to chance, and control is maintained by the firmly established, unalterable influences of the Law of Karma, which in turn is tied into the cycle of rebirth, or incarnations. This is the law of the Cosmic God-Force, which does not bend to accommodate man's whims, wants, ideas, or "private-world" attitudes. Man is permitted to take advantage of those vibrations which he feels are of benefit to him, and to prepare himself to encounter other vibrations which he might consider difficult or unpleasant. Man, however, is not permitted to change the major scope of aspects. There are two things that are never promised in life: the first is happiness; the second is unhappiness. Man, with his petty free will, selects one or the other for himself. One day, man will learn that total freedom and happiness come only when he surrenders his freedom to act in a negative manner.

Man, by his very being, by his very presence upon this earth, is enrolled in a great classroom where the inevitable lessons of his life will be imposed upon him. These lessons in classroom earth can be as exuberant or as dismal as man himself elects to make them. As in every institution of learning, for those at the head of the class there is the dazzling reward of increased consciousness. For those who procrastinate, who are too lazy, too self-indulgent and selfish, there is painful failure and the necessity of picking themselves up and trying all over again. This is truth, and the fact that one is unwilling or unable, at his level of development, to accept it does not alter the situation. Truth cannot be twisted or modified to suit the whims of individuals. Truth is not open to discussion, nor does it have to be proved: Truth is. There is no religion higher than truth, except that truth manifested is higher than truth itself. Karma teaches; Karma does not punish. Those who regard Karma as a punishment are deluded. Nor are there any people on the face of this earth who can say they are not affected by the Law of Karma. Those who do, speak from ignorance, not from enlightenment. This ignorance they impose upon themselves by self-delusion, because they are unable to accept truth. The law has been given time and time again, over the ages, by the masters, including Jesus and Buddha.

In classroom earth there are numerous textbooks for those who elect to open them. Among such textbooks are the studies of the sciences of astrology and numerology. In order to correlate these two sciences with the study of metaphysics the realization must be achieved that *astrology and numerology indicate but metaphysics controls*. Advance notice of the vibrations that control any individual's life is given via astrology and numerology at the time of birth. Despite the strength of these concords, they can be overcome by metaphysical awareness.

There is no necessity for entering upon a long discourse on the antiquity of astrology, which commenced when a man first gazed upon the heavens, noting the movements of the celestial bodies, and asked the question *why*. Likewise, numerology, based upon the sacred science of numbers, is an advanced offshoot of the melodious rhythm of the mathematical precision that controls all creation. The study of either of these sciences is a voyage into the meaning of life. It is a study of man and his relation to the cosmic Power, of the answers to the questions why, where, from where, to where. These sciences are, in themselves, exact and demanding studies; the deeper understanding is the realization of why man walks this path called life which is but a part of his eternal journey to rejoin the God-Force from whence he came.

Man's mission on earth is spiritual comprehension, an awareness of self and its place in the whole. This does not indicate that man must withdraw from the world of form, for it is within this material sphere that man must evolve. But, without sensitive understanding of his basic mission on this plane, man can be subjected to many disruptive experiences.

The sacred sciences are not interesting parlor games, nor is there anything false or misleading in their teachings. Misinformation is often offered by inexperienced would-be professionals, but that does not detract from the sciences themselves. Limited knowledge of a subject does not negate the validity of these subjects. No longer is the mind of man to be held in bondage and limitation by the fears of those who lack comprehension of these truths. We are on the brink of the age of Aquarius, the age of enlightenment. We are on the brink of possessing the great knowledge that will make man free. But man must be prepared to exert sustained effort in order to gain this enlightenment. When or if he does, he will no longer be bound by the prejudices and narrow confines of dogmas that do not permit him to think for himself. The minds of men are going to soar free; they are going to ask questions of others and of themselves.

It is the intent of the author via this text to make people aware and questioning. It is, further, his sincere desire to aid those swimming in the miasma of existence, by providing scope for improving life. As in previous writings, I will present no muted generalizations. The prognosis will be spelled out precisely.

The deeper one delves into the study of any of the occult sciences, the more one realizes and believes in the eternity of God, the cosmic Power, the God-Force. One also comes to a realization of the eternity of the spirit of man, the oneness of man and God. As the reader progresses into the study and observes the trends in this sphere, many questions will be answered if the reader keeps in mind the meanings of the spiritual mission in this life and the understanding that needs to be gained. This life is but one of many excursions that each individual takes for the growth of his soul. The word "soul" is employed here as opposed to the word "spirit," as the Spirit is the unmanifested part of God within each and every one. It needs no growth; the soul does. Never confuse these two.

The mission of man in his spiritual development is to lose fear, give love, render service, and seek enlightenment. This leads to cosmic consciousness, and beyond. The reference to love is not related to the selfish, individualistic love that man thinks in terms of, but, rather, a universal love. Love is an energy that is above mind, and freedom from hate can only be found when love is brought into active manifestation. Diplomacy is a word that is too often employed for hypocrisy. Today, on earth, we have many teachers who follow in the footsteps of Krishna, Buddha, Jesus, and others. These teachers do not shy away from the word "reincarnation." They may be considered unorthodox by the masters of false dogma, but, nonetheless, they are quickly replacing those who shield their eyes from the light of truth. The greatest study and/or science upon this earth is the study of the cosmic Force, which is the only true freedom from all that ails mankind. The greatest gift a person can receive is the gift of truth. In all of creation, for all time, there is one thing that is not possible: it is not possible for the light of God to fail. I do not try to impose my individual way of thinking upon any person, as that is against the law, the only law I follow, the law of the God-Force. I do, however, present you with truth, and ask you to think for yourself. There is a selfish motivation, because in so passing this message I myself will be permitted to advance.

I have also attempted, wherever possible, to separate the spiritual message from the study so that the science may be presented in a clear, occult-free form.

May the blessings of the eternal God-Force be with you.

Kevin Quinn Avery, D.Ms.
New York City
Summer 1976

PREFACE
From Where, and Why

The history of numbers is as old as the recorded history of man. Numerology was in use in ancient Greece, Rome, Egypt, China, and is to be found in the ancient books of wisdom, such as the Hebrew Kabala.

Pythagoras, the "Father of Mathematics," who lived in the sixth century B.C., propounded the theory that nothing in the universe could exist without numbers.

There is recorded evidence that numerology was in use over ten thousand years ago, its origins going back much further than that. Numerology was employed by the priests in the temples of ancient Egypt, also by great Greek philosophers. The actual origins of the science of numerology is open to conjecture, but the foundation of numbers and mathematics is as old as the universe itself.

Now as to the why. It is not necessary for the reader to accept the following theory in order for the numbers to work for him. For those who cannot only accept the theory, but perhaps adapt to it as a firm truth and believe in it, the understanding of the WHY will be no problem.

The theory which this author holds as the truth of all life is that we, each and every one of us, came from the eternal God: that we all are part of the God-Force. Accepting, too, that we have all lived many times before, other lives, in the past, most of us will live again many times in the future. These lives are lived so our spirits or souls may grow, achieve knowledge—above all, mercy, love, and understanding, the final objective being that when we have perfected ourselves, we will rejoin the God-Force, and no further lives in this sphere will be necessary. Heaven and/or Hell is something each of us has created for himself on this earth. Each of us, between our mortal lives, is his own judge, planning his own life with the aim of achieving growth for his spirit, to pay off any past debts of wrongdoing or the misuse of power left over from a previous life. Paying off for past debts is a form of Karma.

The law of the God-Force is all-powerful; what we have sown, so must we reap. For misery or suffering we have caused to others unjustly in this or past lives, so we ourselves must at one time or another experience the same, in order to achieve the ultimate understanding. We ourselves have planned this life, and are now living with the foregoing aims in mind. Each individual, in planning this life, has laid out his own path or destiny. That destiny is revealed in the birthdate and the letters that constitute the name. The most exact of all the "-ology" sciences is numerology. It will point out to each individual particular shortcomings, helping to give a better understanding of life on earth. Karma can be overcome, and when it is, the life of any individual will become far more fulfilling.

The keyword to the foregoing is reincarnation. Today advanced knowledge has made it more than just a theory. Reincarnation has long been the cornerstone of many of the oldest religions on earth. The spirit of man IS eternal.

Each individual may accept or reject the theories of reincarnation and Karma as he sees fit. Whatever your theory, I believe that as you progress in this study and begin to see more of your true personality you will begin to understand for yourself the WHY of your life.

Today, one can walk into any well-stocked bookstore and find several books on the shelves pertaining to numbers or numerology. Volumes concerning numbers are usually full of misinformation, the majority basing their study upon superstition. The texts written by professional numerologists (there are at the present time several good volumes obtainable) are informative studies pertaining to the science of numerology. So, why one more book about the subject? First, almost without exception the texts concerning numerology take the reader only up to a certain point, leaving him with many unanswered questions and a desire to know more. The authors have supplied the average reader with sufficient information to aid him in his daily life, which was the initial purpose of the author. This author, having been a student of numerology for many years, has found the hardest task to be obtaining advanced information, books that would take the study further than the volumes usually obtainable. I, for myself and those who consult me, want to know the whys and wherefores (mostly, what can be expected in the future in more than just a broad, general sense) in order to make life better for those with whom I am concerned. In this book you will be taken deep into the exact science of numerology. The main purpose in writing this text is to aid those who wish to know more of this fascinating subject. This book will begin with the basics, but it will go deeper into the study than other available books do. Beyond the basics, for those who are interested, this text will delve very deeply into the hidden mysteries of numerology. This study will show how to forecast correctly in several ways. For those who can read this volume and gain an understanding through it, there will be more information to be obtained, for the true study of numerology is lifelong.

A second reason this volume is being presented is that modern-day numerologists, at least in print, like to paint everything rosy and pink. Many, despite their own personal knowledge, inform their readers all about the good points of a given set of numbers and leave unsaid the bad points. This text is pulling no punches; it attempts to present both positive and negative in a balanced and intelligent fashion.

One final word: many of these interpretations are the author's own, developed through much hard work and long periods of studying many charts. A few of the charts employed in this book concerning forecasting are the author's creation. The inexperienced reader is strongly advised not to make rash decisions concerning any given set of numbers without first consulting a professional numerologist. The final interpretations rest not in a single number; they are in a set of numbers appearing together. The correct interpretation in many cases takes a qualified expert. For this reason this text is divided into two studies. The first section will be a deep study into the basics, the second will be a study on groups of numbers, letters, and combinations. For those who go into the second part, take your time, think about things, and above all, do not make rash decisions that could later be regretted.

The author will be glad to answer any questions pertaining to this text that can be answered in a short letter, for any or all who may care to send a stamped self-addressed envelope in care of the publisher.

The hope in writing this study is that aid will be made available so that a few people may build a better life, a better understanding, through knowledge of the science of numerology. If only a few are helped on their respective paths, the author will consider the tremendous effort of the book more than repaid.

May the blessings of the eternal God-Force be with you.

Kevin Quinn Avery
New York City
March 1974

CONTENTS

Contents

"The world is built upon the power of numbers"
Pythagoras—sixth century before Christ

The First Study

Chapter 1

YOU AS AN INDIVIDUAL

There is only one you. We live in a world society comprised of many millions of people—but still—there is only one you. You are an individual. There is no other person on the face of this earth who is exactly like you. You may be classified into many different general groupings, but you are still uniquely you. You, and you alone possess your own personality. In many respects, it may appear to be like other people's, but when the very bottom is reached, each individual will stand alone in his own special light.

In this life, you alone are the possessor of two elements that together no other person has. These things are your NAME and BIRTHDATE. Other people may have the same name as yours, many others will share the same birthdate, but to you alone belongs the combination of the two.

The science of numerology is based on these two bits of information. No other information is necessary. With these two facts, determination can be made of the basic patterns of what you are, what you have to work with, what forms your hidden dreams and desires may take, what your problems are, the understanding of these problems, and helping in solving them. Numerology will aid you in becoming aware of what you have been doing, what you are doing now, and what you will be prone to do in the future.

The knowledge of the exact name at time of birth and the

exact date of birth will enable any person skilled in numerology to make a correct interpretation of his own life, or the life of any other person in whom he may be interested.

For the purpose of study in the first half of this text, a fictional person will be created. This name and birthdate will be used throughout the entire first half of this book as the basis of study.

The fictional heroine is going to be:

JANET AUDREY HENDRICH
born SEPTEMBER 24, 1941.

The process will now begin to find out who Janet is, what Janet is, what she is doing, what she would like to do. The reader, of course, may substitute his own name and birthdate, or that of any other person whom he chooses.

In the course of this study many charts will be created concerning Janet. The end result will be a complete personality. The most important of these studies will be the ones pertaining to Janet's Soul Urge, Expression, and Path of Life. As the most important of the three, the Path of Life is based upon the birthdate. This is where the study will begin.

Chapter 2
THE PATH OF LIFE

Within the life span of any individual, his name may be changed several times. The one thing that never will be or can be changed is the date of birth. From this birthdate much information will be gleaned. One of the most important elements in this entire study will be the Path of Life, sometimes referred to as the "Destiny."

The Path of Life along with the three sub-paths known as the Cycles will be with a person all during the life. It will never change. It has positive and negative effects upon the life style or way of life of any given individual.

In numerology all numbers are reduced to a single digit from one to nine. The nine is the ultimate cycle of man. Life revolves around a nine year cycle, divided into nine month cycles, further sub-divided into nine day cycles. If one is so inclined, one may still divide further into nine hour and nine minute cycles.

The following examples are offered:

3		=	3
33	(3+3)	=	6
333	(3+3+3)	=	9
3333	(3+3+3+3) = 12 (1+2)	=	3

Employing the birthdate of our fictional heroine Janet, the following is found:

$$\begin{array}{ccc}
\text{September} & 24 & 1941 \\
\cline{1-3}
9 & 24 & 15 \\
\cline{1-3}
9 & 6 & 6 = 21 = 3
\end{array}$$

September is the ninth month of the year, thus the nine. The day is the 24th $(2 + 4 = 6)$. The year of 1941 is $(1 + 9 + 4 + 1 = 15 / 1 + 5 = 6)$. The totals of all the numbers added together is $(9 + 6 + 6 = 21 / 2 + 1 = 3)$.

THE PATH OF LIFE OR DESTINY
IS "THREE"

There are many numerologists who take the shortcut of not adding nines, this, however, is incorrect. The addition of nine to any other number will result with the same total as if the nine were not added. By taking this shortcut, many hidden numbers are missed that are of importance. All numbers must be taken into account.

All numbers must be reduced to a single digit of from one to nine. There are two exceptions to this rule, an "Eleven," or a "Twenty Two" are never reduced as these are master numbers and must be treated separately. Had the secondary twenty one in the foregoing life path been either an "Eleven" or a "Twenty Two," it would not have been further reduced.

The following is the only correct way to lay out the birth-date:

$$\begin{array}{lc}
\text{SEPTEMBER} & 9 \\
\text{24th} & 24 \\
\text{1941} & 1941 \\
\cline{2-2}
 & 1974 = 21 = 3
\end{array}$$

Misunderstanding is common regarding the correct method of finding the master number. Master numbers are found by adding together the unreduced figures as shown above. Had the secondary twenty one $(1974 = 21)$ been an "Eleven" or "Twenty Two," it would not have been further reduced. By using the first example shown, master numbers are often missed.

A further example is now given using the incorrect way vs. the correct way which is a good illustration of how master numbers are often missed. If the master number does not appear from the addition of the unreduced figures, it does not exist. Master numbers cannot then be attributed to that birthdate, nor arrived at by any other method. In the forthcoming example a birthdate will be employed where a master number does exist.

INCORRECT	January	24	1941		
	1	24	15		
	1	6	6	= 13	= 4

CORRECT	January	1	
	24th	24	
	1941	1941	
		1966	= 22/4

Master numbers are always shown as either 22/4 or 11/2, never as plain 22 or 11.

Having determined that Janet's Path of Life is a "Three," it must be understood exactly what this means.

Any given path of life will have positive or negative effects. Reference is now made to the preface in this text. On the positive side the Path of Life is one that will enable the person to expand his growth, and understanding in a positive way. The Negative would present an obstacle in the way of achieving the full potential of growth. This would be the Karma (if any) attached to the path. It cannot at this point be determined if there is any Karma attached to Janet's path as additional charts will have to be constructed. Throughout this study, the question of WHY is constantly going to arise. Reference to the word "Karma" will have to be employed to correctly answer this question. If there is Karma blocking the way to full growth and potential in a life path, the Karma can be overcome, the path ahead can be cleared for full development.

This study can explain what the life path is, how to determine if there is any Karma present, and to an extent, in what amounts. As for eliminating the Karma, each reader must be his own judge and will know best how to handle the problem.

THE LIFE PATHS OR DESTINY

A "ONE" LIFE PATH: "ATTAINMENT"

POSITIVE: Those who are on a "One" path of life will find the way open for a life of positive action, achievement. Theirs will be a life of individual action, originality, new creations, progress, ambition. They will possess self-confidence, assurance, pride. A full life of activity may be expected. A "One" life path indicates that the person involved will usually be able to stand on his own two feet, will have the desire to be his own person as opposed to being involved with associates or partners.

NEGATIVE: Must learn to fall back on own resources, to make own decisions. Work must be done on the inner self; mind, body, spirit. Must be original, establish new ideas, new ideals, new tactics. Try to break away from the standard trends, be own person. Perhaps the most important lesson to learn is that there are other people in the world besides "self." One must learn to get along, live with others without bullying or imposing unjustly own will upon others.

EXPLANATION: People on this path will strive for self. They will seek attainment in all that they do. It is also possible, and can be determined from other charts that quite the reverse will occur. They may be unable to stand on their own two feet. This is why they have selected a "One" path of life, in order that they may learn self-confidence. (Another possibility is that they may be so laden with self-ego that they have no regard for others what-so-ever, and are on this path learning to subdue their own personality. If such is the case, they will be presented problems in life so that these lessons may be learned.) The main indicator in the majority of cases for people on this path is the striving for self-achievement, self-advancement. It will later be learned how to tell if there are problems on this path and what kind. It will also be learned how to judge this path in relation to other numbers. This "One" path of life standing alone will present, in the main, a person who is a go-getter. Usually very mental, sometimes a promoter. People who put self before others, try to sweep away all on their quest for self-attainment. Those on a "One" life path, if they live it positively will achieve much in life. They will have attainment, and success. They will always be on top, achieving whatever it is that they are seeking, be it financial rewards or other. They will leap to the top quickly in whatever they choose to do. Others will look to them for leadership. If they are on a negative path, roadblocks will be consistently found in their way. (People who oppose them, problems that they cannot solve, delays that keep them from reaching their goal.) Each person has above all free will; there is nothing wrong with attainment, success, as long as others are not hurt along the way. Without taking into consideration any other numbers that might appear to block the positive path, assuming there is no Karma attached to the path, this life path can be summed up in one keyword, ATTAINMENT.

A "TWO" LIFE PATH

POSITIVE: On this path will be found a life of cooperation, the ability to work well with others, and to follow instructions. This will be a life full of gentle love, peace, for the urge of a "Two" path is to give, seek love, and companionship. The best role is that of the peacemaker. As opposed to the "One" path, the tendency will be to stay on the beaten path.
NEGATIVE: The keyword is subservience. The lesson must be learned not to put self before others. To learn cooperation, patience, consideration for others. Must learn to overcome shyness, over-sensitivity.
EXPLANATION: The "Two" path is one where the person affected will strive for marriage; he will not like to be alone, either in business or social life. On the positive side, this person will be an outstanding companion. (If negative, will be found to

be a leaner, a drainer.) Again, without taking any other numbers into consideration, discounting any problems that may be on this path, it can safely be said that this will be a path of marriage or marriages as the "Two" will not and cannot be alone. The positive path will be love, companionship. The negative path will be divorce, failure. The main keyword for this path is ASSOCIATION.

A "THREE" LIFE PATH

POSITIVE: This is perhaps the nicest of all life paths to follow. This is the path of self-expression in the way of peaceful, enjoyable activities surrounded by beauty, inner peace, harmonious atmosphere. This path will lead to many friends, companions. It will be a life full of inspiration, talent, kindness.
NEGATIVE: Must learn the lesson of self-expression, to give freely of the self. One of the biggest dangers to overcome is that of jealousy.
EXPLANATION: The "Three" will be very expressive in the arts. Will be social, outgoing, outgiving, creative. There will be a striving on this path for the creation of something or somethings by self. Unlike the "One" who will strive for power, glory, attainment, money, the "Three" will be more concerned with the product rather than what may be achieved as a net result of the product. The "Three" will live life easy, seek beauty, love. Many "Threes" live, look to live a free sexual life. These people will be creators, originators of many ideas, ideals, for the "Three" is the number of birth. There can be problems on this path, but they are slight, and easy to overcome. The summation or keyword for this path of life is PLEASANT.

A "FOUR" LIFE PATH

POSITIVE: This possibly could be a hard path to follow as it predicts a life of hard work, effort. The outstanding qualities of this path are the abilities of organization, devotion, dignity, trust, and loyalty. Those who follow this path will find, because of their outstanding qualities, much responsibility, trust, is conferred upon them, many times unwanted.

NEGATIVE: The ability to apply one's self to detail work must be cultivated. One must learn to stay put, become the cornerstone, and devote one's self to duty in family, community and country. A particular danger to overcome is that of unjust hatred.

EXPLANATION: As with all the other paths, the "Four" also must be taken into consideration with other numbers. On the whole the life will be limited in many ways. This does not mean that one cannot find happiness on this path. There usually is a happy home, and good business. Those on this path are the cornerstone of the community; they are steadfast; they are the all enduring. It is the "Four" that builds for all of us. He is the rock of the economy. He builds brick by brick, taking his time, making sure everything is done correctly, precisely. He makes few mistakes, either in his own life or the life of others. It would be hard to convince most "Fours" that theirs is not the correct way. They do not consider it either *hard or toil*. Most often they do not understand free souls. The "Four" is often dull, does not fully understand those around him. There is no way of getting around it if the truth is to be told. This is a life of hard work. The keyword is LIMITATION.

A "FIVE" LIFE PATH

POSITIVE: Sometimes a difficult but varied path. There will be frequent changes in all aspects of this life. There will be much variety, and travel. It will be a life of freedom, curiosity, adventure, unattachment, and progress. Above all, it will be the path of constant change.

NEGATIVE: The mis-use of personal freedom. The over-indulgence in sensuality, drink, habit forming narcotics. The "Five" must learn to accept frequent, unwanted changes. Thoughtlessness must be curbed.

EXPLANATION: An entire chapter about the life path of the "Five," could be written. Those born under this sign will live a life of constant change. If they accept and seek this change, they will find success, and everything else that anyone could ever dream of. If they reject this change, they are going to have more misery than a dozen others put together. Theirs is a life of adventure, romance, travel, attainment, and sex. They are quick witted, outgoing, and usually well liked in an instant by others. They are magnetic; they will live more in their life span than a score of others. They will see more, do more, and be exposed to more than any of the other paths. On the positive side this is quite possibly the greatest happiness that one can find in life; on the negative side it is abject misery. The "Five," often classified as the rolling stone, is misunderstood by those that would like to see him stay put. But to "stay put"—is not his life; let the others stay in their ruts, for the "Five" is the path of freedom and all that goes with it. The "Five" must be more careful in his life than others that he does not cause hurt or unhappiness on his way. The "Five" should above all other numbers understand his path well, so that he may plan his life in regards to marriage, business. The "Five" is found to be the most faithful of husbands or wives, once married. The negative aspects of the "Five" are unwarranted sexual excess and all the evils and troubles that go with it. The keyword is FREEDOM.

A "SIX" LIFE PATH

POSITIVE: This path can be one of quick assent to power and greatness in the material, military, or political worlds. It will be a life of responsibility and service. It is very much the path of adjustments. Those following this path will be called upon time and time again to settle disputes, to make adjustments, and to make the final decisions.

NEGATIVE: The positive side is very far reaching, leading to glory and to greatness. Many on this path have been held back from their true destiny because of the negative aspects which are just as far reaching as a matter of balance. The greatest problem to be encountered is adjusting one's self to circumstances, accepting things for their true value, without always looking for perfection in everything. Adjustment is the keyword, particularly in regards to domestic relationships. The willingness to serve family, friends, and country, must be cultivated. One must learn to serve without using tyranny.

EXPLANATION: The path of the "Six" has many aspects. It is a path of greatness, achievement. Many of our greatest statesmen, and generals were on a "Six" path. It is the path of responsibility, obligations, and also the path of love, marriage, sex. The "Six" like the "Two" needs to be married. Unlike the "Two" he of the pair is much more forceful, self-seeking. Those on a "Six" path are usually leaders and looked to for advice from others. On the negative side it is a life of divorce, and romantic problems, especially for those who might have Karma attached to the path. This is often the situation pertaining to women. Like the other paths, the "Six" can be successful or full of discord, it is up to the free will of the individual. It is impossible to make an accurate forecast regarding the "Six" without first delving into other aspects. The keyword for this path is RESPONSIBILITY.

A "SEVEN" LIFE PATH

POSITIVE: The path of the loner, especially concerning matters of the inner self. This is the number of the philosopher, the deep thinker, the dreamer. On this path will be found peace, spirituality, trust, faith, research, wisdom. The "Seven" will find a restful, peaceful sort of life, and will not be too concerned with material aspects.

NEGATIVE: Coldness, aloofness, humiliation, faithlessness, craftiness, must be overcome. Must serve cheerfully, learning to assume problems and troubles of others.

EXPLANATION: This in the first instant foretells of loneliness, poverty. The "Seven" is a deep thinker, a meditator, a loner. He could and most times does make a good priest, min-, ister, or rabbi. The "Seven" will seek enlightenment, knowledge. Many "Sevens" are professors, doctors. It is a path that does not always lead to happy marriage, unless the mate is chosen with care. It is useless to continue with the "Seven" until other aspects are investigated. The keyword is PERFECTION.

AN "EIGHT" LIFE PATH

POSITIVE: This is the path of power, authority, material and financial gains, success in all material aspects. Persons under this sign will be found generous, dependable. There is outstanding inner strength, courage.

NEGATIVE: The keyword is cultivate. There is a need to control love of power, money, power for self, intolerance, abuse, revenge. The need is to cultivate good moral business ethics, the understanding of persons less forceful and dynamic.

EXPLANATION: There are two very powerful aspects to this path. The "Eight" can be a deadly path to follow; it can be an evil path to live. The "Eight" is the number of Karma, associated with the Planet Saturn. Those with a little knowledge of numerology who think that the "Eight" means money, should stop and think twice. More often, the "Eight" means money problems, as opposed to financial gain. This aspect of the "Eight" will be investigated in later chapters. The other aspect of the "Eight" is achievement. The attainment of material rewards, success in big business, with life on a large scale. However, this cannot be predicted with any authority until other conditions are considered. The "Eight" has many aspects, positive as well as negative. The bearers of bad tidings, doom, who forecast the "Eight" path as a life of misery, should likewise think twice. No correct interpretation can be made concerning this path until the other adjoining sub-paths are fully understood. MATERIAL ASPECTS is the keyword.

A "NINE" LIFE PATH

POSITIVE: This is the all-encompassing destiny. Persons under this sign usually are world travelers. Their outlook will be worldwide. Those who follow this path will be understanding, intuitive, full of knowledge, willing to sacrifice. They usually make good husbands, wives, lovers, full of kindness and consideration.

NEGATIVE: The need to hold emotions in balance, the necessity of holding self-ego in check. A few of the pitfalls are fickleness, immorality, daydreaming.

EXPLANATION: A very highly charged emotional number causing unhappiness, loss, and sacrifice. People under this sign are very often aloof, many times condescending and highly intelligent. Their outlook is global as opposed to local. The "Nine" is withdrawn, and must learn to emerge from his shell. It is never-the-less a path of achievement, attainment, success, which the "Nine" often scoffs at. The keyword is EN-COMPASSING.

AN "ELEVEN" LIFE PATH

POSITIVE: This is the master number. It involves a super intelligence, that encompasses few. Those on this path will find revelation, idealism, intuition. The "Eleven" will be very selective of his friends, warming to very few. He can be hard to live with, not always showing the necessary patience, and understanding. The number "Eleven," of course, can be reduced to a "Two" path of life for any who find this master number too hard to cope with.

NEGATIVE: The use of the intelligence to further one's own selfish material ends. In many cases most of the negative aspects will be found in the negative "Two" path. In addition, this path presents a few negative aspects of its own, such as superiority complex, imposition of self will upon others and dishonesty.

EXPLANATION: The master number. The number of the God-Force. Those under this sign are the old souls. They will be given inspiration; their duty and obligation is revelation. If they try to shy away from this, events will force them back into it. If they are self-seeking, which they usually are, they will meet with ruin, having to pick themselves up and do it all over again. This is a very tense, high powered number to live under.

The responsibilities are great; these duties are to mankind. If lived in a positive manner this path will bring fame, fortune, success. The keyword that best describes this path would be IN-SPIRATION.

A "TWENTY TWO" LIFE PATH

POSITIVE: This is the ultimate number. All the super intelligence of the "Eleven" is present, in addition there will be found a universal outlook, towards the ends of immense projects that will benefit mankind. With either the "Eleven" or the "Twenty Two" the positive path is open to become famous. If the "Twenty Two" is too hard to live with, and one wishes to inhibit one's real self, it can be reduced to the "Four" path of life to follow instead. The outlook of the "Twenty Two" does not have room for the daily tasks of just plain living, but is always concerned with things of a bigger scale or larger scope. Usually the honesty found in a "Twenty Two" as well as the sincerity and truthfulness, is absolute. Despite the fact that his head may be in the clouds, the "Twenty Two" feet will remain firmly planted on the ground. This number incorporates all the positive points of every other number combined.

NEGATIVE: Loss of ideals, mixing in the black arts, self-promotion, advancing own ego. The negative aspects of the "Four" also prevail.

EXPLANATION: The big builder, the one who builds dams, skyscrapers. He may also build a peace treaty, or a church. He has all the attributes of the "Eleven," only like the "Nine" his is the global outlook, he is concerned with humanity. This is a number on the main path that often leads to mental turmoil as the energies are difficult to cope with. The keyword is BUILDER.

The life path, while it is the main course of life, will not stand alone, but will have many other sub-paths in operation along with it. The preceding cannot be interpreted in a correct manner alone, without first taking into consideration all the other factors involved. By now some confusion might exist as to the duality of the numbers, but this will be cleared up in subsequent chapters. The life path number is the most important in numerology, it cannot be taken lightly. It is the given path of life, the destiny, the only one that will offer opportunity.

It is common knowledge that a "Five" life path is one of constant change. The questions are, what type of change will it be, is the change going to be for the better or worse in relation to certain aspects? What triggers it, why is a certain person on a given path? When will the changes come, how may the lessons on the path be made easy? At what point in life are various types of changes going to occur? An individual on a "Five" path of life does not need a numerologist to inform him that he is living a life of change; this he already knows. He needs more specific information. This is the duty of the numerologist.

The one question that numerologists hear more than any other concerns what type of problem a particular individual will encounter on his given path, and by what means he can turn that negative into a positive so that he can avoid these pitfalls in the future. The best answer is: learn what the lessons are on the path of life, conquer them, overcome them, and any path will turn into a positive one. People often visit numerologists only when they have problems. A numerologist is not a magician. We cannot take persons out of trouble. We can inform what the problems are, what to expect in the future in both specific and broad senses. We cannot change your life, or the life of those around you, only you can do that. Having the knowledge of what your life is all about, what you have to learn, how you have to live and what the aspects will be on your path in the future, will enable persons using their own free will to make decisions that will change their path into one of happiness and joy instead of misery and strife. Certain things that cannot be overcome can at least be prepared for. One often wonders why one day at the Ritz, the next in the poorhouse. These are the ups and downs of life that have been plotted before birth, that can be prepared for by those with the knowledge. To those scoffers who think numerology or astrology are just interesting games, let them find their own course to follow. The knowledge of life is all around us. Those with the knowledge will have better lives.

The most important piece of information about any individual has now been gained, that of the path of life or destiny. This path of life is with each person from birth until death. It will never be changed, nor can it be escaped from. All paths of life fall into the positive until negative information is forthcoming. As for the negative aspects, further in the study a method will be given to determine if any are present concerning any given path. It must be pointed out that the negative aspects of any path are the ones which are easy for any on that particular path to fall into. The negative aspects are the particular hard ones for an individual on the affected path to overcome. Once more the question of WHY. The overcoming of Karma is never easy; obstacles are to be found upon the path at every turn. If it were pleasant and easy to overcome Karma, it would not be Karma. The negative aspects present, if any, are there to be overcome: they can be overcome.

Our subject of study, Janet, is on a "Three" path of life which promises to be a life of pleasant activities, encompassed by a beautiful atmosphere, full of self-expression. It has not been determined if any problems are attached to the path yet. If any are present, they will be of a minor nature as the negative aspects of the "Three," with the possible exception of jealousy are not of huge proportions, and will not present a major stumbling block on the path.

Chapter 3
THE LIFE CYCLES OR SUB-PATHS

Operating concurrently along with the life path will be three sub-paths known as the Life Cycles. These are the minor positive paths of life. During the span of each an opportunity will be given to the individual to expand some particular type of growth, knowledge. The negative aspects will present the cycle as a time when a specific lesson may be given special attention. The main path of life will always be the ruling force. These three sub-paths will each in turn run concurrently, but the main influence will be that of the destiny.

The first of these cycles is known as the Formative Cycle and will be in force during the years of growth, the teens, on into the twenties, until maturity is reached.

The second is the Cycle of Productivity and will be in operation during the productive or working years, and will remain in force until the early fifties.

The third and final cycle, known as the Harvest Cycle, will take up where the Cycle of Productivity ended, and will continue until death. It is in force during the period of retirement or senior age.

It is now necessary to jump around a little because it is of importance to know the exact year that these cycles will be entered. In order to do so, information will have to be obtained that will not be used until further along in the study. It is, however, important to know the cycles along with the path of life because together they form the influence that will affect the life of any given person.

The information that is needed is the knowledge of the Universal Year and the subject's Personal Year. Further in the text, there will be a complete study into the effects of both of these concerning any given life, which is a most important study, as it deals with short term planning, forecasting. For now all that is needed are the facts, obtained in the following way:

To find the Universal Year, take any given calendar year and reduce it to a single digit.

EXAMPLE: 1973 $(1 + 9 + 7 + 3 = 20/2 + 0 = 2)$
The calendar year 1973 is a "Two" Universal Year.

To find Janet's Personal Year, take her month of birth (September) which equals nine, plus her day of birth (24th) which equals six, plus the Universal Year (Two) and reduce to a single digit $(9 + 6 + 2 = 17/1 + 7 = 8)$.

EXAMPLE: *September 24th Universal Year (1973)*
$$9 + 6 + 2 = 17 = 8$$
The calendar year is an "Eight" Personal Year for Janet.

Before the study of cycles is continued, one further bit of information is necessary, and that is the fact that all life, Universal or Personal, operates in nine year cycles of from one to nine. Each year has a special meaning which will later be investigated. These year cycles begin with one and proceed in numerical rotation until the ninth year. A new "One" year will then follow the "Nine" year and so on.

Having determined that the calendar year 1973 is a "Two" Universal Year, and an "Eight" Personal Year for Janet, the life cycles may be proceeded with.

The first of Formative Cycle is based upon the month of birth. Janet's month of birth was September, so her first cycle will be a number "Nine" . . . . 9.

The second or Productive Cycle is based upon the day of birth. Janet's day of birth is the 24th, so her second cycle will be a number "Six" . . . . 6.

The third or Harvest Cycle is based upon the year of birth. Janet's year of birth was 1941, reduced to a single digit, so her third cycle will be a number "Six" again . . . . .6.

The three cycles combined will of course add up to Janet's main path of life, a "Three."

September	9		=	9	First Cycle
24th	24		=	6	Second Cycle
1941	1941	= 15	=	6	Third Cycle
	1974		=	21 =	"3" Life Path

Determination must now be made of exactly when Janet will enter and be under the influence of any of her three cycles. Among numerologists there are two distinct schools of thought. The first being that an individual will enter his second cycle in a "One" Personal Year, directly following or preceding (whichever is closer) the twenty fifth birthday. This is based upon the theory that a normal life span is seventy five years, which is divided into thirds. This is incorrect. There also has been the following two theories offered in print by numerologists who should know better, both of which are incorrect. First, that the first cycle will be exactly twenty seven years. Second, that a cycle may change in a "Five" personal year as well as a "One" personal year.

Astrology and numerology are closely interrelated, both together are again interrelated with the other sciences. The correct span based on the revolutions of the moon, adapted to numerology is twenty eight years for the first cycle. In this author's opinion numerology is more exact, more personalized than astrology, but from each is learned a little that complements the other. In the final analysis numerology and astrology must stand together. It is also a fact that many of the findings of numerology are based upon astrological findings, and is further true that without astrology, numerology would still be in the dark ages. The first or Formative Cycle ends and the second or Productive Cycle begins in a "One" Personal Year closest to the twenty eighth birthday.

If it begins before, the full effects will not be felt until the twenty eighth birthday is reached. If it begins after, the effects will start to be in force at the time of the birthday, but will not reach full potency until the actual cycle is entered.

Another theory about when the second cycle ends, and the third begins is also incorrect. The common theory is that the third cycle is entered exactly twenty seven years after the second cycle was entered. This is usually the case but the correct time of entry is the "One" Personal Year closest to the fifty seventh birthday. In a few cases if the second cycle was entered prior to the twenty eighth birthday, because of the difference of a few months, the third or final cycle will not be entered until thirty six years have passed. The effects will begin to be felt at about the time the fifty seventh birthday is reached. This is based on the revolutions of the moon taking exactly twenty eight years, four months to make a cycle. The third and final cycle will be entered in the "One" Personal Year closest to the fifty seventh birthday.

For those who wish to be hair splitting the second cycle will be entered in the "One" Personal Year that is closest (either before or after) to the age of twenty eight years, four months. The third cycle will be entered in the "One" Personal Year (either before or after) the age of fifty six years, eight months.

Janet was born in 1941, and in 1973 (September) will be thirty two years old. 1973 is Janet's "Eight" Personal Year. At the age of twenty five in 1966, Janet was in a "One" Personal Year. That is the year that she entered her second cycle on January 1, 1966. The full effects of this cycle would not have been felt until she had reached the age of twenty eight years, four months. This period in between is referred to as a "Cusp" period. Janet will enter her third cycle in 2002 on January 1st, at the age of sixty years, three months. The effects of this final cycle will be felt when she reaches the age of fifty six years, eight months. Janet's is one of those rare cases which has the second cycle in operation for thirty six years instead of twenty seven years. In Janet's case, however, it makes little difference as the second and third cycles are identical, both "Six."

If the month, day, year, digits that were employed to find the cycles turned out to be (each or any) either an "Eleven" or a "Twenty Two," they would not have been further reduced.

At this point, despite the fact that it is not known what each cycle means exactly, it is time to start constructing Janet's life chart, which will be added to as the study progresses.

In the forthcoming chart, Janet's Path of Life (3) has been entered with the keyword Pleasant. There have not been any negative aspects entered because if any exist, they are as yet unknown. The "Three" path of life operates for the entire course of the life, from birth to death. Also under the path of life, have been entered the three sub-paths or cycles with no keywords because they also are unknown at this point. The years at which time the cycles will be entered have been included.

As already discussed, in numerology all numbers operate from one to nine, plus eleven and twenty two. In each study or division the numbers will take on a somewhat different meaning. Regarding the cycles the KEYWORDS of the numbers are as follows. The negative aspects pertain to possible lessons to be learned.

Keywords

	Positive	Negative
1	Individual	Self
2	Association	Subservience
3	Pleasant	Expression
4	Organization	Work
5	Freedom	Change
6	Power/Security	Adjustment
7	Wisdom	Understanding
8	Material	Control
9	Encompassing	Denial
11	Inspiration	Sacrifice
22	Universal	Ideals

BIRTH   FIGURE ⚡1

	PATH & CYCLES		
	3 Pleasant	9	
1966 (25)			
		6	
2002 (61)			
		6	

DEATH

Before delving into the exact meaning of each cycle, it must be brought forward that these cycles have a definite effect upon life. The stepping up from one cycle to another produces positive feelings. For example: a person leaving a "Three" Formative Cycle, going into a "Seven" Productive Cycle would feel a definite uplift. By the same token, should this individual drop down into a "Five" Harvest Cycle, there would result a letdown of emotions and energy.

There is also a certain potency as to how the number is reached. For example: 6 = 6, 24 = 6, 33 = 6. Each of these numbers reduces to a "Six" with the same effect, but the bigger the number that was reduced, the greater the potency, either positive or negative.

An additional example:

$$3 = 3 \quad 12 = 3 \quad 21 = 3 \quad 30 = 3$$

The numbers range in octaves. The thirty being the highest octave, the single three being the lowest.

THE CYCLES OR SUB-PATHS

A "ONE" CYCLE

Formative:

Development of individuality, self resource. It could contain a warning that the child was left to his own devices or was given too much independence. It is also a warning to parents not to repress in the child the very thing he is striving to develop.

Productive:

It foretells inner drive, ambition, achievement, success. It also warns against putting self above others.

Harvest:

As this number carries with it an enormous amount of activity, it does not forecast a restful retirement period, rather one of constant activities.

A "TWO" CYCLE

Formative:

The "Two" being a female number, casts the concern that the child is being raised under the influence of the mother alone. Perhaps, a widow, divorcee. The warning here is not to over-indulge or spoil the child. This will be a period of cooperation, association, friendships, usually early marriage.

Productive:

Cooperation and obedience. The drive will be to form partnerships, alliances, to work well with others. Warning is against pushing the self to the forefront.

Harvest:

This is usually a restful cycle. If you are a man, somewhere you will be under the influence of a woman. People in a "Two" Harvest Cycle find themselves with the urge for collecting stamps, coins, objects, etc. It will be a period full of warm love, close friends.

A "THREE" CYCLE

Formative:

It will be pleasant, full of self-expression. The lead in the school play, local music school show. Music, art may play a big part. As the self reaches the early twenties it will be a gay social whirl.

Productive:

It foretells of the most pleasant of all cycles. This will be easy, carefree, gay, social. There will be many friends, a loving family. It is a period that is outstanding for expressing in the arts, music, painting, acting, writing. Persons in this cycle will be creative, original.

Harvest:

The last cycle will be little different from the second. There will be many friends, many activities. A period of self-expression.

A "FOUR" CYCLE

Formative:

It predicts that studies will come hard in school, the child will have to apply himself. There also may be some sort of restrictive influence that the child has to operate under. In general, life will be hard as opposed to easy, restrictive.

Productive:

This is a period to lay foundations, build firmly. It foretells of a steady, stable influence. It does not predict much travel. This is a period of productivity, hard work, with little time for the carefree life.

Harvest:

This does not forecast retirement or an easy life. There will be some sort of work engaged in, either from necessity or otherwise.

A "FIVE" CYCLE

Formative:

This is a cycle of change, freedom. No particular problems or cares. The warning to parents is to extend the freedom, but to give guidance also, as this number vibrates sex in the wrong sort of way.

Productive:

This is a period of much travel, constant change, new activities, new friends, romance. Complete changes will occur just about every year or so. During this period life changes overnight, usually within an eighteen month period some sort of major change will occur in the life.

Harvest:

This offers much pleasant change, new activities, a considerable amount of travel. A person under this sign may or may not retire, will have little cares either way.

Note:

Regarding the above, the author would like to add a personal footnote for those people under the sign of the "Five." I have as my path of life the "Five," it was also my first cycle. You will find the happiest life that exists if you will learn one lesson, accept change, seek it. Do not misuse your personal freedom, do not worry about the opinions of those who live in ruts. If this is done, there will be a life of attainment, success, happiness, travel. You will see the entire world before middle age. If this is not done, unhappiness will exist in its worst form.

A "SIX" CYCLE

Formative:

The early childhood will be one of duties, obligations, responsibilities. A warning to parents, if possible, try to lift some of the burden. It is too much for young shoulders. This is a restrictive childhood. Around the late teens, some of the pressure will be lifted, there will be romance, possible early marriage.

Productive:

This "Six" middle cycle predicts a period of adjustments, particularly in regards to domestic affairs. The self will constantly be faced with problems from other people. It foretells of a happy home life, if (the if is a big one), the adjustments have been made. There is a warning here against expecting perfection in people.

Harvest:

There is security in this cycle, but also restrictions. The self may be saddled with many unjust, unwanted burdens, adjustments. These burdens should be accepted with a smile.

A "SEVEN" CYCLE

Formative:

A child under this sign will live within himself, be ingoing as opposed to outgoing. Parents should try to draw the child out. As the teens are reached there will be a seeking of knowledge, purpose, inner thought.

Productive:

This is a period of restful growth. A period of study, inner thought. Most people in this cycle do not marry. If it is under consideration, it should be given deep thought. Opportunities should not be reached for, because somehow or other they will be dropped in the lap, but only if not sought after. This is a cycle where the self will work better alone in all respects. It is also a cycle to have and learn faith in.

Harvest:

This predicts a retirement or at least a semi-retirement. Most people in this cycle who work do so from their own study at home. It will be peaceful, restful. There will not be much activity, not too much social life, but the period will be full of wisdom, knowledge.

AN "EIGHT" CYCLE

Formative:

This is a very powerful first cycle, almost too much for a child to handle correctly. Parents should be forewarned not to overindulge the child with excessive allowance. It is a period where the younger person can gain much in the way of achievement, knowledge.

Productive:

It shows immense strides forward in the world of money, finance, big business. It predicts big power, big business, large accumulations of wealth, if handled properly. The power reached in the commercial world could be very high. Individuals in this cycle should push hard, for the tension of the "Eight" will cause inner pressure for forward motion.

Harvest:

This does not predict retirement. There is much that can be accomplished during this period. The vibrations are for money, power, success.

A "NINE" CYCLE

Formative:

This is a hard sign for a young person to operate under due to tension. This is the all encompassing number, and can prove hard to adjust to. Parents will have to exercise a large amount of understanding and love. The bad reactions that might appear in childhood are nerves, emotions, fears. It further foretells of a good educational exposure.

Productive:

The spiritual aspect is present. There are vibrations for success, especially in public life. This is a hard vibration under which to operate. Marriage in this cycle often runs into problems. The feeling is this cycle is all encompassing love as opposed to individual love. It should prove to be a period of freedom, this freedom is necessary to fully exploit the full potential of the cycle. There is little in this cycle that cannot be accomplished if the effort is made to do so.

Harvest:

This will be a period of retirement. It will be a cycle of additional learning and study.

AN "ELEVEN" CYCLE

Formative:

The inspiration of this cycle is far too much for a child to cope with, usually the child reduces it to a "Two," and lives under the lesser sign.

Productive:

A period of inspiration, revelation. A period of greatness, of ideals. Commercial ventures, speculations are strongly warned against during this period.

Harvest:

Certainly a period of retirement. A period of reading, perhaps writing. The inspiration of course will always be there.

A "TWENTY TWO" CYCLE

Formative:

As there is no twenty second month, there is no formative cycle pertaining to this number. This is for the very best as there is no young person capable of living with this number.

Productive:

A period of top leadership, huge achievements. Warning: nerves and emotions can play havoc.

Harvest:

Plan to keep active. The vibrations are strong for being high strung, nervous.

In every cycle there are fine outstanding qualities, many fine aspects to enjoy. An understanding of the personal cycle will aid in taking advantage of certain strong points, backing away from other considerations. Unless the negative aspects of any given number are overcome, the positive cannot be realized. The Cycles can prove to be a fine guide pertaining to work selection.

If one of the Cycles agrees with the main path of life (identical numbers), then the lessons to be learned will be made easier because they will be spread over a wider range. The Cycles or sub-paths are for the purpose of expansion, growth, knowledge. They will have a big effect during the course of their operations on the main path of life.

Janet's chart can now be added to in a positive way. The word security has been used in describing the middle and last cycles. This is because pertaining to females in a "Six" Cycle, this is the keyword that usually applies. At this point readers should have absorbed the basic meaning of all the numbers, should be able to select their own keywords that best fit.

The main vibrations throughout Janet's life are going to be pleasant. The secondary vibration that will be in force from birth to age twenty five will be encompassing, which means that during her formative years, Janet might be nervous, high strung, emotions may run a little high. This number will expose Janet to many influences, much knowledge and experience. By the time she reached her late teens, Janet should have achieved a high level of intelligence. The signs were strong for good education. From age twenty five, and for the rest of her life, Janet will constantly be troubled with making adjustments of one sort or another, in particular to adjustments that will primarily be concerned with her home and family. An educated guess can be

FIGURE #2

BIRTH	PATH & CYCLES		
	3 Pleasant	9 Encompassing	
1966 (25)			
		6 Security	
2002 (61)			
		6 Security	
DEATH			

made at this point that Janet will marry young. If she can cope with the adjustments, she should have a happy secure home. The latter part of her life may prove to be restrictive.

A good example of how numbers affect each other, would be to take a life with a destiny of "One" which is aggressive, self-seeking, place it next to a "Seven" cycle, which is quiet, retiring. The "Seven" is a period for introspection. True, the main path of life will prevail, but the path will be toned down heavily. These two opposing numbers could well cause problems in the life. It could also be the turning point where the self chooses another road to follow, more in keeping with the cycle. Full explanation will be made in the second study of this text pertaining to the interpretation of opposing numbers. For the present time, concern must be applied with the basics.

Chapter 4

THE VIBRATIONS OF THE BIRTHDAY

The calendar day upon which an individual was born, will have a strong vibratory force upon the life. This force will be particularly strong during the middle or Productive Cycle, as the cycle was derived from this number. The vibrations of the master numbers (11 & 22), will be felt throughout the entire life. It will be a help in understanding the birthday vibrations if it will be remembered that the numbers range in octaves, as already discussed.

THE VIBRATIONS

The "1" numbers (birthdays on the 1st, 10th, 19th, 28th).

Persons born on any of the above dates will naturally be in the "One" Cycle of Productivity. These number "Ones" will have the force of the "One" vibration: forceful, ambitious, a self-starter. In addition each birthday has its own features.

1st   Mentality, logic, independence, apt to repress emotions.

10th   Creative, with all the qualities of those born on the first in a higher octave.

19th   This number runs the entire span of numbers from one to nine. This could be a period of ups and downs for those in their middle cycle. It would range from the dizzy heights to the bottomless pit. However, because of all the attributes of this number, the person possessing it would be quick to recover from any pitfalls.

28th   Affectionate. This number comprised of the subservient "Two" and the forceful "Eight" would lead towards material leanings, fast, close friendships.

The "2" numbers (birthdays on the 2nd, 11th, 20th, 29th).

The "Two" is the friendly number, leads to associations, partnerships, alliances.

2nd   Emotional, nervous, moody.

11th   The master number, highly emotional, large amounts of nervous tension, very high mentality. Determination, quick reactions, ideals. Apt to go to extremes without reason, especially where the emotions are concerned.

20th   Exactly like those born on the second only more so. This is the extension of the "Two" to a higher octave. The moods could go very deep. There is a very strong inner drive for friends, family, marriage.

29th   Inspired, dreamer, homelover. This number will have most of the attributes of those born on the eleventh, as two plus nine equal eleven.

The "3" numbers (birthdays on the 3rd, 12th, 21st, 30th).

Pleasant, cheerful, social.

3rd   Self-expression, restlessness, intensity.

12th   Brilliance, imagination.

21st   A combination of the third and twelfth birthdays.

30th   The highest vibration of those born on the third.

The "4" numbers (birthdays on the 4th, 13th, 22nd, 31st).

4th   Substance, drive, productivity, stubbornness.

13th   Discipline, adaptability.

22nd   A master number, spirituality, a dreamer, nervousness, intuition.

31st   At times unreasonable. All the attributes of the thirteenth in a higher octave.

The "5" numbers (birthdays on the 5th, 14th, 23rd).
Constant change in every respect.

5th   Versatility, quick mentality, good adjustment, sociable.
14th   Creativity, an adventurer.
23rd   Sensitivity, understanding.

The "6" numbers (birthdays on the 6th, 15th, 24th).

6th   Inner driving force, ability, love.
15th   Attraction, cooperation, knowledge, demonstrative.
24th   Energy, restlessness, activity.

The "7" numbers (birthdays on the 7th, 16th, 25th).
Solitude, aesthetic, ideals.

7th   Love, intuition, intelligence.
16th   Aloofness, philosophy.
25th   Similar to the 16th, on a higher octave.

The "8" numbers (birthdays on the 8th, 17th, 26th).
Accumulation, exploitation, material aspects.

8th   Productivity, progressiveness.
17th   Conservative.
26th   Generosity, cooperation, expansiveness.

The "9" numbers (birthdays on the 9th, 18th, 27th).

9th   Artistic, literary, successful.
18th   Variety, greatness.
27th   Forceful, responsible.

The foregoing was a rather simple breakdown of the key-words for any given birthday, so it will be expounded a little. The "One" numbers are the active, ambitious persons who strive, usually via mentality, to get ahead in life. The "Two" numbers are those who would be far happier working in association with others or perhaps being employed, as opposed to self-employment. The "Three" numbers, which are all outgoing, friendly, social, would find their success in a life where such talents could be put to good use, such as salespeople, etc. The "Four" numbers are the real doers, the workers, the builders, upon which enterprises are built. The "Five" numbers crave change, constant activity, with a touch of adventure. The "Six" numbers are the real drivers, the pushers, the ones that get things done. The "Sevens" are the dreamers, the moralists. The "Eights" function best in high powered enterprise, big business, while the "Nines" operate best on a level that is far reaching, international.

These are the inner abilities that would best be applied in the selection of a profession or type of life. A person with a "Seven" path of life, a "Nine" Cycle would function well as a writer, perhaps one traveling world-wide to collect material. Should this same "Nine" Cycle oppose a "One" path of life, an ideal pursuit would be that of a statesman, a diplomat. There are many thousands of careers, professions, various types of work to be found today. Each person must make his own selection, but if he is guided by the middle cycle, the path of life, the vibrations of the birthday, he will be able to find one that would be best suited to his particular vibrations, one in which he would be successful. These foregoing factors should be referred to in connection with the important movements in life, such as work, where to live, marriage.

Having discovered by the vibrations of Janet's birthday that she is an idealist, will be seeking perfection in life, a portent of trouble exists when these vibrations come up against her "Six" cycle. She will have to adjust to meet the situation, realize that life, people, are not all perfect. This could present Janet with a problem as she will be seeking a rainbow in a relationship that does not exist. She is full of energy, restless, will be seeking activity. Janet will not be content with being a "sit at home" housewife. She will seek other interests as well, perhaps even a career of some type to give her an additional interest in life.

Chapter 5
CHALLENGE OF THE BIRTHDATE

Depending upon which day a person is born, he or she will have a specific challenge in life to cope with, outside of other challenges. The challenge will be in operation during the entire life, but will be hardest felt during the Productive Cycle when the birthday itself comprises the cycle.

In order to find the challenge, the numerical value of the date of birth is taken (day only), and one number is subtracted from the other. Presented here is the entire spectrum of challenges.

1st	Single Digit	No Challenge
2nd	Single Digit	No Challenge
3rd	Single Digit	No Challenge
4th	Single Digit	No Challenge
5th	Single Digit	No Challenge
6th	Single Digit	No Challenge
7th	Single Digit	No Challenge
8th	Single Digit	No Challenge
9th	Single Digit	No Challenge
10th	$(1-0=1)$	The Challenge is 1
11th	$(1-1=0)$	No Challenge (Specific)
12th	$(2-1=1)$	The Challenge is 1
13th	$(3-1=2)$	The Challenge is 2
14th	$(4-1=3)$	The Challenge is 3
15th	$(5-1=4)$	The Challenge is 4

16th	$(6-1=5)$	The Challenge is 5
17th	$(7-1=6)$	The Challenge is 6
18th	$(8-1=7)$	The Challenge is 7
19th	$(9-1=8)$	The Challenge is 8
20th	$(2-0=2)$	The Challenge is 2
21st	$(2-1=1)$	The Challenge is 1
22nd	$(2-2=0)$	No Challenge (Specific)
23rd	$(3-2=1)$	The Challenge is 1
24th	$(4-2=2)$	The Challenge is 2
25th	$(5-2=3)$	The Challenge is 3
26th	$(6-2=4)$	The Challenge is 4
27th	$(7-2=5)$	The Challenge is 5
28th	$(8-2=6)$	The Challenge is 6
29th	$(9-2=7)$	The Challenge is 7
30th	$(3-0=3)$	The Challenge is 3
31st	$(3-1=2)$	The Challenge is 2

It is necessary to bring forward that a "One" Challenge derived from the birthdate of the 12th, is more potent than the same "One" Challenge derived from the birthdate of the 21st. In short, the lower the octave of the birthdate, the higher degree of potency the Challenge has. (I.e., negative effects are always minus, positive effects are always plus.)

There are two numbers which have a Challenge of "Zero," the "Eleven," and the "Twenty Two," both of which are the master numbers. A Challenge of "Zero" is a little different than "No Challenge." The "Zero" is all of the Challenges rolled up into one. Those who have the master numbers will face all of the Challenges in return for their gift of inspiration, revelation. No particular Challenge is going to present a great problem, however, as opposed to those who have specific Challenges.

THE CHALLENGES

One   To Individualize.
Two   To give cooperation.

Three   Not to scatter energies.
Four   To apply self to work, not to feel oppressed because of it.
Five   To overcome inertia, to accept change, to use freedom correctly.
Six   To adjust to responsibilities.
Seven   Self-discipline, obtain faith.
Eight   To learn correct use of money and power.

These Challenges are lessons to be learned aside from all others, and are going to cause tension on the life path until they are overcome.

Chapter 6
THE BIRTHDAY GIFT

In the balance of life, nothing is taken away without something being given. In the preceding chapter, it was found that twenty out of the thirty one birthdays carried a challenge with them. To those with the challenge an aid will be given to overcome the challenge or make living with it easier. This is sometimes referred to as the complimentary challenge. This author prefers to call it the birthday gift.

The gift is found by subtracting the challenge from the ultimate number of nine. Again, the entire chart will be offered for those affected.

10th, 12th, 21st, 23rd
The Challenge is One $(9 - 1 = 8)$ The Gift is 8

13th, 20th, 24th, 31st
The Challenge is Two $(9 - 2 = 7)$ The Gift is 7

14th, 25th, 30th
The Challenge is Three $(9 - 3 = 6)$ The Gift is 6

15th, 26th
The Challenge is Four $(9 - 4 = 5)$ The Gift is 5

16th, 27th
The Challenge is Five $(9 - 5 = 4)$ The Gift is 4

17th, 28th
The Challenge is Six $(9 - 6 = 3)$ The Gift is 3

18th, 29th
The Challenge is Seven $(9 - 7 = 2)$ The Gift is 2

19th
The Challenge is Eight $(9 - 8 = 1)$ The Gift is 1

THE GIFTS

One	Attainment
Two	Intelligence
Three	Creativity
Four	Growth
Five	Stability
Six	Success
Seven	Knowledge
Eight	Material success

What an individual may have lacked in his birthday vibrations, he had to make up as a Challenge, but in return was given something else that he needed.

Janet has a "Two" Challenge (derived from her birthdate of the 24th). She is going to have to learn cooperation and association, especially in her middle cycle. If she wishes that happy, secure home that is her destiny, this challenge must be overcome.

She has received a gift of "Seven." This will lead her into philosophical fields, endow her with much knowledge, wisdom, and faith, especially pertaining to the God-Force, as "Seven" is the number of God.

Chapter 7

THE ATTAINMENT

Running concurrently with the cycles, but overlapping them is the Attainment. The Path of Life is the main course that a given life will follow. The Cycles or Sub-Paths are the secondary course that will affect the life. The Attainments represent the high point a life may reach at any given point in that life. They also forecast the changes that will occur as the life unfolds. The Attainments are going to have a very direct influence on the life.

In the course of life there will be four separate Attainments. At the point in time where one of these segments change at about the same time as a Cycle changes, there will be evidenced in the life a change, perhaps of outlook, fortune, ideals, emotions, or interest. Whatever the change, there will be one; and it will be determined by exactly what the given cycle and/or Attainment happen to be.

If there are negative aspects in the life that pertain to a given Attainment which have not been overcome by the time the Attainment is in force, the full potential of the Attainment cannot be reached.

The basic cycle number is nine and there will be four Attainments, so four is multiplied by nine, for a total of thirty six. From this is subtracted the destiny (path of life) number. Janet has a "Three" destiny, so the new total will be thirty three. This supplies the fact that the first Attainment will be from birth to age thirty three. The second Attainment will start where the first leaves off, and will be in operation for exactly nine years. For Janet this will be from age thirty three to age forty two. The third Attainment will operate also for exactly nine years; in Janet's case, this will be from age forty two to age fifty one. The last and final Attainment will be from age fifty one until death. The Attainment changes always take effect on the birthday. The greatest effect of the Attainment is felt when the "One" Personal Year is reached.

To further clarify this, in order to find the ages of the Attainment changes, multiply four times nine for a total of thirty six, and subtract from it the path of life number. This will be the age where the first Attainment ends, and the second begins. The second Attainment will be for exactly nine years, as will the third. The fourth and final Attainment will operate from the ending of the third until death.

To find out exactly what these Attainments will be, Janet's birthdate of September 24, 1941 will be employed, reduced to its single digit form (9-6-6).

The first Attainment will be the month added to the day.

$9 + 6 = 15 = 6$ ATTAINMENT # 1 6

The second Attainment will be the day added to the year.

$6 + 6 = 12 = 3$ ATTAINMENT # 2 3

The third Attainment will be the sum total of the first and second Attainments added together, reduced to a single digit.

$6 + 3 = 9$ ATTAINMENT # 3 9

The fourth Attainment will be the month added to the year.

$9 + 6 = 15 = 6$ ATTAINMENT # 4 6

EXAMPLE of correct method to find pinnacle/attainments:

Birthdate Sept. 24, 1941

FIRST ATTAINMENT: 9
                                        + 24
                                        ‾‾‾‾
                                        33 = 6

SECOND ATTAINMENT: 24
                                        + 1941
                                        ‾‾‾‾‾‾
                                        1965 = 21 = 3

THIRD ATTAINMENT: 33
                                        + 1965
                                        ‾‾‾‾‾‾
                                        1998 = 27 = 9

FOURTH ATTAINMENT: 9
                                        + 1941
                                        ‾‾‾‾‾‾
                                        1950 = 15 = 6

Via this method, the attainments having master numbers will not be missed.

These attainments may be either easy or difficult. They may contain a Karma lesson if their numbers correspond with one of the lessons in life.

If one of their numbers agrees with the Life Path, this path will become very smooth, many opportunities will be presented. If one of their numbers agrees with the Soul Urge (to be discussed in future chapters) everything that is desired or wanted in life will be made available. If one of the numbers agrees with the Expression (also to be discussed in a future chapter) opportunities will be presented to help along the lines of the Expression. These extra benefits will only be in force during the period that the particular agreeing Attainment is in operation.

Again a return is made to the basic interpretations of the numbers, with very little change. Presented are the keywords

for the Attainments with very little change from either the Life
Path or Cycles.

One	Individual, attainment.
Two	Association, alliances.
Three	Pleasantness, self-expression.
Four	Organization, achievement.
Five	Change, freedom.
Six	Responsibilities, obligations, success.
Seven	Knowledge, wisdom.
Eight	Achievement, material aspects, power.
Nine	Greatness, achievement, completion.
Eleven	Inspiration, success, fame.
Twenty Two	Universal, accomplishment.

Above are the positive aspects. The negative aspects will
remain exactly as described in the chapter regarding the Path of
Life. (With the positive aspects many of the interpretations of
the Cycles and Main Path will pertain.)

Now to offer a little deeper insight into these Attainments. In
the professional world of numerology, these Attainments are
known as the Pinnacles. (Life Pinnacles.) The word Attainment describes them better, for they are what is given in life. If
the life is lived in a positive manner they will give rich rewards.
If the life is lived in a negative manner, they will bring disaster.
The first Pinnacle or Attainment is known as the Pinnacle of
Attainment. The second is known as the Pinnacle of Obligation.
The third is the Pinnacle of Foundation. The fourth is the Pinnacle of Retrospection. The second and third, with heavy accents on the third are the most important. This is when the
groundwork is laid for the remainder of the life.

The first half of this text is a base for study into the second
part. In many cases throughout the first study only keywords
are used instead of entire explanations. In the second half of
this study will be laid out the entire spectrum: the meaning of
each number, and how to interpret it.

Regarding Janet, her first Attainment will be a "Six." During
the ages of birth to thirty three, she will be going through a pe-

riod of responsibility, will be given the opportunity to attain and meet these responsibilities. From age thirty three to forty two, she will have an Attainment of "Three," which will be pleasant, self-expressive, creative. Since it matches her path of life, which was pleasant to begin with, during this period life will, indeed, become very pleasant for her; she will be present with opportunities to attain things that are of interest to her. From age forty two to fifty one, Janet will have the all encompassing "Nine" as her attainment, and will be offered much exposure in her chosen field. There is a very good chance Janet will reach prominence in whatever she will be doing. From age fifty one, and for the rest of her life, Janet will once again be affected by the responsibility of the "Six." It would seem that Janet has received more than her share of the "Six." There is just a little hair splitting difference between the two "Sixes" in her sub-paths, and the two "Sixes" in the Attainments. On the brighter side, she certainly has a pleasant path of life, one that will be full of harmony, beauty. To give this even greater force, one of her Attainments will also be the same "Three," thus creating even more harmony, beauty, into her life. The "Nine" of her early sub-path might prove to be a little hard for Janet to cope with in the tender years, but is certainly good training ground for what lies ahead in her third Attainment. Janet's life is starting to unfold a little more with each study.

As the Attainment is a fixed path of life, it will be added to Janet's chart. The reader will note that for the Attainments, the age was used instead of the date. This is because the Attainments change on the birthday, while the cycles change on January first of the calendar year.

A further informative description of the Attainment Pinnacles is now offered.

"One"

This is an ideal Pinnacle to have at the start of life. This is not a good Pinnacle to be saddled with in the latter part of the life. A "One" Pinnacle falling into the second, third, or last positions will indicate new beginnings, a rebirth, a destruction of the old

FIGURE #3

BIRTH	PATH & CYCLES		ATTAINMENT	
	3 Pleasant	9 Encompassing	6 Responsibility	
1966 (25)				
		6 Security		
Age 33				
			3 Pleasant	
Age 42				
			9 Greatness	
Age 51			6 Responsibility	
2002 (61)		6 Security		
DEATH				

way of life, sometimes material as well as emotional. Those who have a "One" Pinnacle in the middle course of their lives must be very careful not to lose that which is most important to them in life.

"Two"

Not a good Pinnacle to begin life with as it indicates the loss of the father through death, divorce, separation or long term travel away from home. If the father is at home and no loss or separation exists it means that a strong domineering mother influence is exerted. In other aspects it is ideal. This Pinnacle anywhere in the life span will bring warm friends, close associations, good marriage, both bad and good emotions.

"Three"

An ideal Pinnacle in any position. This will bring an expanded social life, tremendous self-expression, especially in the creative arts. It will bring friends, romance, love, sex. It will bring success and fertility in most aspects.

"Four"

In any position will bring a period of limitation. Certainly a period of intense work. A very good time to build solid foundations.

"Five"

A period of complete personal freedom, constant travel, frequent change. Things started under this sign will not usually be of a permanent nature. The personal sex appeal will be great and many aspects will be presented in this situation.

"Six"

A period of responsibility and adjustment. A period of marriage, love, romance. If positive, a period of success, security. If negative, a time of strife, divorce, trouble.

"Seven"

A time of loneliness, a period of being alone. A good time for study, meditation, introspection. This is not an ideal Pinnacle in any position especially for those who may have problems with this number, which so many do. Marriage during this Pinnacle will not lead to happiness. Marriage before this Pinnacle will be arrived at will cause no particular problem during the Pinnacle and will usually stand the strain of the "Seven." The most difficult position in which to find this Pinnacle is at the final position in the life span.

"Eight"

A time of successful material aspects. Quick ascent to power if the life is positive. A time of worry and concern over finances during the duration of the Pinnacle if the life is negative.

"Nine"

A period of huge accomplishments, a time of success in business. There will be considerable long range and foreign travel. Personal matters such as love affairs and marriage usually do not lead to happiness during this Pinnacle. It will also be a time of loss and sacrifice in many matters.

"Eleven"

A time of great inspiration. A period of almost positive success.

"Twenty Two"

Huge accomplishments. Great creativity. If the life is negative, a period of mental trouble, injustice to others.

In the opinion of this author the Attainment/Pinnacles are perhaps the single most important ingredient outside of the Path of Life. They will greatly affect the Path one way or the other. In some cases the potency of any given Pinnacle may in itself over-ride the Path of Life in certain aspects.

Chapter 8

THE ATTAINMENT CYCLES

The Attainment Cycles operate in conjunction with the Attainment. For each individual they are the same. Nine years is the cycle of man. Nine times nine is the ultimate. The number of each one of these cycles will have different effects upon the Attainments as they intersect with the Attainments. The reaction upon the Attainment will depend upon the number of the Attainment, and the number of the intersecting Attainment Cycle.

The true value of the Attainment Cycles is for interpreting tones or currents attached to the pinnacles. In order to present a correct base for study, the Attainment Cycles are outlined here. The important feature is to discover at which point any given Attainment intersects with an Attainment Cycle.

Each individual will have individual Attainments based upon the birthdate comprised of any combination of the numbers, in any order. The Attainment Cycles which are fixed and are the same for each person, are as follows:

THE ATTAINMENT CYCLES

From birth to age 9	Number One	Individualization
From age 9 to age 18	Number Two	Association
From age 18 to age 27	Number Three	Self-expression
From age 27 to age 36	Number Four	Work
From age 36 to age 45	Number Five	Freedom

From age 45 to age 54	Number Six	Responsibility
From age 54 to age 63	Number Seven	Introspection
From age 63 to age 72	Number Eight	Material aspects
From age 72 to age 81	Number Nine	Encompassing
From age 81 to age 90	Number Ten	Rebirth
From age 90 to age 99	Number Eleven	Inspiration

The cycles tell a story that is quite in keeping with life. From birth to age nine, the self is indeed concerned with growth, attaining for the self. From age nine to age eighteen is the time of dates, friendships, associations, team work. At age eighteen, the childhood pastimes are left behind; the self takes a broader look at the world, seeks self-expression, achievement, originality. This is the growing up period. At age twenty seven, one feels life drifting on, and begins to settle down to business, take things seriously, lay a foundation for later life. This is certainly a period of work. At about age thirty six, the self, now firmly settled in the business world, starts to look around, wants more out of life than work. He seeks travel, change, in short he wants personal freedom. From age forty five to age fifty four, is usually when the greatest responsibilities come in life. From age forty four upwards into the sixties, the self has a chance to rest awhile, meditate. The self is concerned with the spirit, seeking and gaining wisdom. From age sixty eight to the seventies, he comes out of his shell, once more becomes concerned in the world of form. In the later seventies, he is no longer local in outlook, he is concerned with the entire world. This is the completion period. In the eighties, he has already lived a full life, a complete cycle of nine times nine. Now is the rebirth, with all the knowledge and wisdom of the past life behind it. Those who live up into the nineties are no longer interested or concerned with the world of form; they are looking for inspiration, revelation.

Chapter 9

THE LIFE CHALLENGES

The Life Challenges are lessons that must be given special attention during the entire course of the life. They are a great indication of what is lacking in the self. These Challenges are not to be confused with Karma lessons, they are entirely separate. Failure to overcome these Challenges will have serious consequences, upon the Life Path, Cycles, Pinnacles.

There will be three challenges to be met and overcome. Two are minor challenges, the other is the major challenge. The major challenge will be in force for the entire span of life. The first minor challenge will be felt hardest in the first half of the life, but the vibrations from it will continue onward. The second minor challenge must be given special attention during the last half of life, but again, vibrations from it will be felt in the early years as well.

Using Janet's birthdate reduced to single digits (9-6-6), subtract the month digit (9) from the day digit (6). One from the other, the lesser from the greater.

$$9 - 6 = 3 \qquad \text{First Minor Challenge} \quad 3$$

Subtract the day digit (6) from the year digit (6), one from the other.

$$6 - 6 = 0 \qquad \text{Second Minor Challenge} \quad 0$$

The first minor challenge is subtracted from the second minor challenge, one from the other, to find the major challenge.

$$3 - 0 = 3 \qquad \text{Major Challenge} \quad 3$$

An inverted pyramid form can be used for this process as follows:

$$
\begin{array}{ccccc}
 & 9 & 6 & 6 & \\
\text{1st Minor} & 3 & & 0 & \text{2nd Minor} \\
 & & 3 & & \\
 & & \text{Major} & &
\end{array}
$$

THE CHALLENGES

One

The ego, the desire to impose one's own will upon others must be held in check. At this point it is hard to get the correct interpretation until the name is dissected, but the challenge will be the foregoing or the following. There might not be enough inner drive, individuality.

Two

To learn to cooperate with others, to take and follow directions. To gain a little humility. One could also be leaning too hard upon others, following their lead blindly. One must learn to cooperate without leaning.

Three

The need to get out in the world more, meet people, there needs to be more self-expression. Life cannot be lived entirely within self.

Four

The challenge could go either way. It is the challenge of not applying self to work, details, or too much attention is paid to the details.

Five

The ability to accept change must be developed. Things, people must be let go of. The "Five" also deals with the senses, the warning is very plain not to over-indulge in sensual activities, especially those that are immoral, unorthodox.

Six

The lesson to be learned is to accept things, people, for their true value. Not to seek a perfection that does not exist, to give and take in life with other people. To be able to spring back after a disappointment. The "Six" of course deals with responsibility. The strong emphasis in the challenge deals with the home, marriage.

Seven

The pedestal must be left. The warning is not to live too much within self, not to stand back and watch the world go by. One must learn to give of one's self. One must develop patience, achieve understanding. The self must have faith.

Eight

This again can go either way, it is either an over concern with material aspects, money, power, or not enough concern.

Nine

It would be impossible to arrive at a "Nine" with the method employed. The "Nine" deals with human compassion, emotional understanding of fellow men. Anyone lacking in this aspect is in very sad shape.

Zero

The "Zero" deals with the entire span of challenges. All must be given attention with no special emphasis concerning any particular one aspect.

If these challenges agree with a life cycle, a life pinnacle, the main path of life, they must be given acute attention. If they are not overcome, destruction and ruin will follow in the particular agreeing path or sub-path. The major challenge will present the most difficulty. The two minor challenges will present their own set of problems, but do not carry the importance of the major challenge.

In every realm, the numbers have a meaning. In the realm of the body, or health, each number represents a part of that body or health aspect. The challenges are a key indication of trouble that might arise in the life with any particular type of illness. This special trouble must be watched very closely if the challenges agree with one of the life paths.

Presented below is a short list of the numbers in regards to health aspects:

1   Heart, head, senses.
2   Kidney, stomach, nerves.
3   Throat, liver.
4   Teeth, circulation.
5   Sex organs, nerves.
6   Heart, neck.
7   Glands, nerves.
8   Stomach, nerves.
0   Any place in the body.

Before progressing further, the challenge will be employed to outline how one of the most frequently used forms in numerology is done. This is a further explanation of the pyramid used prior in this chapter. The pyramid is used either up or down, either adding or subtracting.

Employed will be Janet's birthdate numbers reduced to their single digit form.

9   6   6

From the nine, the six will be subtracted, for a total of three. From the six, the last six will be subtracted, for a total of zero. The first number is subtracted from the second *or* the second number is subtracted from the first, the lesser from the greater, the same applies with the six and six.

9   6   6
3   0

The three and the zero are subtracted one from the other for a total of three, the pyramid is complete.

9   6   6
3   0
3

The three and the zero being the secondary influences or minor challenges. The final three being the major challenge.

Besides the "Zero" which is a warning to Janet to be careful in all her dealings, Janet's only other concern will be with the "Three." The effects of this "Three" are going to be very heavy in the early years of life, but will be spread a little to take some of the pressure off. Janet's challenge is the challenge of expression. This is her main life path. This challenge has to be overcome fast or the entire life *will* go negative. (Janet's path or destiny is to do exactly what must be overcome, and will prove a problem.) Just how big this problem is will be determined when her name is analyzed. This challenge might well be a warning to Janet not to scatter her energies, not to withdraw in the latter part of her life when she could become burdened with the responsibilities of the "Six."

Janet's chart may now be expanded with the addition of the challenges, pinnacle/attainment cycles.

In a small percentage of charts a fourth challenge may be found which acts as an additional minor challenge that will be in effect for the entire life. While this fourth or additional challenge is only found in a small minority of charts, it would be well for the reader to understand how it is arrived at.

To find this additional Challenge, if any, the month of birth is subtracted from the year of birth (one from the other.) In most cases the figure arrived at will be the same as the Major Challenge and may be forgotten. If a new number shows up

BIRTH

FIGURE #4

Age	PATH & CYCLES		PINNACLES & CYCLES		CHALL.	
Age 9	3 Plea.	9 Encom.	6 Responsibility	1	MAJOR 3	
Age 18				2	Self-Express.	
1966 (25)						
Age 27		6 Security		3	First Minor 0	
Age 33						
Age 36			3 Pleasant	4	Second Minor 3	
Age 42						
Age 45			9 Greatness	5		
Age 51						
Age 54			6 Responsibility	6		
2002 (61)				7		
Age 63		6 Security				
Age 72				8		
Age 81				9		
Age 90				10		
Age 99				11		

DEATH

that is not one of the three challenges then the life affected will
have an additional problem to overcome.

The following example is offered below first using Janet's
chart which does not possess a fourth challenge and then using
a chart which does.

```
            9    6    6
  Janet       3    0
                 3
                 3        Same as Major
                          Challenge. Fourth
                          Challenge does not exist.

            1    3    9
  Other       2    6        First & Second Minor
                 4          Major
                 8          Additional Minor
```

Chapter 10

THE PERSONAL VIBRATIONS
(Year—Month—Day—Monthly Cycle)

All life operates in cycles of nine. Nine years, nine months, nine days, even nine hour and nine minute cycles. The strongest personal vibrations are those of the year. To find the personal year for any individual, the month of birth is added to the day of birth, with that total being added to the Universal Year.

The Universal Year for any given calendar year is found by adding all the numbers in the year together, reducing to a single digit.

> EXAMPLE: 1973 $1 + 9 + 7 + 3 = 20 / 2 + 0 = 2$
> The year 1973 is a "Two" Universal Year.

To locate Janet's Personal Year in 1973 is as follows:

> *Birth Month (Sept.) Birth Day (24th) Univ. Yr.*
> 9   +   6   + 2 = 8
> 1973 is an "Eight" Personal Year for Janet.

Each year from one to nine will have its own vibrations. These vibrations cannot be avoided, but the knowledge of same will help any person to take advantage of certain points at given times and avoid pitfalls. A particular year may be excellent for one aspect but poor for another, the following year may prove to be a complete turn-about.

One individual in a certain personal year will be attracting one set of vibrations, while the same year, another individual will be attracting a different set of vibrations, if the second individual is in a different personal year.

THE PERSONAL YEAR VIBRATIONS

A "One" Year

The keyword is beginning. This is the ideal year to start all new projects. This is the year to assert one's own personality. To create new ideas, institute new plans. This is the year to be positive, forge ahead. It is not the year to try and end anything. The personal vibrations are good. This is the most important year in the cycle as it lays the groundwork. What is started this year may well last the cycle. There will be little outside help offered, the self will have to go it alone, but there will be little hindrance from outside sources affecting this year. People under this sign will find many new things entering their lives, in many cases a move of home. In some cases, an entirely new life will begin.

A "Two" Year

The keyword is cooperation. This is the year to pull in your horns, to smother the personality a little. An ideal year to work with others, put their ideas to use. This is a bad year to try and forge ahead on your own, or to impose your personal ideas upon others. The personal vibrations are poor. This is the year one can find new friendships, the vibrations are strong for marriage or divorce. They are equally as strong for harmony or discord. Some of the benefits from what was planted in the first year will be in evidence this year. Many will be met during a "Two" year to help the self along its path.

A "Three" Year

The keyword is social. This is the ideal year to renew old friendships, form new ones. The year for expressing self in the arts or music. This is the year to set the pace for personal activities along the lines of self-expression, club functions, etc. The personal vibrations are good. This should prove to be a pleasant year in all respects. Friendships, business should be successful, life should be happy. This is the best year outside of the "One" year to put new ideas into being. This year, however, can be rather upsetting in the emotional area, as it is a personal time when the inner emotional self will have to be dealt with. Additionally, problems carried forward that should have been settled in the "Nine" year can erupt here, as well.

A "Four" Year

The keyword is work. The year to keep one's nose to the grindstone. Matters pertaining to business or job should be carefully watched or things could get out of hand. Keep all affairs in perfect order. Be careful of health, attend to the small details. The personal vibrations are very poor. This could be a year of loss if not watched closely, it could bring with it hard times. It will prove to be a year of hard work. By applying oneself to the work, some of the hard aspects of this number can be avoided.

A "Five" Year

The keyword is change. This is the year to put new methods into old operations. A year to fix up the old dwelling or perhaps obtain a new one. Personal freedom will be at its peak, take advantage of it, seek personal change, it will not be hard to find this year. The personal vibrations are very good. Many changes will come into the life under the sign of the "Five." A move of home perhaps. In a "Five" year, one move usually leads to another, a change in every respect including, perhaps business, travel, or a new romance. The vibrations are a little shakey, things started in a "Five" year are not always of a permanent nature. Married people must guard against becoming involved in outside love affairs.

A "Six" Year

The keyword is adjustments. This year is ideal for collecting monies due you. It is also a good year to make adjustments with creditors. It could be the year when the self is called to task by those whom he owes. It is an excellent year for marriage, but also a good one for divorce; be forewarned: give that little bit extra at home. It could be a year of happy domestic affairs, but there will be adjustments to be made in the home. The personal vibrations are poor. This is the ideal year to purchase a new home or add to the old one. There will be a lot of responsibility, adjustments this year.

A "Seven" Year

The keyword is rest. A good year for just loafing around if the bankroll permits. A fine year for study, self improvement. A good year to give some thought as to your mission in life, what you wish to accomplish. A very bad year for investments or speculations of any sort. A bad year to start a new business. A good year to spend some time alone, get the thoughts in order. The personal vibrations are both bad and good: bad for everything connected with material affairs, good for all else. This is a year when anything can happen. The self will be alone a lot of time during the year, emotions are sometimes badly affected.

An "Eight" Year

The keyword is money. This is the year to invest, the year to put loose dollars to work. This is the correct time to take advantage of every single opportunity that appeals to you to increase your personal wealth. Forge ahead as much as possible, but be careful, this is the year that Karmatic debts are usually collected. The personal vibrations are excellent for material aspects, not so good for others.

A "Nine" Year

The keyword is finish. This year start nothing new that is wished to be continued. A good year to take care of unfinished business. A good year to check on the health. Nothing should be carried past the year into the new cycle, necessary things excepted. Nothing new should be started this year or it will finish before the end of the year. This is a good year for study, writing. An excellent year to end associations or dealings with those that are getting you down. The personal vibrations are both good and bad. This year will bring finish in many respects. It will be an emotional year. It will be a year the self is called upon to sacrifice, usually lose something. It could be a year of complete ruin in every respect. A very bad year to change jobs, unless the wish is to finish. Those who have not lived the past cycle in a positive manner will find themselves at this time exactly where they were nine years ago. Many times completely wiped out, financially and emotionally.

While all cycles are of a nine year period, it is possible to have an "Eleven" year instead of a "Two" year or a "Twenty Two" year instead of a "Four" year.

An "Eleven" Year

This is the year to put new ideals into practice. This is not the year to seek personal accumulation. This is a good year for personal achievement in religion, writing, the arts, etc. It has a lot of the vibrations of a "Seven" year and a "Two" year combined. The personal vibrations are very bad for material matters. Under this sign will come many new ideas, much inspiration, personal revelation. A tense, nervous, high strung year. Vibrations are good for non-material matters, if the person is not self-seeking.

A "Twenty Two" Year

All the vibrations of the "Eleven" year, even more so. Projects undertaken will fail, unless they benefit the community or mankind in general. The personal vibrations again are very bad for material aspects, excellent for projects which will be a public service.

The major changes in life will come in the "One," "Five," "Nine," personal years. The biggest losses will occur in the "Seven," "Eight," "Nine," personal years. The hardest times will come in the "Four," "Eight," "Nine," personal years. Love affairs or marriage will be strongest in the "Two," "Five,"

"Six," personal years. The "Seven" and "Nine" personal years will be the most emotional.

The vibrations will be strongest from the first of the year until the end of September when they will start to wane. A cusp period will be in effect for the last three months of the year with the old getting weaker, the new getting stronger.

The full effect of the year will be felt when the "One" Personal Month is reached.

The primary or strongest personal vibrations will be those of the personal year. The secondary vibrations or influence will be those of the personal month.

The personal month is found by adding the digit of the personal year to the calendar month digit.

EXAMPLE: *October Personal Year (1973-Janet)*
$$10 \; = 1 + 8 \quad = \quad 9$$

For Janet, October, 1973 will be a "Nine" Personal Month in an "Eight" Personal Year.

What is now in operation is a miniature nine month cycle operating within the year. The vibrations are almost the same for the months as they are for the year.

For Janet, while she is in an "Eight" Personal Year which calls for investment, this would be a bad month to take advantage of any new ideas regarding investment, as the sign of the month calls for finish, loss.

The vibrations of the months are strongest from the fifth to the twenty fifth. When the personal month agrees with the Destiny number, the particular month could prove to be a very pleasant one. This also holds true with the personal year agreeing with the Destiny.

Within the month cycle, there is a day cycle. To find the Personal Day, add the Personal Month digit to the calendar day.

EXAMPLE: *Date Personal Month (October–Janet)*
$$22nd = 4 + 9 \qquad = 13 = 4$$

Thus the 22nd of October, 1973 would be a day of work, in a month of finish, in a year of material aspects for Janet.

THE PERSONAL DAYS

A "One" Personal Day is a good day for appointments, business deals, etc.

A "Two" Personal Day is good for associations, agreements, perhaps that big date that was looked forward to.

A "Three" Personal Day is ideal for self-expression in all forms.

A "Four" Personal Day, the self should be applied to work, do nothing else.

A "Five" Personal Day is the best for personal contacts, travel, change, advertising.

A "Six" Personal Day is the best for apartment or home hunting. Purchasing for the home. Start nothing under the sign of the "Six" that will not be completed. This is a bad day for travel.

A "Seven" Personal Day is ideal for self-meditation rest. Good for a family outing.

An "Eight" Personal Day deals with material aspects.

A "Nine" Personal Day is a day of finish, start nothing new, plan nothing ahead.

It is not advisable to start anything new on days with bad vibrations, save these items for the days when the vibrations call for success dealing with that aspect. To go against the numbers is to court disaster.

The calendar date or the number that was reduced to find the personal vibrations must also be looked into. The higher the octave, the greater the degree of potency. The original number itself, many times, acts as a hidden number or influence. These hidden vibrations will be discussed in the second study in this text.

A small chart for this date discussed could be set up as follows:

1973	8
October	9
22nd	4
ESSENCE	$\overline{21} = 3$

The essence of the day is going to be pleasant. A pleasant day of work, finish, money matters. The essence of the entire scope is very important, as well as the numbers above the essence.

The foregoing was rather a brief outline of what may be expected under different vibrations. To get an exact picture, the Universal Vibrations as well as the Excursion Vibrations (both to be discussed in future chapters), must be taken into account.

If the birthdate of another person is known, the Vibrations for this person may be calculated and added to one's personal vibrations, a fairly accurate picture of what relations will be for any given time will be presented.

EXAMPLE:	*Janet*	*Unknown Friend*		
Year	8	1	=	9
Month	9	5	=	5
Day	4	2	=	6
Essence	$\overline{3}$	$\overline{8}$	=	$\overline{2}$

The vibrations for the entire year will be that of some sort of finish between the two friends. The monthly vibrations will bring some sort of change into the relationship. The day vibrations will bring an adjustment between the two. The final combined essence of "Two" calls for harmony or discord. Perhaps love or sex if the friend is a man. If the friend is a woman the friendship is valued, she should be avoided on this date, if possible. The "Two" will bring harmony where there is discord; it will also bring discord where there is harmony. The "Two" alone calls for association, friendship; the numbers adding up to the "Two" (9-5-6) do not call for harmony. The strongest vibrations are those of the year, the month being secondary, the day following last.

Now presented in capsule form is what may be expected in any given personal year.

"1" Year   New beginnings.
"2" Year   Cooperation, association, new friends, marriage, divorce, romantic interests.
"3" Year   Self expression, new ideas, new creations; social, friendly, successful time. Personal emotions.
"4" Year   Hard work, possible hard times.
"5" Year   Major change, possibly one or more moves of home.
"6" Year   Responsibility, obligations, love, marriage, divorce, purchase of a new home.
"7" Year   Loss, bad emotions, possible lack of funds, knowledge, wisdom. Success in other matters.
"8" Year   Material aspects, either good or bad. Possible that the self will be called upon to atone for past errors.
"9" Year   The finish, the completion. Loss, sacrifice, bad emotions, misery. Could also bring rich rewards if the life has been lived in positive manner for the past eight years.

A Personal Year at time of birth will always agree with the Destiny number.

Hour Cycles will not be discussed in this text, but for those who are interested, the hours are found in the same manner as the months, days. Thus the hour of Midnight to 1 A.M., would be the first hour and is added to the Personal Day in order to find the Personal Hour. There are books on the market that claim to be written by numerologists that maintain for everybody that this hour is a "One" hour. They are incorrect. This is a "One" universal hour. For personal vibrations, the hour is found exactly as are the days, months, years.

An important element to be taken into consideration is the composition of the personal year.

Personal years are comprised of the birth digit (month and day of birth) known as the Achievement. (To be discussed in a future chapter.) To the birth digit, as discussed, is added the universal year or outside pull. The relationship of these two numbers as well as the individual ability to cope with the achievement must be given prime consideration (i.e. the effect the achievement will have in positive or negative aspects when in conjunction with the universal pull).

Thus an individual, for example, who is positive eight, could still fare badly in an eight personal year if he/she were Karmic six and six were the achievement coupled with the universal two. (This foregoing will be plainer as this study is progressed into.)

There is another personal vibration that is very telling in life, the vibrations of the month cycle. Each person will have three cycles per year and, in a nine year period, will return back to the starting point. The first cycle runs from the birthday for exactly four months. The second cycle is in operation for the next four months. The third or final cycle is in operation for the remainder of the year until the next brithday.

Janet was born on September 24th, her first cycle would be from September 24th to January 24th. The second cycle would be from January 24th to May 24th. The third cycle would be in operation from May 24th to September 24th.

The first monthly cycle will be the same each year; it usually denotes Karmic trouble, and is there for the purpose of learning. If this is true, which can be determined from the name, then special attention must be paid to this cycle, especially in the matter where the Karma is concerned, or it is going to bring bad times.

The second and third cycles will run in numerical order with the numbers progressing each year. If positive they will bring good vibrations in the areas to which they pertain. If there are problems with these numbers, this is the time, the self will be hit with trouble in the respective area, so that the lessons may be learned.

First Cycle:

Subtract the age at last birthday from the calendar year, reduce balance to a single digit. Janet will be 32 in 1973. The 32 subtracted from 1973 results in a total of 1941. $(1 + 9 + 4 + 1 = 15 / 1 + 5 = 6)$ Janet's first monthly cycle which will be the same each year is a "Six." An easier way to do this, is take the year of birth, reduce it to a single digit.

Second Cycle:

Subtract the path of life number from the current year's date. Janet's destiny number is "Three." Subtracting the "Three" from 1973, results in a total of 1970 which is reduced to a single digit. $(1 + 9 + 7 + 0 = 17 / 1 + 7 = 8)$

Third Cycle:

To find the third cycle, add the first two cycles together, reduce to a single digit.

First Cycle   6
Second Cycle   8
Third Cycle $\overline{14} = 5$

These monthly cycles will present to the individual opportunities, both positive and negative during the course of their operation for conditions that will be in keeping with the number of the cycle. They react within the personal year much like the sub-paths relate to the main life path.

A form of interpretation can now be made as to the various aspects affecting Janet during 1973. Discounting any problems, also discounting the day aspects as they change too rapidly for this type of forecasting, the following chart can be constructed.

YEAR	1973 8		
MONTH CYCLE	1/24 to 5/24 7	5/24 to 9/24 4	9/24 to 1/24 6
MONTH	Jan Feb Mar Apr May Jun Jul Aug Sept Oct Nov Dec 9 1 2 3 4 5 6 7 8 9 1 2		
ESSENCE	8 9 1 2 9 1 2 3 6 7 8		

It will be noted that Janet's first two cycles used the numbers "Seven" and "Four" instead of the "Eight" and "Five" already calculated. This is because it was necessary to backtrack into 1972, because both of these first cycles preceded her birthday of September 24th. The cycles operate from birthday to birthday, while the year, month vibrations operate on the calendar basis.

The essence was obtained by adding the year, plus the cycle, plus the month. The essence contains very important values.

The period of October to December will be concentrated upon. The first vibration is that of the "Eight," which is on the cusp, going out, especially in November, which is a "One" Personal Month. The new influence, also felt on the cusp, will be that of the "Nine." The monthly cycle indicates that during this period Janet is going to be concerned with responsibility, obligations, marriage, divorce, love, domestic affairs. October is a month of finish, with the new incoming year vibrations, which also calls for finish, emotions are going to run high. November calls for associations, cooperation, marriage, divorce, love affairs. During the month of October, Janet under the influence of finish, with the secondary influence of the "Six" will be giving serious thought to moving her personal residence, will be considering ending a love affair or marriage. The essence of the October period is also "Six," making this more than a strong possibility. Janet has too many "Sixes" in her life chart for the "Six" not to be Karmic. I suspect that she has a deep problem with this part of her life, has not at this point in life learned to make the necessary adjustments. The over-riding "Eight" is the number of Karma, and is giving way to the finish of the incoming "Nine." The essence of the month is finished, the vibrations for November are the emotional "Seven." Janet is going to have bad emotions, feel loss, over what she did in October. It is, of course, a month of new beginnings for Janet. In December Janet will be seeking new associations, will run into problems with the essence of "Six." This small forecast was made without taking into consideration the Universal Vibrations, or other important information. The chart, however, speaks for itself in this matter.

The question always arises, that since the individual has freedom of choice, how can numerology predict with such certain forecasts. In numerology, the main vibrations are taken, especially in trouble areas, one number is joined with the other numbers to make a determination. The life path has been laid out, the individual does have freedom of choice. Assume that Janet was married during the period forecast, it would seem like a divorce was in order. Marriage is not the legal papers of the bureaucrats, it is the joining of a man and woman in their minds. Divorce likewise is the separation of the pair, also in the minds. If Janet was negative, the signs would have brought an actual divorce. If she has learned her lessons, learned to accept the responsibility, make the adjustments, this trouble would be reduced to nothing but a big family squabble. If such were the case, Janet would never have left the home. The month of November with its new beginnings would have restored peace in the household. If Janet had really conquered her problems, it would have been nothing but a period of adjustment and adaptation for her. The period was not a good one in any case and created some sort of problem for Janet.

From what has been seen of Janet so far, one of the dead give-aways is the double sub-path of "Six," Janet has had serious problems with this number in past lives. Janet would have an indication to shy away from responsibility, adjustments. This author has sort of put his head on the chopping block by making this forecast without reference to the Inclusion chart, but the signs are too strong to be ignored.

The warning is again put forward, until a complete knowledge of the numbers is obtained and understood, no individual should try to make any sort of serious forecast pertaining to his own chart, or to those of others.

As a final offering in this chapter, there is now presented a rendering of positive points, negative points, pitfalls, vibrations, attractions, influences, of the Personal Year and Month Cycle. When the Path of Life (Destiny) number agrees with a Personal Year, the vibrations and attractions will be doubly strong.

ONE

Personal year:

Everything pertaining to this year is excellent. This is a new life, a new beginning. The entire cycle will be built upon what is done this year. Do not repeat the same mistakes that were made in the last "One" Personal Year. The opportunity for a new life in all respects will be presented this year. Vacillation will meet with destruction. The cornerstone of the nine year cycle has to be laid correctly. Willpower will be rewarded. Phoney promotions will fail. Arrogance will not be tolerated.

Month cycle:

The opportunity to assume command, take charge, gain control or leadership, will be presented. All dealings with men will be beneficial. The self must take the leading steps forward.

TWO

Personal year:

There will be opportunities presented this year, but only if not sought after on an active basis. If the first year was lived in a correct manner, much will be in evidence in a "Two" year. Patience and cooperation must be employed this year. On the domestic front, this year will present problems in the home.

Month cycle:

Success will only come from working in association with others. All dealings with women, either social or business, will be successful.

THREE

Personal year:

If the seed was planted firmly in the "One" year and cultivated in the "Two" year, the "Three" year will bring rewards and success. There will be new relationships come into the life this year. Self-expression and positive action will be rewarded. Overspending, gloom, moods, will put a heavy damper on this year. There could be evidenced a loss this year, if things were not cleaned up and let go of in the previous "Nine" Personal Year.

Month cycle:

This will be a successful four months, providing assets are not squandered. The vibrations are outstanding for dealing with the public. Social life will be at an all time high. New friendships will be formed. A good time to start a new romance.

FOUR

Personal year:

Nerves will be tense. This is the year that the efforts of the past three years must be perfected. All details must be attended to. Nothing must be overlooked. Opportunity will only come from concentrated effort, tending to one's business. Laxity will bring ruin. No changes must be made this year of any sort. All changes will bring destruction. Outside of a normal vacation, do not plan any trips for this year.

Month cycle:

This will be a restrictive four months, but the work and toil must be suffered in order to build up the foundation. Attend to all details in the home and work.

FIVE

Personal year:

For those who have run into problems in the past four years, who have met with adversity because of negative actions, now is the time to try and salvage what is left. Take advantage of the "Five" vibration, change everything that needs to be changed. For those who have lived the past four years in a positive manner, this will be a period of happy change, travel. A time of romance, sex, personal freedom. For those who have been positive, make no unnecessary change this year, either in home or job. To do so would be to court disaster, for one change will lead to another. The good will turn into bad. Start nothing new this year as it will not last, instead use this period for expansion, change within what is already in progress. For those who have been negative, if you will treat this "Five" year as a "One" year, seek change in all, the bad will turn into good. What you plant now will be realized in your "Seven" year. There will be no mis-use of personal freedom tolerated this year. The sex life must be watched by all. Over-indulgence in the wrong kind of sex will bring problems. Enjoy all the sex you care to, but see that no individual is hurt by it, or no promises are made without the intention of keeping same. This mis-use of sexual freedom will guarantee the individual loneliness and misery in the "Seven" year. A warning to all, this could be the year when someone close to you betrays you.

Month cycle:

If decisions are carefully made they will bring pleasant change into the life. This will be a time of travel, new friendships.

SIX

Personal year:

This is the year that marriage and/or divorce could be in the offing, either for you or someone close to you. This is the year the vibrations are outstanding to purchase that new home you have been thinking about or to add to the present one. There will be responsibility presented this year. If the cycle has been positive, it will be in the form of advancement, promotion. There will be no need to be concerned with finances this year, if the life has been positive. The funds for all that is needed will be made available. The home life will be happy and secure. The home itself will be comfortable, perhaps outstanding. Those who have been negative will be presented with responsibilities that will not be to their liking. In addition there will exist domestic trouble. Do not unjustly impose self-will upon others this year. To present it in a blunt manner, unless you are sought out for advice, keep your nose out of other people's business, keep your advice to yourself. Those in a "Six" year whose interference causes problems for others, putting out something that will bounce right back on them in the "Nine" year.

Month cycle:

The "Six" of course deals with love and marriage. The "Six" or Venus offers financial protection as well. This is a period of obligations. You will receive more than your just share, see that others close to you benefit.

SEVEN

Personal year:

This is the time for introspection. The time to perfect the nine year cycle. It is not the time to brood over past errors. It is the

time for positive thinking. This period should be used for looking over the past six years in a positive manner, correcting mistakes, realizing within the self the errors made. The vibrations
are perfect for a trip or holiday for as long as one wishes. Some
thought should be given during this year as to the mission in
life. Spiritual aspects, study, teaching, writing, will all meet with
success. For those who have been positive, this will be a year of
inner peace, harmony, love. For those who have been negative,
it is too late at this point to pull out. All ventures into the material world will fail, you must live the best way possible. For the
negative, this is a period of misery, poverty, loneliness. Brooding or crying about it is only going to make it worse.

Month cycle:

Delays may be in evidence. The life will be slowed down. A
good time for agreements, alliances. For those who live positively, this may be the time of unexpected gifts.

EIGHT

Personal year:

This year deals with material aspects. It will usually bring pay-
ment of all monies justly due you from this cycle. For those
who have been positive, it will bring advancement in personal
power, increase in material wealth, new contacts, new business
agreements that will lead to larger scopes. This is often the year
women marry "well." For the negative it will bring financial
loss or limited income. This is also the period of Karma. The
"Eight" is associated with the Planet Saturn. For those who
have hurt others in a spiritual way the debt was collected in the
"Seven" year. For hurt in an emotional way it will be collected
in the "Nine" year. For all other type of unjust actions, including mental and physical hurt to others, it will be collected this
year. A warning to all: modesty must be displayed this year.
Show-offs will be struck down. No arrogance will be tolerated.

Month cycle:

Every opportunity will be made available to you in every respect. Again, arrogance will not be tolerated.

NINE

Personal year:

This is the completion. This is a year of travel, many trips. This is the time to clean the slate for positive action for the new cycle. Carry nothing forward that should be left behind. This is the year to look for the inner spirit within self. The time for self-honesty. No waste will be tolerated this year. A loss or sacrifice may be needed this year, not always material, many times emotional, sometimes both. A loss of things or people could come about. Death could occur to someone close to you. This is also a period for introspection of the past cycle. A time for study, writing. For those who have been positive, this is a period of greatness, attainment, riches, achievement, advancement, knowledge, success, happiness. Make no plans what-so-ever. Save them for next year. For those who have been negative, this is a year of loss, divorce, ruin, bankruptcy, emotional upheaval, misery, unhappiness, sacrifice, tears. Make plans for a new life next year. All loss or gain this year will be in proportion to the positive or negative aspects of the past cycle, all hurt caused others unjustly during this period will now be collected in proportion.

Month cycle:

Attainment and success will come in this period to those who will help others along their way. All self-seeking will end in ruin.

The duality of the Personal Years may be a little plainer at this point. The foregoing was the "Cycle of Man." The presentation might have been a bit strong, but it was the intention to present the truth of the Cycle of Man in as straight-forward a manner as possible. This Cycle will not bend, give, adjust, reconcile. Every nine years, man has the opportunity to adjust to the Cycle.

The Month Cycles operate within the Personal Year presenting the opportunity for advancement pertaining to a particular aspect every four months. The Year Vibrations will take precedence. Challenges must be overcome in order to reach the full potential of the Month Cycles.

Personal Months operate within the year and present a month influence. Personal Days operate within the months. Pinnacles and other yearly vibrations (to be discussed in a future chapter) operate concurrently with the vibrations outlined in this chapter.

Learn and understand the Challenges, overcome them. Pay particular attention to a Challenge if the number is the same as a personal cycle number. The overcoming of the Challenge will make the Cycle positive.

Chapter 11

THE UNIVERSAL VIBRATIONS
(Year—Month—Day)

It is understood that all things operate in cycles of nine. As a
personal individual operates in his own cycle, so does the universe. A city, country, corporation, will also operate in their
own respective cycle. The Universal Vibrations are those of the
outside world. In most cases the Universal Vibrations will be
stronger than Personal Vibrations, this must always be taken
into consideration when dealing with individual charts. It has
been discovered that by knowing, understanding personal vibrations, advantage may be taken of the strong points, caution exercised with the weak ones. We must all live in the world, there
is no other place to go. An understanding of Universal Vibrations with their over-riding pull, will enable individuals to make
more accurate personal decisions, bring into play an additional
set of numbers for use with personal charts, in order to secure a
better understanding.

The method employed to find the Universal Year has already
been discussed, but once again an example will be offered.

The year 1973 is a "Two" Universal Year.

$$1 + 9 + 7 + 3 = 20/2 + 0 = 2$$

These Universal Vibrations when coupled with Personal Vibrations and the numbers come into operation together can
affect the life, either for the good or bad.

Considering the Universal Vibrations alone, they operate

with the same meaning of the numbers to a large extent as do
Personal Vibrations, with the exception that it is on a worldly
scale. In a "One" year the world is starting new beginnings in
many respects. The vibrations of a "Two" year are treaties, discord, harmony, alliances. More marriages will take place in a
"Two" year, as will divorces. In most other matters there is inertia present. Regarding material matters, the world will offer
little resistance to individuals in a "Two" year. The vibrations
of a "Three" year are mainly for expression in the medium of
the arts, theater. There is usually a rush at box offices by the
general public. An overflow crowd will gather at public recrea-
tion areas, jam beaches, resorts. Vibrations of the "Four" year
will be hard, the pull on individuals will be hard, work will be
in evidence all over. The cycle progresses for the world as it
does for the individual. The "Five" year will bring changes, the
"Six" year will bring adjustments, peace treaties, war, another
run of marriages. The "Seven" year will be restful, the world
will awaken to the spirit of God, churches will be crowded. The
"Eight" year can bring large scale famine, epidemics, etc. It will
bring large exchanges of currency, big business on an international scale. The "Nine" year will bring finish, completion, universal projects, as the fruits of the previous eight years will be
realized, sales will go up on material published concerning religion, occult matters. There will be a run on church services.
The "Eleven" will also result in a wave of interest concerning
the Spirit and the occult. Many new ideals will be put forward
during the transit of the "Eleven." The "Twenty Two" year will
bring large projects to build hospitals, libraries, schools, etc.

The Universal Month is found in the same manner as the
Personal Month. The Universal Year is added to the calendar
month.

October   Universal Year (1973)
10 = 1 +   2   =   3

October, 1973 is a "Three" Universal Month.

The Universal Day is likewise found in the same manner. The Universal Month is added to the calendar day.

22nd   Universal Month (October, 1973)
$$22 = 4 + \qquad 3 \qquad = \qquad 7$$

October 22, 1973 is a "Seven" Universal Day.

For the world, October 22, 1973, is a year of inertia, in a month of expression, in an aesthetic day.

To determine what Janet's vibrations would be with the world at large on this date, the following could be constructed.

	Janet		*Universe*		
1973	8	+	2	=	1
October	1	+	3	=	4
22nd	5	+	7	=	3
Essence	5	+	3	=	8

Janet's vibrations with the world at large for the entire year will be one of new beginnings. The secondary influence felt during the month of October will be that of work. The vibrations of the day call for pleasant aspects. Janet's overall essence for the day will be that of material aspects. The "Eight" is derived from the "Five" and "Three." The material aspects will be pleasant ones for Janet. Had the "Eight" been obtained from two "Fours," it would have been a bad day to engage in material aspects. The main vibration of the Universal Year with material aspects is inertia. Janet's Personal Year calls for forward movement in the world of finance. The universal vibrations do not present any problem to her in this aspect.

The Universal Vibrations must always be taken into account with the Personal Vibrations. The year 1973 is one where peace treaties will be signed, or broken. It is a year when new companies will be formed, old ones will go bankrupt. It is a strong pull that could bring any individual new friendships, marriage, divorce, sex. It is a year when the voice of women is heard more than usual.

All things are relative, and must be kept in correct proportion. A set of numbers that would bring a business tycoon a new fortune, a general a great victory, will bring to average "John Doe" an achievement in keeping with his life, i.e. small raise in pay, a successful venture. Everything must be kept in proper balance. There is no reason why "John Doe" cannot become more than "John Doe"; but on the climb upward all must be kept relative.

One of the favorite studies for forecasters is the life of Napoleon Bonapart. His path of glory, victories, bloodshed, ultimate defeat, make a good trail for the student to follow. The numbers which defeated Napoleon at Waterloo and sent him into exile, would bring the average person a loss in keeping with his daily life.

The vibrations of the year, month, day, must likewise be kept in proper proportion. A "One" Personal Year will bring new starts, new creations. The "One" Personal Month, will present a period of self-advancement. The month will not necessarily bring new beginnings as will the year; it is possible that it might, but the vibrations are towards opportunities for self-advancement being presented. The vibrations of the Personal Day will bring a chance for self-assertion, if the individual wishes to take advantage of the vibrations.

Chapter 12

THE PINNACLES AND CHALLENGES
(Year—Month—Day)
AND THE CYCLE OF PERIODICITY

Discussed in previous chapters were the Attainment/Pinnacles, Challenges, which play major roles upon the main path of life. Within each year, month, day, there will be similar Pinnacles, Challenges, of a much smaller scope. As the life cycle operates with the major (life) Pinnacles, Challenges, so do these minor Pinnacles, Challenges, operate within the cycle of the year, month, day, returning to their original position every nine years.

THE PINNACLES AND CHALLENGES
OF THE YEAR

To obtain the base numbers, The Universal Year digit, The Birth Digit (month and day only), and The Personal Year digit will be needed.

The Universal Year (1973) is "Two" (2). Janet was born in September (9), on the 24th day (6), totaling a single digit of "Six" (6). In 1973, Janet is in an "Eight" (8) Personal Year. The base line is 2/6/8.

The first Pinnacle which will be in operation from January 1, to March 31, is found by adding the Universal Year (2), to the birthdate digit (6), for a total of "Eight" (8). The first Pinnacle is an "Eight."

The second Pinnacle which will be in operation from April 1, to the end of June, is found by adding the birthday digit (6), to the Personal Year (8). $(6 + 8 = 14 = 5)$

The second Pinnacle is a "Five."

The third Pinnacle which will be in operation from July 1, to the end of September, will be found by adding the totals of the first two Pinnacles together. $(8 + 5 = 13 = 4)$

The third Pinnacle is a "Four."

The fourth Pinnacle which will operate from October 1, to December 31, will be found by adding the Universal Year (2), to the Personal Year (8), which totals ten, reduced to one. $(2 + 8 = 10 = 1)$

The fourth Pinnacle is a "One."

The length of operation of each of these Pinnacles is identical for all. The first Pinnacle is in operation for January, February, March. The second is in operation for April, May, June. The third for July, August, September. The fourth Pinnacle will cover the last three months in the year.

The meanings, vibrations of the Pinnacles will be exactly as described in the chapter concerning the Attainments.

The Challenge will be in effect for the entire year, with a major Challenge, two minor Challenges, exactly as the main life Challenge. The first minor Challenge must be given more attention during the first half of the year, while the second minor Challenge must be watched closely during the second half of the year, but the vibrations from both will be felt throughout the entire year. The major Challenge will be in operation for the entire year and is the main challenge of the year. The main life Challenges will always take precedence.

The same set of numbers is used to find the Challenges, as was used to find the Pinnacles. (2-6-8)

The first minor challenge will be found by subtracting the Universal Year from the Birth Digit (one from the other, the lesser from the greater). The Universal Year (2), will be subtracted from the Birth Digit (6), for a total of "Four" (4).

The first minor challenge will be a "Four."

The second minor challenge will be found by subtracting the

Birth Digit, from the Personal Year (one from the other, the lesser from the greater). The Birth Digit (6), will be subtracted from the Personal Year (8), for a total of "Two" (2).

The second minor challenge will be a "Two."

The major challenge will be found by subtracting the first minor challenge from the second minor challenge (one from the other, the lesser from the greater). The second minor challenge (2), will be subtracted from the first minor challenge (4), for a total of "Two" (2).

The major challenge will be a "Two."

The correct way to write or indicate these challenges (or any challenges) is 2/4-2.

Presented now in Pyramid Form is the entire spectrum of the Pinnacles and Challenges.

The base line is 2/6/8. Universal Year/Birth Digit (month and day)/Personal Year.

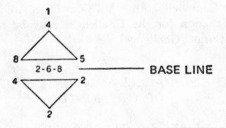

To find the Pinnacles.　First,　$2 + 6 = 8$
　　　　　　　　　　　　Second,　$6 + 8 = 5$
　　　　　　　　　　　　Third,　$8 + 5 = 4$
　　　　　　　　　　　　Fourth,　$2 + 8 = 1$

The fourth Pinnacle was found by adding the Universal Year to the Personal Year.

To find the Challenges.　First,　$6 - 2 = 4$
　　　　　　　　　　　　Second,　$8 - 6 = 2$
　　　　　　　　　　　　Third,　$4 - 2 = 2$

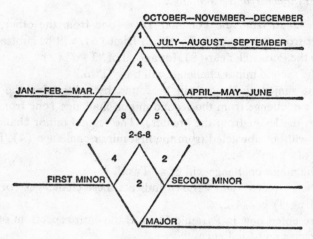

Presented now is an ideal form to use for the Pinnacles and Challenges. The spaces inside each pyramid may be used for notations affecting that period. (NOTE—This form was devised by Florence Campbell, author of "Your Days Are Numbered")

The explanation for the Challenges may be found in the chapter concerning Challenges.

THE PINNACLES AND CHALLENGES OF THE MONTH

The first number needed will be that of the current month reduced to a single digit. The month of October will be employed. October (10 = 1)

The second number required will be that of the Personal Year. Janet's Personal Year (1973) is an "Eight" (8).

The third number needed will be that of the Personal Month. October, 1973, will be a "Nine" (9) Personal Month for Janet.

Using the pyramid, the Pinnacles and Challenges for the month of October, 1973 will be found. These numbers will be added and subtracted in exactly the same manner as the ones were for the year.

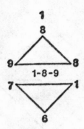

The first Pinnacle which is in operation for the first seven days of the month is a "Nine" (9).

The second Pinnacle which is in operation for the second seven days of the month is an "Eight" (8).

The third Pinnacle which is in operation for the third seven days of the month is an "Eight" (8).

The fourth Pinnacle which is in operation for the remainder of the month is a "One" (1).

The two minor Challenges are "Seven" (7), and "One" (1).

The major Challenge is "Six" (6).

All the challenges will be in operation for the entire month.

THE PINNACLES AND CHALLENGES OF THE DAY

The first number required is that of the calendar day, reduced to a single digit. The day of the 22nd will be employed. (2 + 2 = 4) Single Digit "Four" (4).

The second base number needed is that of the Personal Month. October, 1973, is a "Nine" (9) Personal Month for Janet.

The third number needed will be that of the Personal Day. October 22, 1973 is a "Four" (4) Personal Day for Janet.

Employing the pyramid the Pinnacles and Challenges for the day will be found.

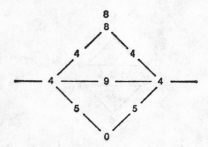

The first Pinnacle which is in operation from Midnight to 6 A.M. is a "Four" (4).

The second Pinnacle which is in operation from 6 A.M. to Noon is a "Four" (4).

The third Pinnacle which is in operation from Noon to 6 P.M. is an "Eight" (8).

The fourth Pinnacle which is in operation from 6 P.M. to Midnight is an "Eight" (8).

The two minor Challenges are both "Fives" (5).

The major Challenge is a "Zero" (0).

Following is Janet's Personal Vibrations for October 22, 1973.

	Personal	Challenges	Pinnacles
YEAR	8	2/4-2	8-5-4-1
MONTH	9	6/7-1	9-8-8-1
DAY	4	0/5-5	4-4-8-8

The days operate within the month cycle. The months operate within the year cycle. The years operate within the main life cycle. The Life Cycle presents the strongest vibrations. Do not put overemphasis upon the day vibrations, as they operate within the year overtones. Remember it is possible for positive/negative to coexist. For correct day forecasting it is necessary to understand day cycles, which will be presented in Chapter 39.

THE CYCLE OF PERIODICITY

The Cycle of Periodicity is much like the Pinnacle Cycles as described in a separate chapter. It operates within the year as the Pinnacle Cycles operate within the life. It is fixed and will be the same each year. The dates will vary from individual to individual. There are seven separate cycles, ranging from One to Seven. (Based on the original seven planets.) The entire scope of the cycle begins on the day after the birthday, and is complete the day before the following birthday. Each cycle operates for exactly fifty-two days.

The effects of the Cycle of Periodicity is exactly the same as the effects of the Month Cycles, Pinnacle Cycles, or Life Cycles (sub-paths).

Now offered is a chart for Janet for October 22, 1973, using all the pertinent information concerning the year, omitting the main life information. This is presented so readers may get an idea of what to look for, work with, and be concerned with on any given day. The chart will not be interpreted, this will be saved for the second study in this text concerning the relationship of numbers. If the day were eliminated from this chart and the chart were being run for a month or longer, the major Challenges, major Pinnacles, Sub-Paths, Path of Life, and other factors would have to be taken into consideration.

A DAY IN THE LIFE OF JANET—October 22, 1973

PERSONAL YEAR	8	Material Aspects
UNIVERSAL YEAR	2	Association/Cooperation/ Marriage/Divorce
PER. YEAR PINNACLE	1	Self Assertion/Creation
PER. YEAR CHALLENGE	2/4–2	Major: To Cooperate Minor: To Cooperate Minor: To Work

MONTH CYCLE	6	Responsibility/Obligation/ Marriage/Divorce
PERIODICITY	1	Beginning/Self
PERSONAL MONTH	9	Finish/Completion
UNIVERSAL MONTH	3	Pleasant
PER. MONTH PINNACLE	1	Self Assertion/Creation
PER. MONTH CHALLENGE	6/7–1	Major: Responsibility/ Obligation Minor: Introspection Minor: To Achieve or Subdue
PERSONAL DAY	4	Work
UNIVERSAL MONTH	7	Aesthetic
PERSONAL DAY PINNACLES	4–4–8–8	Work/Material Aspects
PERSONAL DAY CHALLENGE	0/5–5	Major: All the Challenges Minor: Change, Personal Freedom

Not taken into account were any aspects of Karma that might be present. It will be noted what a large assortment of numbers have to be considered just for one day.

There are conflicting numbers present which will not be gone into at this point. The day will be pleasant enough for Janet if she will pay attention to her challenges.

The important feature to keep uppermost in the consideration is that this is just an average day in the life of an average person. All things must be kept relative.

For correct interpretations, no factor can be overlooked, nothing can be omitted. The 22nd of October, 1973 for Janet is just another day; for a general planning to give battle, the aspects would be a little different, the chart would be enlarged, and intense study made of its aspects.

Vincent Lopez in the opening chapters of his book, "Numerology," cites several correct predictions that he made concerning the fate of nations, which came to pass. Professional numerologists make correct predictions concerning nations, businesses, individuals, as a matter of course, every day. The study of numbers is power derived through knowledge. Sepharial in his book, "The Kabala of Numbers," had this to say: "I conceive it quite possible, nay, even probable, that the higher intelligences who guide the destinies of mankind may employ them (numbers) as an universal language in order to signal to our minds something concerning the trend of things which is essential to our welfare."

Pythagoras said "The world is built upon the power of numbers," that numbers are the key to the understanding of the world.

The writing of this text itself is the fulfillment of a forecast made to this author almost a quarter of a century ago by a numerologist, when the author was age sixteen and had no intention of writing about anything, let alone numbers.

The destiny of man is pre-determined; man is allowed, permitted, freedom of action, will, only within the confines of that destiny.

If one will adjust to the things that he wishes to do in keeping with the personal day and the personal day pinnacles, one will find what he is seeking. To seek it at other times is a waste of effort.

If a person is lonely, in a strange town, seeks companionship, perhaps love, the time to go seeking is on a five or six personal day during a two, five, or six daily pinnacle. The fives will lead to love affairs without much foundation. The six will lead to permanent relationships. For those who scoff at this proposal, try seeking on a seven or four day and see what you come up with.

The final offering in this chapter will be a chart, omitting days, of the yearly vibrations for Janet in 1973.

THE YEAR 1973
(for Janet)

1973	YEAR	PINNACLES	CYCLE	PERIODICITY	MONTH	M.P.
	8	8	To 1/24	2	9	9
Jan.			6	To 2/28	UM 3	8
	U.Y.		T0 5/24	3	6/7-1	8
	2		7			1
	Chall.				1	1
Feb.	2/4-2				UM 4	9
					1/6-7	1 3
				To 4/21	2/11	2
Mar.				4	UM 5	1
					1/5-6	3 5
		5			3	3
Apr.					UM 6	2
				To 6/12	1/4-5	5 7
				5	4	4
May					UM 7	3
			T0 9/24		1/3-4	7 9
			4		5	5
June				To 8/3	UM 8	4
				6	1/2-3	9 2
		4			6	6
July					UM 9	5
					1/1-2	2 4
				To 9/24	7	7
Aug.				7	UM 1	6
					1/0-1	4 6
					8	8
Sept.					UM 2	7
			T0 1/24	T0 11/15	1/1-0	6 8
		1	6	1	9	9
Oct.					UM 3	8
					6/7-1	8 1
					1	1
Nov.				To 1/7	UM 4	9
				2	1/6-7	1 3
					2	2
Dec.					UM 5	1
					1/5-6	3 5

Chapter 13

THE UNDERTONES OF THE PERSONAL VIBRATIONS

In the past few chapters have been presented a complex variety of vibrations that will affect the life. Now the situation will be involved even a bit further. It was promised in the beginning of this text to go deep and that is what is being done.

A personal month has vibrations according to the number assigned to that month. The vibrations are strongest from the fifth to the twenty-fifth of the month. For the first two thirds of any particular month there will be in operation an undertone, setting the texture for that particular month. This texture or undertone will draw the essence of the month in the direction of the undertone.

The undertone will end on the "One" Personal Day closest to the twentieth of the month.

To find the undertone the foregoing month is added to the present month.

EXAMPLE: In 1973 the month of July is a "6" Personal Month for Janet. The month of August is a "Seven" Personal Month for Janet. The "Six" is added to the "Seven" for a total of "Four."

July   August
  6   7   =   13   =   4

The undertone for the first two thirds of August will be "Four."

What this means exactly is that Janet in the month of August will be concerned with matters of the inner self. She will be spending much time in study, meditation, thinking. She will probably spend more time alone during the course of the month than usual. These are the vibrations of the "Seven" of the month of August for Janet. The undertone of "Four" is going to bring Janet's thoughts around to work, to building something of lasting value. Despite the month vibrations of "Seven," Janet may during the first part of August be more concerned with her job than usual. The inner thinking or self-meditation, at any rate is going to be centered around her job and perhaps building new foundations in the home and/or social life.

These undertones apply to each month. They also apply to each personal year. The foregoing year is added to the present year to reach the undertone of the year. Regarding Personal Years the undertone will be in effect for the first part of the year until the "One" Personal Month is reached.

To further complicate matters, there is one exception to this rule which this author has found to be very evident in all life. The exception is "Nine" added to "One" which totals "One." In "One" Personal Months and "One" Personal Years this undertone is not in effect. Instead there exists an overtone of the foregoing "Nine." Thus while a "One" Personal Year is a year of new beginnings until the "One" Personal Month is reached in October there will exist an overtone of finish despite the new vibrations of "One."

With a knowledge of numerology any individual can, within the mind, and within moments, arrive at positive conclusions regarding any matter. This is what the author refers to as surface scanning. To go into a deep study of any individual or any matter will take a set of several complex charts. This author when deeply researching some important matter will use as many as a dozen complex charts. Many of these charts will be a maze of numbers running in all directions. This author has found the use of color on his charts a tremendous help in arriving at the correct conclusion without missing any elements. It was not the author's intention to go into matters such as color in this text but a brief rendering of color in association with numbers will be given in as much as the use of color may help the beginner in arriving at conclusions pertaining to charts. If color is to be used, it might as well be the correct color.

One	Red	"One" is Fire. Wearing red will attract "One" vibrations to the individual. It will also give off the "One" vibrations.
Two	Orange	"Two" is Water. The color that attracts or gives off the emotional togetherness of the "Two" vibration is Orange.
Three	Yellow	"Three" is Fire. The birth, the expression. The color of "Three" is yellow. If your love interest has a "Three" Soul Urge, send her yellow roses and watch the results.
Four	Green	"Four" is Earth. The color is green.
Five	Tan	"Five" is Air. The color is light brown, reddish brown or tan.
Six	Blue	"Six" is both Air and Earth. The emotional color of love or security is blue.
Seven	Purple	"Seven" is Water, the spirit, the number of God. The Royal color of purple is for number "Seven."
Eight	Gray	"Eight" is Earth. The color is black or gray.
Nine	Gold	"Nine" is fire. The color is reddish gold or pure gold.
Eleven	Pink	"Eleven" is air. The color is flesh or pink.
Twenty Two	Brown	"Twenty Two" is water. The color is red brown or brown.

There will be additional renderings of personal vibrations later in this volume. For correct interpretation all the numbers must be taken into consideration. The more there is to work with, the better will be the forecast.

This author once had a so-called professional numerologist inform him that she could arrive at a conclusion for anything using just one master chart. This is nonsense. Surface information can be arrived at by using the master, but for correct forecasting several charts will be needed. The lack of knowledge that exists even among professionals in the world of numerology is sometimes pathetic.

There also exists an undertone in the months of October, November, December. These three months will have the vibrations during any given year identical to the months of January, February, March, but will in addition, have their own respective undertones, as well as the supplementary undertones "Ten," "Eleven," "Twelve." These three numbers (10, 11, 12) will be discussed in detail in the second half of this book.

Chapter 14

THE HIDDEN NUMBERS AND
PLANETS IN RELATION TO NUMBERS

There are all around hidden numbers which play a direct influence upon life. These numbers add to what we already have, make our path easier by their presence. Numerology and Astrology are very closely intertwined, one such set of numbers can be found in the signs of the Zodiac.

Aries	=	1	Libra	=	7
Taurus	=	2	Scorpio	=	8
Gemini	=	3	Sagittarius	=	9
Cancer	=	4	Capricorn	=	10 = 1
Leo	=	5	Aquarius	=	11
Virgo	=	6	Pisces	=	12 = 3

The "Eleven" of Aquarius was not reduced. A word must be mentioned about master numbers. Their potency or the type of effect they will have upon any given life is relative with where they are found. The greatest effect will be if found on the main path of life, in the birthdate.

Pertaining to the subject of Astrology, the planets can be reconciled with the numbers. There are no hidden numbers in Astrology but we will give the reader familiar with Astrology a good indication of how to interpret numbers. The effect of the numbers crossing each other in numerology is similar to the planetary transits of Astrology.

The number "One" is associated with the Sun.

The number "Two" is associated with the Moon.

The number "Three" is associated with Jupiter.

The number "Four" is associated with the Earth, and the negative aspects of the Sun.

The number "Five" is associated with Mercury, in some aspects with Mars.

The number "Six" is associated with Venus.

The number "Seven" is associated with Neptune, and the negative aspects of the Moon.

The number "Eight" is associated with Saturn.

The number "Nine" is associated with Mars, in some aspects Uranus, also with all of the other planets.

The number "Eleven" is associated with Pluto.

The number "Twenty Two" is associated with Uranus.

In advance forecasting the following formula should be employed:

> "1" Positive Sun
> "2" Positive Moon
> "3" Jupiter
> "4" Negative Sun
> "5" Mercury
> "6" Venus
> "7" Negative Moon
> "8" Saturn
> "9" Mars

There are some professionals who will take exception to a few of the above planetary assignments, but that is neither here nor there. In the last several books I have read, no two have agreed. It is my considered opinion that the above is the most correct interpretation possible. In many cases a planet will operate in aspect with more than one number. I believe that this is where the confusion arises with professionals. The numbers are understood, the planets are understood, it is just a matter of correlating the two.

The main path of life is associated with the Sun, all else revolves around it. The Karmic Lessons are associated with Saturn. The Soul Urge is the Moon, the first vowel is the planet Venus.

Another set of hidden numbers can be found with the birthdate. Janet was born in a three personal year, in a three personal month, on a nine personal day. The essence of these numbers is "Six." The "Six" that seems to have so much effect in Janet's life. The "Six" of the Planet Venus.

Chapter 15

THE ALPHABET VALUES

Up to this point, all studies have been based upon the date of birth. Now the efforts will be concentrated upon the name. Using the date of birth it was discovered that Janet has many interesting aspects. Now it will be found that the name and the birthdate are going to tie in, to give a complete picture. A strange occurrence is going to come to pass. Using the information from the name, it will be found that it ties into her life path, cycles.

Each letter in the alphabet has a numerical value from one to nine, as follows:

1	2	3	4	5	6	7	8	9
A	B	C	D	E	F	G	H	I
J	(K)	L	M	N	O	P	Q	R
S	T	U	(V)	W	X	Y	Z	

The letter "K" has the value of eleven.
The letter "V" has the value of twenty-two.

In addition to numerical values, each letter will have different meanings, meanings that form the personality, future, past, of any given individual.

All professional numerologists agree with the foregoing chart. There are however, a few exceptions to this. In the days of early numerology, most charts stopped at the number "Eight."

The value of a letter is not in its numerical sequence in any given alphabet, but by the sound that it makes. This will be taken into consideration in the second part of this text. When Pythagoras was constructing his charts, there was no English language. Each race must be interpreted through its own respective language. This is also a warning to readers not to try to interpret charts for those born in a foreign country and using a foreign language, unless there is knowledge of the glyft/phonetic sounds. The foregoing chart stands for those born in the English speaking world in the last few hundred years. In contradistinction to those who maintain that the numbers cease at "Eight," this author would like to reply that all cycles operate in series of "Nine," the ultimate number of man. There is something more for man after the base materialism of the "Eight." There is the ultimate knowledge, universal love. Interpretation must be made with a set of numbers whose charts are made from the alphabet for which it was devised. When the chart of Pythagoras is employed, the numbers that apply to that given chart will be put to use, or rather not the numbers themselves, but the associated sounds. When interpretation is made for the modern day, English speaking world, it must be in the range of from "One" to "Nine."

Too much confusion, misunderstanding, and lack of knowledge exists today in print. Too many fine, outstanding, knowledgeable astrologers try to use numerology for interpretation when they know nothing about its secrets or mysteries what-so-ever. Numerology and astrology are inter-related, but the study of numerology is a science unto itself. Pythagoras was a genius, his charts contain many lessons for modern day numerology, but while these charts were fine for the ancient Greeks, they do not pertain to our alphabet sounds in the English alphabet in relation to numerical value of the letters.

This writer has just finished studying one volume written by, for lack of a better word, an author. In this text the author is dooming all with a life path of "Four" or "Eight" to eternal misery and suffering. True, these are hard numbers, but the positive aspects of either is large, especially with the "Eight."

Each person or author is entitled to his own opinion, but there is no excuse for the misleading of innocent readers, affecting their emotions and lives, by those with insufficient knowledge. If some of these so-called experts had investigated a little further they would have found that Pythagoras used many charts, including several which made profuse use of the "Nine."

The letters S, T, U, V, W, X, Y, Z, R, are known as the "Testing Letters" being the highest octaves of their respective numbers. These letters will present special problems in relation to the numbers which will be gone into in detail in the chapter regarding the Letter Transits or Excursion.

Chapter 16

THE SOUL URGE AND SOUL URGE CHALLENGE

The Soul Urge is exactly what the name implies. It is the urge, longing of the inner soul or self. This urge will of course be known to the person affected, but need not necessarily be expressed. Vera Scott Johnson in her book "The Secrets of Numbers" calls the Soul Urge the "Motivation." No single word better describes the Soul Urge.

The Soul Urge is found from the vowels in the name. A-E-I-O-U. In addition "W" is a vowel if united to another vowel, and sounded as one. The letter "Y" is also considered a vowel, if preceded by another vowel, or if there is no other vowel in the syllable.

To find the Soul Urge, lay out the name, place the vowel value on the top of the letters in the following manner.

6	7	5	= 18 = 9
6	16	14	= 36 = 9
1 5	13 57	5 9	= 36 = 9
JANET	AUDREY	HENDRICH	

The above method is the only correct manner to lay out the numbers. Following this procedure, the seeker will be able to obtain all necessary information, as well as locate numbers with special meanings that might be hidden behind the Soul Urge.

Janet has a number "Nine" Soul Urge.

THE SOUL URGE

A "1" Soul Urge:

Wants to dominate. Wants to be the leader. Prefers to be a loner. Seeks praise, and opportunities to create praise. Is mostly interested in the large, overall plans, as opposed to the details. Is usually capable of doing large or great things. Could be impatient and/or boastful. Wants to create on a large scale. Wants to succeed.

A "2" Soul Urge:

Seeks association, partnership, craves love, understanding. Is able to follow much better than lead. Seeks marriage, companionship. Likes comfort but is not ambitious. Is friendly, but sensitive. Is emotional, gives love, affection.

A "3" Soul Urge:

Is friendly, outgoing, social. Wants to self-express. Seeks happiness, beauty in all people, surroundings.

A "4" Soul Urge:

Craves order. Is a lover of tradition. Is steady, craves regularity in home and work. Gives and demands dependability.

A "5" Soul Urge:

Demands personal freedom in every respect. Is a constant seeker after change in all matters. Loves to travel, follow the easy road in life. Is impatient. Is usually above average intelligence. Is able to adapt to any type of situation. Seeks many varied interests.

A "6" Soul Urge:

Is a lover of family, home. Seeks to be a peacemaker. Is usually found to be very understanding, willing to listen to problems of others. Able to accept responsibility.

A "7" Soul Urge:

Prefers to live within himself. Is philosophical, intelligent, intellectual. Keeps inner thoughts to self. Loves to be conservative. Lives in the clouds, not down to earth, puts self above menial work. Hates revolutionary new ideas. Seeks silence, quiet, meditation. Much prefers to live alone.

An "8" Soul Urge:

Is the lover of big business, large accumulations, is the seeker of power, wealth, and huge success. Gives out confidence, courage.

A "9" Soul Urge:

Is the seeker of knowledge. Is self-sacrificing. Wants all to benefit from his knowledge and experience. Always ready to teach or give without thought of self.

An "11" Soul Urge:

Is selective in his associations. Is keen to gain and impart knowledge about his ideals, God. The "Eleven," being a master number pertaining to revelation and inspiration, is known as the "Messenger of the God-Force." Forms and sticks to his ideals. Has broad outlook upon life.

A "22" Soul Urge:

This is the ultimate of the two master numbers. This is the number of the person who wishes to build for humanity. Of the two master numbers, "Eleven" and "Twenty Two," the "Twenty Two" is the less self-seeking. Both numbers possessing unusual high intelligence. Ideals are of the highest, but is able to live a down to earth life.

Janet with her number "Nine" Soul Urge has a great inner desire to learn, to teach. An occupation that would serve her inner self best in life would be that of a teacher, nurse, writer.

Janet's Soul Urge can be looked into even deeper with the

numbers behind the "Nine." It is comprised of the "Eighteen," a combination of the "One" and the "Eight." It could have been comprised of a "Two" and a "Seven," etc., but it is not. These numbers "One" and "Eight" combined give us a very good picture. This shows strong willpower, the desire to be at the top, above all a dislike of taking advice.

The secondary set of numbers in the Soul Urge are "Six," "Seven," "Five." These are the numbers that will comprise some of the instincts that Janet will have in her Soul Urge. She will long for marriage, a happy home. The inner self will seek wisdom, knowledge, she will want her personal freedom, crave change. Behind the "Seven" and "Five" are the "Sixteen" and "Fourteen," these two numbers will be reserved for discussion in Karma in a later chapter.

The final influence is the total span of numbers consisting of 2 "Ones," 3 "Fives," 1 "Three," 1 "Seven," 1 "Nine." Each of these in turn will go to make up part of Janet's Soul Urge. The three "Fives" are very indicative of a strong desire for personal freedom, change. The two "Ones" are for the attainment of self. There is no doubt that Janet is a headstrong person and does not like to be crossed. In numerology all numbers must be taken into account to give a final accurate interpretation.

THE CHALLENGE

The Challenge in Janet's Soul Urge is found by subtracting the value of the first letter from the value of the last letter. The first vowel is "A" with a value of "One." The last vowel is "I" with a value of "Nine," so the Challenge will be "Eight." The first vowel is subtracted from the last vowel, or the last vowel is subtracted from the first, i.e. the lesser from the greater.

The Challenges in the Soul Urge are just about the same as the Challenges in the Birthday, only this time they do not apply to the path of life, they apply to the inner feeling within self. Janet's Challenge of "Eight" is the Challenge to achieve, to grow, to gain control, use proper management.

BIRTH

FIGURE #5

	PATH & CYCLES		PINNACLES & CYCLES		CHALL.	S.U.
	3 Plea.	9 Encom.	6 Responsibility			9
Age 9				1	MAJOR 3	
Age 18				2	Self-Express	
1966 (25) Age 27		6 Security		3	First Minor 0	
Age 33						
Age 36			3 Pleasant	4	Second Minor 3	
Age 42						
Age 45			9 Greatness	5		
Age 51				6		
Age 54			6 Responsibility			
2002 (61) Age 63		6 Security		7		
Age 72				8		
Age 81				9		
Age 90				10		
Age 99				11		

Encompassing Challenge (8) Material Aspects

DEATH

Demonstrated below is an ideal way to lay out the Soul Urge taking all aspects into consideration.

The symbol for the Soul Urge is a circle. To indicate that Janet's Soul Urge is "Nine," a circle may be drawn around it on

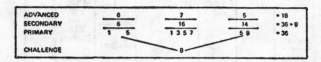

the chart. The Soul Urge is the Sun within the self. It is the drive, the center, the ambition.

More information has been gained for Janet's main chart, and thus we can supplement it further. The keyword that will be employed is "Encompassing."

The Soul Urge is not a fixed path of life as the others are on the chart, but plays a major role in the decisions one will make along the fixed path.

Chapter 17

THE QUIET SELF AND CHALLENGE

Using the consonants in the name, the Quiet Self will be found, sometimes referred to as the Quiescent Self, the Impression, the Inner Self, the Latent Self. The total of these letters will be what is vital within the self to achieve, to create, and to *accomplish* what is necessary to be accomplished in this life. This is the part of self that is the planner, builder, dreamer. This core is not expressed to friends or family, in many cases it is not even evident or realized by the self. These are the secret inner dreams of the self, many times brought to the surface in daydreams.

To find the Quiet Self, a return is made to the name layout, and the value of the consonants is entered below the name.

```
      6              7              5          18
      6             16             14          36=9
   1   5      1 3       5 7     5       9       36
   J A N E T  A U D R E Y   H E N D R I C H
   1   5   2       4 9      8   5 4 9    3 8    58=13=4
      8                        37             58=13=4
                   13
      8              4             10          22=4
      8              4              1          13=4
```

Janet's Quiet Self is the number "Four."

The keywords that apply for what the Quiet Self will activate in order to achieve and/or the secret dreams are as follows:

Number	"1"	Leadership
Number	"2"	Association, Companionship
Number	"3"	Self-Expression
Number	"4"	Work, Building
Number	"5"	Freedom, Change
Number	"6"	Responsibility
Number	"7"	Learning
Number	"8"	Material Aspects
Number	"9"	Service
Number	"11"	Inspiration, Revelation
Number	"22"	Constructive

The Quiet Self is not active except in the secret dreams of the self. Many times, a person will visit his Quiet Self in his daydreams. Thoughts are deeds, deeds are action.

Janet dreams about building a good solid foundation in home and career. This will always be of importance in Janet's life. As she dreams, thinks, wants, so shall she do.

The master number "22" which comes through as a secondary calculation cannot be attributed to Janet's Quiet Self as it was not derived from the original span of numbers. It does give Janet an opportunity to work up to this aspect regarding the Quiet Self, if she so elects.

As in the Soul Urge, the main number must be looked behind to find the secondary influence, also the individual numbers that go to make up the sum total must be inspected. Janet's secondary dreams are of money, power, the attainment of self. Going further back to the "Nines," there exists a love for humanity, a drive for knowledge. With each of the numbers, there is added something to Janet's life, dreams. The stronger the influence of the numbers, the stronger the urge or pull.

The Challenge in the Quiet Self is found in the same manner as the Soul Urge. Subtract the value of the first and last letters, one from the other, the lesser from the greater to arrive at the

Challenge. Janet's Challenge is "Seven," which was obtained by subtracting "One" from "Eight." Janet has the challenge to overcome aloofness, coldness, fear, doubt in her inner self. She must obtain faith.

The entire spectrum of the Quiet Self is shown following:

Challenge:

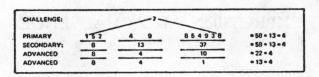

A square, the symbol of the Four Square, the limitation, may be placed around the "Four." The Quiet Self, because it is not active, is limited, contained.

The Quiet Self also makes another contribution to knowledge. It is usually correct in describing the appearance of any given person by its number. The following rendering is offered:

One	Tall, thin.
Two	Quiet, elegant.
Three	Attractive, heavy.
Four	Plain, simple, sometimes heavy.
Five	Short, lively, magnetic.
Six	Comfortable looking, jolly.
Seven	Thin.
Eight	Well dressed, prosperous looking.
Nine	Gentle, understanding.

Chapter 18

THE EXPRESSION AND CHALLENGE

The Expression is the sum total of the Soul Urge and the Quiet Self added together.

The Expression is exactly what the word means. This is what the self is expressing to the people whom it comes into contact with. This is the single element in the life that comes through, broadcasts itself to others.

The Expression is the sum total of what each individual has to work with in life. In it is contained all of the positive and negative factors that comprise the individuality. The Expression should always be—when studied—taking into consideration the type of work that one will engage in. Using the Expression as a guide, each person will quickly be able to arrive at the type of work that is best suited to his own expression; or if preferred, instead of the word expression, the word personality may be employed.

Returning to Janet's name, the Expression will be added in. In addition, the entire gauntlet of numbers will be run in a single row under the name. The reason for this is that, again, hidden numbers behind the Expression must be sought. The Expression is the sum total of all the numerical values of the letters in the name.

Janet's Expression is that of "Four," the same as the Quiet Self.

6	16 = 7	14 = 5	= 18 = ⑨
1 5	1 3 5 7	5 9	
JANET	AUDREY	HENDRICH	= 13 4
1 5 2	4 9	8 5 4 9 3 8	
8	13 = 4	37 = 10 = 1	= 13 = 4
1 1 5 5 2	1 3 4 9 5 7	8 5 5 4 9 9 3 8	= 94 = 13 = ④
14	29	51	= 94 = 13 = 4
5	11	6	= 22 = 4
5	2	6	= 13 = 4

The symbol used for the Expression is that of the Triangle. The Triangle of birth, symbolizing the birth of the Expression from the marriage of the Soul Urge and the Quiet Self.

THE EXPRESSIONS

A "1" Expression:

One who stands alone, one who leads. Ambitious, creative. The desire to achieve, create.
Negative—Egotism, imposition of self will upon others.

A "2" Expression:

One who works well with others. One who cooperates in associations, in partnerships. Usually married.
Negative—Leaning too much upon others for emotional or other needs.

A "3" Expression:

Is outgoing, self-expressing, social, friendly. An originator in art, music, fashions, drama, etc.
Negative—Boastful, life of the party type.

A "4" Expression:

The worker, the down to earth routine, the follower of the nine to five o'clock group. An admirer of solid works, through time tested methods.
Negative—Brooding, stern, repressed.

A "5" Expression:

The free spirit, the seeker of constant change in all activities of life. The traveler. Outgoing, knowledgeable.
Negative—Irresponsible and over-indulgent, especially in regards to sensuality.

A "6" Expression:

The home builder, one who is able to assume responsibility. Understanding, stability.
Negative—Jealousy, interference.

A "7" Expression:

The one who is interested in philosophy, the meaning of life. The seeker after the truth of the "whys" and "wheres" of the spirit. Living within one's own self, keeping one's own secrets.
Negative—Coldness, aloofness, sadness.

An "8" Expression:

The seeker after material wealth, success in big matters, big business. The fast moving, hard hitting top executive. Wealth.
Negative—Hardness, self-ambition, hunger for power.

A "9" Expression:

The searcher after truth, the teacher. The one with the global outlook who hates being confined to small places, small situations; must have room to move around in, build on a large scale.
Negative—Impracticality, bitterness.

An "11" Expression:

The one who digs deep. Inspiration, revelation, knowledge.
Negative—Self-superiority, fanaticism.

A "22" Expression:

The great builder, great idealist, great creator. Large vision, inspiration, faith.
Negative—Big-time operator, promoter.

The Expression is what there is to work with in life, and is one of the prime considerations for the type of work to be engaged in. The Soul Urge is the motivator, or what moves the self, what is being sought. The Quiet Self is one's dreams, what one would like to be accomplished.

The Challenge in the expression is found by adding together the Challenges of the Soul Urge and the Quiet Self. In Janet's case it is "Eight" plus "Seven" which reduce to a single digit of "Six." Janet must learn responsibility, especially in regard to her business life.

With Janet's expression of "Four," her personality calls for a job that is regular, solid. Taking into consideration her Quiet Self, it is found that she wishes to build something solid, lasting, with permanent effects. Janet's Soul Urge is to learn, to teach. What better profession could Janet find in life than that of a teacher; it meets all of her wants, needs, desires.

Looking into the secondary numbers in Janet's Expression, there is an "Eleven" present. That will give her added intelligence in her chosen work, inspiration. From the "Six" the desire for a solid home, solid job. With the "Five" the expression of freedom, change, are once again present. The total sum of all the numbers will be left for the chapter concerning the Inclusion.

There was no intention of going into symbols in this text, but what has been started might as well be finished.

The following is the complete set of symbols for the numbers, one to eleven plus twenty two, with their meanings explained, as they pertain to the "Numbers of Life."

The span of these numbers is, in itself, perhaps the best interpretation for numbers offered. This is the sum total of man's reason for existence. This is the true interpretation of the numbers in regards to man.

The Soul Urge is the soul or motivation. The expression is all the letters in the name and thus the personality.

One of the troubles that exists today in modern numerology is that so many different, well-informed people call the same element by various names. To further complicate the matter one person may refer to one element by one specific name that an-

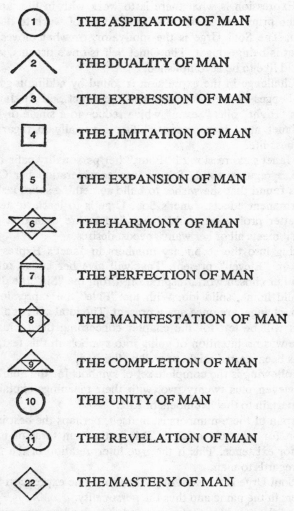

1 THE ASPIRATION OF MAN

2 THE DUALITY OF MAN

3 THE EXPRESSION OF MAN

4 THE LIMITATION OF MAN

5 THE EXPANSION OF MAN

6 THE HARMONY OF MAN

7 THE PERFECTION OF MAN

8 THE MANIFESTATION OF MAN

9 THE COMPLETION OF MAN

10 THE UNITY OF MAN

11 THE REVELATION OF MAN

22 THE MASTERY OF MAN

THE SYMBOL FOR THE PATH OF LIFE WOULD BE /\/\/\

other person associates with a different element. The important thing is that when the bottom is reached all agree with the interpretation in pretty much the same manner as their associates, and that the same element is recognized as such, no matter what it might be called.

There are today in the United States countless numbers of dedicated professional numerologists who not only understand the numbers but try to help their fellow men with their knowledge. Every once in a while someone comes along who is so completely off track that it must be commented upon. Each individual is entitled to his own opinion or interpretation. This is what makes the world go round. This author did not write this text to pan other professionals. There are on the market numerous volumes by outstanding experts in the field of numerology, however, one bad book can offset a lot of good ones. I have just read a well written text by what appears to be a rather well informed numerologist that goes into considerable detail, most of which is correct, and which, I feel, has made an outstanding contribution to the printed world of numerology in many ways, with but one exception. This author claims that the Quiet Self is the expression. The label which he assigns is actually insignificant, rather it is his interpretation which is inappropriate. The Expression called by any name is the total personality or make-up of the self. The Quiet Self is the inner person, the dreams. All the letters in the name are needed to find the personality or expression. The total of the consonants in the name cannot in any way comprise the total personality.

Chapter 19

THE INCLUSION

This chart is the knowledge and sum total of experience for all past lives lived, or what the self came to this earth with, for this life. It is the key of what we are, what will be expected from us during the course of our life in this sphere. This is, perhaps, the most important chart in this study. Based on the number values of the letters in the name, it is going to tie in with the numbers arrived at from using the birthdate. For those of you who do not accept the theory of reincarnation, the eternity of the soul, mind, spirit, it will be a personality chart that will come very close to home in all cases.

Using Janet's name, the following is found:

J A N E T A U D R E Y H E N D R I C H
1 1 5 5 2 1 3 4 9 5 7 8 5 5 4 9 9 3 8

There are nineteen letters with the following breakdown:

Value of One	3
Value of Two	1
Value of Three	2
Value of Four	2
Value of Five	5
Value of Six	0
Value of Seven	1
Value of Eight	2
Value of Nine	3
Total	19

Devise the following chart, place the total of each group of numbers as indicated in its respective position:

1	2	3
4	5	6
7	8	9

ARRANGEMENT FOR
PLACEMENT OF EACH
GROUP OF NUMBERS

3	1	2
2	5	0
1	2	3

COMPLETED

THE MEANING OF THE NUMBERS

Number One:

The ability to rely upon self, own resources. The ability to originate, create; self-assurance, aggressiveness, pride, ego.

A lack or shortage of this number means that the self is unable to stand alone, does not have enough confidence or self-drive. If this number is overly out of proportion, it would mean that the self is probably too dominant, would try to inflict own desires upon others.

The number "One" is known as the Ego Number.

Number Two:

The ability to work well in relation to others. To cooperate, associate, in domestic, other phases of life.

A lack or shortage of this number would mean that the ability of association, cooperation, is not present. Also over-sensitivity. An over-abundance of this number would mean the self is much too reliant upon others; and is quite possibly an emotional, physical, and mental drain upon family and friends. This could be an indication that the self might have homosexual tendencies.

The number "Two" is known as the Subservient number.

Number Three:

The ability for self-expression. Outgoing, social, friendly. This number relates to tremendous self-expression in the creative arts.

A lack or shortage would indicate that the self is withdrawn, not at all outgoing. An over-abundance means that the self could be a party seeker, without aim, boastful.

This is known as the Self-Expression or Social number.

Number Four:

The ability to work, to apply self to details.

Shortage or lack, would mean that the self dislikes work, especially menial or detail work.

Over-abundance indicates that the self has a tendency to smother itself with too many details or mundane tasks.

This is known as the number of Work.

Number Five:

The ability to accept change. The knowledge of the correct use of personal freedom. A desire for change.

A shortage or lack of this number would mean that the self is not able to accept change, would no doubt repress those close to him with jealousy, etc.

Over-abundance indicates the mis-use of personal freedom, the possible hurt of others by employing said freedom to the detriment of others. A seeking of change without reason. Usually an over-indulgence in matters of sex.

The "Five" is known as the number of Change and/or Freedom.

Number Six:

The ability to accept things for what they really are. The ability to accept responsibility, to adjust to situations, especially domestic.

Lack or shortage means that there is little ability to accept things for their true value. A seeking for perfection especially in marriage. A dislike of responsibility.

Over-abundance means the inner self is overly concerned with family and duties.

The "Six" is the number of adjustment.

Number Seven:

Shows a keen mind interested in facts. The number "Seven" being the number of God, shows a knowledge, acceptance of religion and/or God. This also indicates understanding and compassion.

A lack or shortage means that the self has little concern about faith or religion, might even go overboard in the other direction. Impatient, impulsive, with lack of inner faith.

Lack of "Sevens" is common; the lack will find most persons pursuing inner knowledge, or faith.

An over-abundance of this number is very rare.

The "Seven" is the number of Wisdom.

Number Eight:

When in proportion, it shows the correct interest in material aspects as well as an appreciation for their true value.

Few or insufficient eights represent a lack of concern for these elements. Also often indicates an over-whelming drive towards the accumulation of finances.

An over-abundance means the self is much too interested in money, power, the gathering of personal wealth.

"Eight" is the number of money or material aspects.

Number Nine:

When the nines are in proportion they show that the self cares for humanity, the woes of his fellow men.

A shortage of nines, which is rare, would indicate a person who has not yet obtained the knowledge of human caring or compassion.

An over-abundance sometimes causes the self to be very determined to do things his own way, whatever that might be. It also indicates an over-concern with problems of the world to the detriments of the self.

The "Nine" is the number of Humanity.

A correct proportion is determined by the number of letters in any given name.

The ideal proportion based on a total of eighteen letters would be as follows:

3	2	2
2	2	2
1	2	2

The lessons or Karma to be learned are not going to come easy, but until they are learned, any given life is going to be full of misery, as well as cause misery to others. Those with a lack of "Sixes," such as in Janet's case, will be presented with a happy marriage, a good home, a fine husband. They will sooner or later, within themselves, for reasons that are only plain to them, wish to reject this marriage, and in most likelihood will do just that. Life will teach them a lesson. At some future date they will bitterly regret what they have lost and given up. They will find neither happiness nor a good marriage again, unless they make amends. Their life will be full of misery, and unhappiness. The worst aspect of the situation is the unhappiness that they will bring to others. Those with a lack of "Sixes" will continually find responsibility and obligations waiting for them. Those with no "Sevens" will be presented with loneliness and poverty, until they learn to have faith. Those with no "Eights" will be presented sooner or later with a substantial sum of cash, which they will promptly squander, and regret the loss of later. So it goes, up and down the line. The chart of the Inclusion is without a doubt one of the most important charts in numerology. From it is learned what the lessons or Karma in life are. It can now be seen why Janet has so many "Sixes," and one can almost determine the amount of trouble, misery, and suffering Janet is going to bring to those closest to her. What she gives, she will receive. The law of the God-Force does not budge one inch. There is no just cause on earth for leaving a marriage, unless one has been deserted, or one has left with the permission of the spouse, and in so leaving has not brought emotional, mental, physical, or spiritual hurt. The subconscious mind, which feels no hunger, no pain, is the conscience of the God-Force, and will attract to us all the things necessary to make sure we learn our lessons the hard way, if we refuse to learn them of our own free will.

The God-Force has one law, one law only. No intentional hurt, physical, mental, emotional, spiritual, shall be caused to another living being without just cause. Just cause is not a fine point. It will not be stretched to cover revenge. One is free to dispose of the vermin that would infest one's home. One is free to discipline one's pet; one is not free to abuse that pet. There is little use in continuing. The law of the God-Force, is the Ten Commandments rolled up into one law. Those who choose to break this single law will find themselves in the same set of circumstances as they inflicted upon others, so that they may fully realize, understand, what their actions have caused.

This author is a numerologist, not a religious fanatic, or an evangelist. The further one delves into the numbers of life, the more one understands the law of the God-Force. There is no separation between the two.

The question of WHY has been answered to this author's satisfaction. The study of numerology is in itself a study of the God-Force.

Janet's chart indicates the following. The ego with 3/19 is in good proportion. The subservient "Two" is not strong enough, and Janet would have a tendency to dominate most personal relationships. The "One" being the positive number, the "Two" being the negative, Janet could have a problem in a romance or marriage until she gains some cooperation. The social number (3) is in good balance, and shows little problem. The ability to work (4), to apply self to details is also good. Janet will have little problem with this in life. The number "Five" is in over-balance, showing that Janet will always be a seeker of constant change in every respect as the "Five" is the pivot number. Janet will demand her personal freedom in life at all costs, and will not be smothered or put down by jealousy. The number "Six" is entirely lacking in Janet's chart. This is her Karma. She will have no ability to accept things for what they are, and will be seeking perfection. She will have a great dislike for responsibility. Janet is going to have a hard time adjusting in a marriage, and will need to marry a man who is most understanding and tolerant, or the marriage will end in divorce through Janet's departure. Returning to the "Ones" and "Twos," coupling them with the "Six," indicates that Janet must take extreme care in whom she marries. The man of her choice should be aware of her intense drive for personal freedom. The number "Seven" is not as bad as it looks, most persons do not possess this number at all. It is true that the "Seven" could be better, but Janet does possess the drive or inner search for faith. The number "Eights" are just about perfect, and Janet will attract finances to herself. With three "Nines," she may be just a bit heavy in this aspect. The understanding of humanity is present, but so is the inner drive to do her own thing. Janet could very easily be imposed upon by others.

Now to refer to the chart that has been building for Janet. Her main path of life is "Three." The "Threes" are not going to present a problem to Janet in her life, her main path is Karma free. With no lessons to be learned on her main path, she will be entirely free to follow her destiny of self-expression and creativity with little hindrance. All lessons distract from any path of life until they are overcome or learned. There is always present the free will to reject or accept the lessons. Those who can accept will find their lives richly rewarded. Those who cannot accept will soon learn that Hell is truly on this earth. Janet's main path of life is going to be pleasant, full of warmth and beauty. The Main Challenge in life for Janet is "Three." She has no problem in overcoming this, but its presence is an implicit warning to Janet on her main path of life not to scatter her energies. The Challenge is one of the most important things to be taken into consideration on any given path. Janet's first cycle of "Nine" is also Karma free as the "Nines" are in a good balance, she will be free in her formative years to grasp the all encompassing knowledge that she will be exposed to. At age twenty five Janet is going to run into serious problems. Her next two cycles are both "Sixes." She is getting a double dose, because of the complete lack of "Sixes" in the Inclusion.

The cycles were formulated from the birthdate, the chart we are now concerned with has been formed from the name. Yet one is working out against the other. Janet is going to be hit with what she considers unwanted responsibilities, especially in her domestic life. Life will most certainly present to her a set of problems, where she will have the opportunity to overcome her shortage of "Sixes." If Janet is married, and she will be, she is going to have a great deal of adjusting to do, which will come very hard for her. Taking into consideration her desire for personal freedom, the urge to divorce is going to be very strong. This "Six" represents marriage/divorce. It may be assumed that Janet will be married, at least by the time the Productive Cycle is entered. The positive path of the "Six" will give Janet a happy secure home, the opportunity to take full advantage of her main path of life. If Janet rejects the positive path and cannot make the adjustments, she is going to find herself on the negative path, her life full of problems. The first point of Attainment is again working on the missing "Six." Janet was, no doubt, more than most young girls, presented with a set of problems, responsibilities in her early life with which to learn responsibility and adjustment. How well she learned would have been up to Janet herself. The abundance of the "Six," indicates that Janet has had this problem in previous lives. The second attainment (3) having no Karma will be a very pleasant period for Janet. The point of attainment matching the Soul Urge, Janet should realize her innermost dreams, desires, during this period. The third attainment, also having no Karma should present to Janet a period of vast knowledge, will bring to her great success, achievement in her chosen field, if, repeated if, she is able to lead a positive path in the "Six" cycle adjoining the attainment. Each particular attainment has to be read in conjunction with the adjoining cycle, the main path of life. The final attainment is again coming back to the same old problem of the "Six." If by now Janet has learned to make adjustments, accept responsibility, it will be a pleasant period of a secure, happy home. If not, it is truly going to be hell on earth as adjoining the "Six" attainment is a "Six" cycle for a double dose again. The Challenges will present no major problem in her life as the Challenge of "Three" is mainly a warning not to scatter the energies. With the "Zero" Challenge Janet is going to have to be extra careful in all respects, especially during the second half of her life. The Soul Urge, of course, contains no Karma lessons. It is on the main chart, as its influence or drive is great on the life path.

The Pinnacle Cycles are the indicators at which point in life various changes are going to occur. This will not be interpreted or forecast at this point, but will be saved for the second study.

Janet's main chart can now be completed. The Expression and Quiet Self may be added to the bottom, as they too have an influence upon the life, but not to the degree of the Soul Urge. The Karmic lessons can be added to the chart and it is now complete. The author, who devised this chart, calls it the MAIN INDICATOR OF LIFE.

The Inclusion can inform the numerologist how the individual will operate in any aspect of life. What the reaction will be towards love, marriage, home, family, business, job, travel. The ability to give and take or the inability to do same. If the inclusion is coupled with the Soul Urge there will be a vivid un-

FIGURE #6

BIRTH	PATH & CYCLES		PINNACLES & CYCLES		CHALL.	S.U.
Age 9	3 Plea.	9 Encom.	6 Responsibility	1	MAJOR 3	
Age 18			KARMA	2	Self-Express	
1966 (25) Age 27		6 Security		3	First Minor 0	
Age 33						
Age 36			3 Pleasant	4	Second Minor 3	
Age 42		KARMA				
Age 45			9 Greatness	5		
Age 51				6		Encompassing Challenge (8) Material Aspects
Age 54			6 Responsibility	KARMA		
2002 (61) Age 63		6 Security	KARMA	7		
Age 72				8		
Age 81		KARMA		9		
Age 90				10		
Age 99				11		
DEATH	EXPRESSION (4) Work-QUIET SELF (4) Work					

derstanding rendered of any person's likes, dislikes, tendencies, habits.

As a brief rendering to exhibit the foregoing, the pivot number of "Five" will be used as an example. Those with insufficient "Fives" will have a strong tendency to be jealous. They will be mis-trustful, abhor change, dislike travel, will not understand or accept the personal freedom of those closest to them. The sex drive will not be strong. If the shortage of "Fives" is compounded by lack of "Sixes," these people will have an urge to dominate the home. All numbers pivot off the "Five," so when a shortage of "Fives" exists reactions will be strong, but will vary from individual to individual, depending upon the percentage and structure of the surrounding numbers.

An over-abundance of "Fives" will react in the opposite way. There will be an over-concern with sex. Change will be sought, travel will be looked forward to, jealousy will be nonexistent but in return these people will insist upon their own personal freedom as well.

Using the over-abundance of "Fives" as a point of illustration, we will couple it with the various Soul Urges, and study the reactions each particular relationship will have on love and sex.

The "Five" over-abundance in itself will present a strong sexual drive, a craving for sex, in many cases a craving for variety.

With a "One" Soul Urge—Aggressive, domineering.
With a "Two" Soul Urge—Passive but demanding.
With a "Three" Soul Urge—Pleasant, but often the unusual is sought.
With a "Four" Soul Urge—Limited to standard and accepted methods.
With a "Five" Soul Urge—Anything can happen. Tremendous drive.
With a "Six" Soul Urge—The emotions must be involved, there must be a feeling of love and companionship.
With a "Seven" Soul Urge—Will not wish to become involved in a permanent type arrangement.

With an "Eight" Soul Urge—No regard what-so-ever for others. Aggressive to the point of ruthlessness. Not interested in anything but self-satisfaction.

With a "Nine" Soul Urge—Understanding, selfless, but suffers much within self.

With an "Eleven" Soul Urge—Reacts as a "Two" with tenseness added.

With a "Twenty Two" Soul Urge—Reacts as a high octave "Four."

The "Fives" could be expounded in just this one aspect for an entire book. Coupled with an over-abundance of "Twos" in—disproportionate—relation to the "Ones," this aspect will present a bi-sexual, homosexual, or lesbian with intense drives.

Chapter 20

THE HIDDEN PASSION, SUB-CONSCIOUS SELF, ECCENTRICITY

The Hidden Passion, sometimes called the secret desire, probably best described as the intensity number, is found by examining the Chart of Inclusion, and picking out the single element with the most numbers attached to it. It is possible for an individual to have more than one Hidden Passion. This is not at all like the Soul Urge. This is the one single element in a person's life which is an overpowering drive.

Before selecting the Hidden Passion, because of the over-abundance of "Fives" found in most charts, the sum of two must be subtracted from the total number of "Fives," especially if the "Fives" are a dominant influence.

Referring to Janet's chart, the Hidden Passion is THREE, FIVE, NINE (arrived at after subtracting two from the total of the "Fives"). Janet has three hidden passions. These hidden passions present a very intense drive in the self and must be watched so that the self does not go overboard because of their over-emphasis.

The numbers one to nine have the same meanings as in other charts. For the Hidden Passion, they are as follows:

1. Drive for self.
2. Drive for association.
3. Drive for self-expression, originality.
4. Drive for work.
5. Drive for change, personal freedom.

6. Drive for achievement, position, responsibility, home, marriage.
7. Drive for knowledge, wisdom, understanding.
8. Drive for money, power, material aspects.
9. Drive for universal knowledge, all encompassing love. Drive to do one's own thing.

Regarding Janet, her drive, hidden passion, intensity, is for self, personal freedom, change, for doing her own thing. By now, all should have a pretty clear picture of Janet, so there is really no need to dwell on this subject any further.

The Sub-Conscious Self is the reaction that a person would have when presented with a problem or emergency. It is also the first thing that would enter a person's mind when presented with a new idea or project. The Sub-Conscious Self is found by subtracting the number of Karma lessons from the number nine. Referring to the Chart of the Inclusion, add up the groups where there are no numbers present, subtract this figure from nine.

In Janet's case, she has no "Sixes," but all the other numbers are covered, so one will be subtracted from nine, with the result that Janet's Sub-Conscious Self is "EIGHT."

THE MEANING OF THE SUB-CONSCIOUS SELF

1,2,3. As these numbers are never found in this chart, we will begin with the number Four.
4. This shows five lessons. The self in this case would be lost in detail. The reactions would be very weak. Vacillation would be the keyword for anything referred to this type of person.
5. The self would be irresponsible, tense, nervous. There would be much activity, with nothing much being accomplished.
6. The first thought would be of home and loved ones. Once this aspect was securely positive, this person would radiate love and understanding for others.
7. Would be aloof, unconcerned. Would refer things to the inner self, and hope for the best. Might rely upon drink.

8. Dependable, solid, could be relied upon in most any situation. Would first refer things to the material aspects.
9. This shows no Karma lessons. This person would be resigned, impersonal, probably show little concern, as most things in life are not of importance to this individual.

The Eccentricity is the way in which a person would react to a specific unpleasant problem that appeared, to him, unsolvable, or to a situation that he did not care for. This is different from the Sub-Conscious Self, in as much as the Eccentricity deals with everyday associations, or, how the life is lived on a broad basis.

The Eccentricity is found by adding the Key to the day of birth, reduced to a single digit. The Key will be discussed in the following chapter. The Key is the total of all the numbers in the first name.

J A N E T
1 1 5 5 2 = 14 = 5

Janet's Key would be "Five." Janet's birthday is the twenty fourth reduced to a single digit of "Six," so the Eccentricity is found as follows:

Key   Birthday Digit
5   6   = 11/2

Janet's Eccentricity would be a "Two," however, hidden behind the "Two" is the master number "Eleven," so in addition to the Eccentricity of the "Two," Janet would receive inspiration, and insight along this particular line.

EXPLANATIONS OF ECCENTRICITY

1. Would refer everything to self. Would stand alone, try to conquer, achieve.
2. Would seek companionship. Would try to rely upon others.
3. Would be original, create new ideas.

4. Would refer everything to work.
5. Would refer all to change, personal freedom.
6. Would refer things to home, family. Would accept the responsibility, obligations.
7. Would refer things to the inner self, meditate.
8. Would refer all to material aspects.
9. Would take the broad outlook for the concern of all.

Chapter 21

THE CORNERSTONE, BALANCE NUMBER, KEYS, AND FIRST VOWEL

The cornerstone is exactly what it implies. It is the foundation upon which the life is built. The cornerstone is found by using the first letter of the first name.

The "J," the first letter in Janet's first name, has the value of "One." Thus the number "One" becomes the cornerstone of Janet's life, the "One" being self or self-asserting, etc.

It will not be necessary to present a chart for the cornerstone as the reader by now should know exactly what each number means.

The Balance Number is the number that the self can fall back on in emergencies. This number is exactly what it says. It is the balance of the self, or what the self seeks to stand firm.

The Balance Number is found by taking the initials of all three names, reducing them to a single digit. Janet's initials are "J"–"A"–"H." The "J" has the value of "One." The "A" has the value of "One." The "H" has the value of "Eight." Added together the total is ten, which is reduced to its single digit form of "One."

EXAMPLE: J A H
$$1 + 1 + 8 = 10 = 1$$

Janet would rely very heavily upon self. The octave of her "One" is derived from the higher ten. Again, no chart will be necessary for the balance number.

The first key which is known in numerology as "The Key" is found by reducing all the letters in the first name to a single digit, as outlined in the foregoing chapter, as for example:

$$\text{J A N E T}$$
$$1 \ 1 \ 5 \ 5 \ 2 = 14 = 5$$

The Key is the indication as to how the life will be lived. In Janet's case the life will be lived with constant change, personal freedom. The numbers behind the Key can also be looked into. Two "Ones," two "Fives," one "Two." Self, attainment, personal freedom, change, marriage, divorce, sex, association.

The beauty of numerology is that everything eventually checks out.

The Second Key, sometimes referred to as the "Key Letter" is found by using the first initial of the last name (sur-name). Janet's last name begins with an "H," so her second key would be the number "Eight." The best description of this key is that this is a particular element that will be strived for.

The first vowel to be found in any given name is of importance. The first vowel is an important character trait of the self, a give away in many cases to the inner self.

The first vowel will not be dealt with too deeply in this chapter as a more thorough explanation will be given in the chapter concerning letters, again in the second study. The sound of the first vowel in conjunction with the surrounding letters is important in obtaining the correct interpretation, as well as the first vowel itself. For the time being, presented below in brief is a short explanation of the First Vowel. A true picture of particular traits will be obtained if the "W" and "Y" are eliminated as vowels.

A   Highly mental, original. The value of "One," all the drive of the "One."

E   Active, with accents on the physical.

I   Highly emotional.

O   Emotional, but tends to hold emotions within self. Secretive, self-contained.

U   Intuitive. Great emotional strain, self-sacrifice.

A complete chart for Janet of other pertinent information as discussed in this chapter and the foregoing one, would be as follows:

Cornerstone	1	Balance	1
Sub-Conscious	8	Key	5
Eccentricity	5	2nd Key	8
Hidden Passion	1/5/9	First Vowel	A

Most readers at this point should not need an interpretation of the above, but it is offered anyway.

The life will be built around self, self will be the most important factor to Janet. She will have an intense drive to get ahead, to achieve. She will be very concerned with home, family, will seek her own early in life. Above all, she will have her personal freedom, seek variety, change, as well as travel. There will be an intense inner desire to obtain knowledge, teach. She will always rely upon herself before others, will live her life with constant change and personal freedom, in all aspects. She will seek the material aspects of life, in home, business, and other areas of life. Money will be important to her, as will security. Her first vowel makes her creative, original, independent, mental, inspired, progressive. She must go forward but will not be driven. She will follow her own desires, and intuition, and will not be prone to take advice from others. She will be strong of will, energetic, ambitious, a lover of truth, and justice.

Chapter 22

OTHER CONCORDS

(The Achievement—Capstone—Life Number—
Age Digit—Name Cycle—Birth Element—
Chaldean Vibrations—Keystone—Name
Characteristic)

Several other points of information may be obtained that are
very telling regarding the life of any individual.

THE ACHIEVEMENT

This is obtained by adding the month of birth to the day of
birth. Using the birthdate of September 24th, the Achievement
number would be "Six" $(9 + 2 + 4 = 15 = 6)$.

The Achievement is WHAT must be accomplished in life.
This is one of the primary reasons for the existence of the self.
A good description of the Achievement would be that it is the
primary mission of the life. Until the Achievement is obtained
there will be tension in the life causing negativity.

As the above birthdate employed was Janet's, it is she who
must achieve the number "Six," responsibility, adjustment, cooperation, especially in regards to marriage.

The basic meanings of the numbers would apply to the
Achievement. Until the Achievement in any life is obtained, understood, and accepted, the negative aspects of the Achieve-

ment number will be in evidence throughout the individual's life.

THE CAPSTONE

The Capstone is the last letter in the first name. The first name, being the main attracting and outgoing vibration in life, the Capstone is the completion. The aspects of the Capstone indicate the manner in which the individual or personality of the self will react to daily life.

It is better to treat the Capstone for interpretation as a letter instead of its numerical digit. The same would apply to a great extent with the Cornerstone. The Capstone in the name of Janet would be "T."

The "T" indicates emotional feelings, either for good or bad, a striving for understanding, knowledge. The "T" is somewhat Karmic and pertains to lessons to be learned in life.

Again, the basic interpretation of letters and numbers would apply to the Capstone. A "Seven" Capstone would indicate a personality with a very strong indication towards drink. A "Nine" Capstone would show a person who suffers much emotionally, does not find much happiness in personal affairs, as the "Nine" is universal as opposed to individual. A "Three" Capstone would show creativity, originality, but the letter must be looked into. A "Three" derived from an "L" would indicate a person who is accident prone; derived from a "C" it would show outgoing tendencies, a free flowing personality.

THE LIFE NUMBER

The Life Number is found by adding the Path of Life number to the Expression number. This Life Number will become a power motivator in the life.

Janet's Expression is a "Four," her Path of Life number is "Three," the Life Number would be a "Seven" (4 + 3 = 7).

This Life Number will draw to Janet and create within her an intense desire for knowledge, wisdom, spirit and faith.

An additional example will be offered:

Expression 9
Path of Life 5
$$\overline{14} = 5$$

In the above example the Life Number would be Karmic as it contains one of the four Karma numbers left over from past lives. In the above, until the correct use of personal freedom is understood and accepted, the life will be negative, delays and obstacles will be encountered in life so that the lesson may be learned and accepted.

The Life Number and the vibrations from it must not be underestimated. This single vibration is what the entire life and destiny will pivot from. Interpretations from the Pinnacle/Attainments would fit closely to the Life Number and this would operate throughout the life span.

THE AGE DIGIT

The Age Digit is very informative when applied to any Personal Year. Unless an individual has a birthday in late December or early January, during the course of any calendar year he will be two separate ages. The Age Digit is found by reducing each age to a single digit and adding together.

EXAMPLE: *Year 1973*
Age before birthday in 1973 $39 = 12 = 3$
Age after birthday in 1973 $40 = 4 = 7$
Birth Digit $\overline{10} = 1$

The "Ten" is perhaps more informative than the "One." The number behind the digit must be looked into. "Ten" could be considered a form of master number, as could "33," "44," etc.

It will be assumed that in the above example the person affected was in a "Nine" Personal Year. The Age Digit will in

no way overcome the vibrations of the "Nine," but informs that
during the course of the year there will be much activity and
new starts made. The "One" especially derived from the
"Ten" of rebirth when found in a "Nine" Personal Year usually
means an end to the old way of life. In short it could mean destruction of the old life, a very trying, emotional, suffering year
full of tears while the rebirth is being experienced.

THE NAME CYCLE

The Name Cycle is obtained in a simple manner. The total
number of letters in the complete name at time of birth are
counted.

EXAMPLE: Mary Ellen Jones = 14 Letters = 5

What this means is that every fourteen years there will occur
in the life incidents of major importance, either for good or bad.
Every five years there will occur incidents of minor happenings.

This author has found this method not to be as informative
as it should be. The author has found the similar chart presented in the chapter pertaining to Ancient Numerology based
on the birthdate much more correct for use in this type of
forecasting.

Not withstanding, as many modern numerologists employ the
Name Cycle in their charts, it is presented here.

Dealing with the letters, a few well informed numerologists
will span the life with a single transit of letters and apply each
letter to a year. They further hold that when the last letter in
any single name appears, it will be a critical time in the life.

EXAMPLE: Mary Ellen Jones

The "M" would apply to the first four years and stand alone.
The "A" to the next year, the "R" to the following nine years,
the "Y" to the next seven years. When the first name is complete the second name would begin to be employed, letter by
letter, as the preceding name. At the end of the second name,

the third name would be put to use, and, when this process would be complete, it would begin again, the first name now following the last name.

The aspects of the letter itself are far more important than the numerical digit of the letter.

This author will agree that the last letter in any name when found in the Excursion will present a critical year, but does not employ the single transit of letters in his own charts.

BIRTH ELEMENTS

This will be of little informative help in numerology charts outside of additional information pertaining to personality and soul. Again, this author does not make use of the birth elements as they serve really no worthwhile purpose. They are presented here because many numerologists who were initially interested in astrology seem to feel that they are important.

The day of birth alone is used and reduced to its single digit of from one to nine, plus the master numbers of eleven and twenty two. Only three elements are employed using this method, Air, Water and Fire. Those with a day digit of "3," "6," "9" would be Air. "1," "5," "7" would be Water. The remaining digits "2," "4," "8," "11," "22" would be Fire.

While on the subject of Elements, the symbols for the four Elements will be presented.

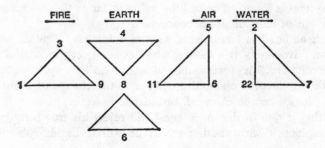

Employing the Fire symbol as an example, the "One" would be the cornerstone, the "Three" the key, and the "Nine" the capstone.

CHALDEAN VIBRATIONS

The study of the Chaldean Quaballah is a study of numbers and not a study of numerology. It is true that many correct predictions can be made using this method, especially those predictions pertaining to places as well as people. This study of numbers blends very closely with many aspects discussed in the Saga of the Numbers because all numbers have a foundation in the ancient Tarot. The employment of this Quaballah for use in the daily lives of individuals is worthless except in matters of predictions. It informs very little about the problems or mission of life.

The proponents of this theory make much use of the words "lucky" and "unlucky." This author is not knocking this method, as many correct interpretations have been made employing this system, and the students who follow this course are outstanding in their sincerity. The main use of this system when applied to individuals is to see if the birth number and name number are in harmony. These two numbers are then used as a guide for where to live, where not to live, what to avoid. In this manner it is successful. Charting these numbers, the numerologist will arrive at correct predictions on important issues in the life either fortunate or unfortunate. On the whole, however, this system is found to be of little value as far as the inner soul, drive, etc. of individuals are concerned.

This author has just finished reading a book by a rather well known advocate of this theory, who has been very successful in his predictions. The forementioned author, in all ways a sincere individual, devoted one entire chapter to the change of a birthdate. Names can be changed, birthdates, however, cannot. It is true that if one in the inner mind will reject his true birthdate and replace it with another which he will force his sub-conscious to accept that a major change will occur. This however is Metaphysics, not Numerology.

In the Chaldean method the birth number is found by employing the day of birth only, reduced to a single digit. The compound number behind the digit is also looked into. Thus a person born on January 1st, 1900 would be a "One" Birth Number, found by using the day of birth only, the 1st.

The following is the Quaballah for letters:

1	2	3	4	5	6	7	8
A	B	C	D	E	U	O	F
I	K	G	M	H	V	Z	P
J	R	L	T	N	W		
Q		S		X			
Y							

EXAMPLE:

```
M A R Y    E L L E N    J O N E S
4 1 2 1    5 3 3 5 5    1 7 5 5 3
    8        21 = 3       21 = 3
            14 = 5
```

The name number would be "Five."

These extra studies were brought forward in this chapter to give the reader a deeper insight into the study of numerology.

Knowing just the first name, month and day of birth of any individual will reveal a telling amount of information concerning this person, the cornerstone, first vowel, key, eccentricity, first two cycles, first pinnacle, achievement, personal year, etc.

THE KEYSTONE

In a first name with an odd amount of letters the middle letter is the Keystone and gives off additional personality characteristics. In a first name with an even amount of letters no Keystone exists. Thus in the name of "James," with five letters, which has an odd count, the Keystone would be the middle letter of "M." In the name of "Herman," which has an even amount of six letters, there would be no Keystone.

A   Indicates mental ability.
B   Indicates gentleness and constructive mannerisms.
C   Indicates creativity.
D   Does not always follow through with opportunity presented.
E   Very analytical.
F   Fixed and dogmatic.
G   Usually laboring under awesome burdens.
H   Keen business intellect.
I   Inspirational.
J   Justice-minded.
K   Always willing to help out others.
L   Well balanced in most aspects.
M   Very active.
N   Lover of humanity.
O   Introspective.
P   Intense love of power.
Q   Uplifting to those around.
R   Often a catalyst.
S   Shrewd.
T   Quick intelligence.
U   Self-protective and self-centered.
V   Cautious.
W   Scatters in too many diverse directions.
X   Courageous.
Y   Gentle.
Z   Full of revelation.

NAME CHARACTERISTIC

Counting the total number of letters in the full name at birth gives more additional insight. The name of Janet Audrey Hendrich has 19 letters, thus her name characteristic is "19." This may be interpreted as the fadic "1" or for advanced students may be interpreted as the compound "19."

A very basic interpretation of the compound numbers is

hereby offered. However, these interpretations apply more to Life Path than to Character.

10 Possesses self-confidence, usually carries out plans. Very often known for good or evil.

11 Gentle, imaginative, artistic, and romantic. Warns against hidden dangers and deceit from others if found in life path and great difficulties to contend with in life.

12 Very often sacrificed by others.

13 Symbolizes upheaval and the unexpected.

14 Everlasting movement and sexuality. Is open to danger because of others.

15 Benefits from others.

16 Indicates weakness, and often catastrophes. Brings disappointment in personal relationships.

17 Spiritual. Often secures fame. Brings financial success.

18 Inner strife because of materialism warring against spirituality.

19 Brings success, happiness, and honor.

20 Not fortunate with material aspects.

21 Brings success in later part of life.

22 Indicates false judgment.

23 Success, help from people in places of influence. Very fortunate.

24 Gains from the opposite sex. Warns of danger from large animals.

25 Indicates obstacles in early life, but success in later life. Those who vibrate to the "25" are very fortunate upon water.

26 Indicates prosperity through public affairs.

27 Brings authority and power.

28 Full of contradictions.

29 Brings uncertainties and often deception and betrayal from others. Warns of problems caused by opposite sex.

30 Can be fortunate or unfortunate depending upon other aspects.

31 Indicates loneliness and material stress.

32 Indicates close friends but often a lack of morality. Closely connected with magic.

33 Conservative, but in negative aspects is connected with riots and treason.

34 Indicates secrecy and also mystical.

35 Indicates inheritance and easy material living.

36 Brings authority and success but with many ups and downs.

37 Considered fortunate in personal relationships.
38 Very often brings separation and divorce.
39 Brings good health and long life with fortunate personal relationships.
40 Conservative with finances. Very literary.
41 Can be very detached from earthy things.
42 Religious and helps others. Often connected with untimely and violent death.
43 Connected with war, armies, strife, and uprising. Considered unfortunate.
44 Indicates success in almost any undertaking. Often brings success in material world coupled with loss in personal life.
45 Indicates early marriage and a life of justice.
46 Very inspirational and indicates success through originality.
47 Indicates danger from water. Somewhat unstable in all aspects.
48 Usually brings happy marriage, but is often too self-indulgent.
49 Very successful in political matters.
50 Indicates adventure but with no mishaps. Brings success and renown often through public life.
51 Usually indicates military aspects.
52 Often indicates withdrawal from the mainstream of life.
53 Fortunate. Indicates success through service in public aspects.
54 Brings respect, but often crippling in physical body.

These compound vibrations, of course, continue into infinity, but the above offering should serve to shed insight into just about anything the novice student will run into.

Before closing this chapter, I feel that not enough attention was paid to the Life Power Number, so I desire to point out strongly that this is one of the most important sources in numerology and cannot be treated in a light manner. It is the source from which all other aspects spring, the Life Path or Destiny being just the road one follows, the Power Number being the very source of direction.

Chapter 23

THE SPIRITUAL INITIATION

The Spiritual Initiation is what the inner self is being exposed to in this life as a form of life lesson.

This is found by adding the Expression, the Soul Urge, the Path of Life, and the day of birth together, and reducing them all to a single digit.

                EXAMPLE (Using Janet's numbers)
                        Soul Urge   9
                        Expression   4
                        Life Path   3
                        Birthday (24th)   6
                                            ―――
                                            22/4

Janet will experience in life conditions that will involve her with humanity in a large way to teach her to build and create for others. The lesson to be learned here is that foundations must be laid for mankind as well as for self.

The basic interpretations of the numbers will apply to the Spiritual Initiation.

To expound a little further on the foregoing chapters, the Cornerstone, Key, Capstone work in relation to each other: the Cornerstone being the base upon which the life is built, the Key being the manner in which the life is lived, and the Capstone being the end results of activities or endeavors. Employing a triangle form and using Janet's numbers the following is devised.

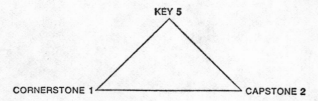

These three digits, all obtained from the first name alone, spell
out the entire mode of existence. In everyday living Janet's life
will revolve around self and will be lived with a sense of personal freedom and constant change. The end result of all activities will be emotional and will be concerned with others, who
will be counted on to aid Janet with her problems.

Chapter 24

THE UNPAID DEBTS

Concealed behind the final numbers in the name and birthdate can be found, occasionally, what are known as "hidden numbers." These concealed numbers are actually the master numbers, the "Eleven" and the "Twenty Two," and therefore signify revelation, inspiration, and knowledge. The "Twenty Two" is sometimes called the number of the medium. In addition to the two master numbers, there are four numbers of importance for Karmic purposes. These numbers are the Thirteen, Fourteen, Sixteen, and Nineteen. These four numbers represent unpaid debts from a previous life which will have to be paid in this life. This perhaps will answer the question of many who inquire why did such and such have to happen to them, or what did they do to deserve some unpleasant incident. For those who still will not accept the theory of unpaid Karmic debts and reincarnation, they are free to explain away these unanswered life questions in any fashion that they so desire.

Constructed will be another chart which will be complete in one stroke. Janet's name will be laid out, in correct fashion, along with her birthdate. The Karmic numbers and master numbers will be underlined wherever found, in the Soul Urge, Expression, Path of Life, and Quiet Self.

The numbers will now be disposed of one by one, starting with the master numbers. Within the Quiet Self is the master number "22." This does not give Janet a "22" Quiet Self as the original set of numbers did not add up to "22." The implication

6	7	5	18=9
6	16	14	36=9
1 5	1 3 5 7	5 9	36=9
J A N E T	A U D R E Y	H E N D R I C H	=13=4
1 5 2	4 9	8 5 4 9 3 8	
8		37	58=13=4
	13		
8	4	10	22=4
8	4	1	13=4
1 1 5 5 2	1 3 4 9 5 7	8 5 5 4 9 9 3 8	94=13=4
14	29	51	94=13=4
5	11	6	22=4
5	2	6	13=4

September	9=9	9
24th	24=6	6
1941	1941=15	=6
	1974=21	21=3

of the hidden "22" is that she can progress within her Quiet Self to this master number, if she so chooses.

In the Expression is also found the master number "22," in the same fashion as *it is found* in the Quiet Self. The same explanation would pertain. *Similarly,* Janet does not have a "22" Expression either.

Also, within the Expression is found the master number "11." This particular master number is in a much stronger position than the foregoing "Twenty Twos." This does not present Janet with an "Eleven" Expression either, but this number will be strongly in evidence along the lines of the Expression.

In the Quiet Self are found three "Thirteens," the strongest ones being those which directly reduce to the "Four." The Quiet Self is the dream self of the individual. These numbers are just warnings, usually below the threshold of consciousness, informing Janet, perhaps in dreams, that things do not come easily, and must be worked for.

Behind the Expression, in many prominent places, is the number "Thirteen." The "Thirteens" all bear the same relative placement, so it is only necessary to be concerned with one of these numbers. Janet has a number "Thirteen" as an unpaid debt in the Expression.

The life path is clear of any numbers what-so-ever.

In the Soul Urge are the Karma numbers "Sixteen" and "Fourteen." Both of these numbers represent unpaid debts from a past life for Janet.

Returning to the Expression, there is also the number "Fourteen" present here. This is another unpaid debt.

Janet's Unpaid Debts

Number 13—Expression
14—Expression
14—Soul Urge
16—Soul Urge

Those deeds which were left unpaid from a previous life, and which must be balanced out this lifetime, are signified by the general term "Karma." For those of you who may be Bible students, an intimation of this concept is contained in the Biblical phrases: "What you sow, so shall you reap," and "An eye for an eye, a tooth for a tooth." Long have these quotations been insufficiently interpreted. We live in a civilized world, an orderly society, where there must be rules, as well as enforcement of these rules, but no man has the right to sit in judgment upon another, although we must, of course, contain those who would be a menace to a decent orderly way of life, there is only one judge, the Supreme Being, or you may call him God, or the God-Force, or Cosmic Law, but under that law we will all judge ourselves, mete out our own punishments, or rather expose ourselves to certain situations wherein we must learn certain lessons, so that in experiencing the same situations which we have visited upon others we may achieve an understanding, a more comprehensive knowledge of life.

If the Karma Number is found in the Soul Urge it is going to interfere with the personal life of the individual affected, in collecting its debt this subconscious Karmic force will upset his dreams, his hopes, and his emotional cravings.

If found in the Expression, the Karma Number is going to interfere with the outer life of the person affected, interfere with his business, his job or other facets of life which are signified by the Expression.

If the Karma Number is found in the Main Path of Life, it is going to interfere with the entire life in every manner.

The Thirteen:

When this number is found, it is usually because the individual did not apply himself to work in a past life, but instead sat by, letting others do his share of the work. The warning in this life is to apply one's self to work, and all the details that go with work, especially in the material plane. It further denotes a fear of death which must eventually be overcome.

The Fourteen:

When this number is found, it is because of the misuse of personal freedom in a past life, especially in matters concerning sexual appetites.

The forecast includes accidents, sickness, sudden death. It will bring broken love affairs if found in the Soul Urge. If found in the Expression, it will bring disappointment in material matters. If found in the Path of Life, it warns of loss of the things closest to the self: home, business, family, loved ones, sweethearts. As the "Thirteen" reduced to the "Four" meaning work, so the "Fourteen" reduces to the "Five," meaning the misuse of personal freedom, so that this lesson must be learned the hard way, in order that personal freedom will be correctly understood.

The Sixteen:

The "Sixteen," of course reduces to the "Seven," the "One" being "self," the "Six" being love, marriage. It is the Karma of illicit love affairs that in previous lives, caused hurt to others. The "Seven," being the spirit that the "Sixteen" must be reduced to, signifies the spirit of true love, the spirit of God.

If found in the Soul Urge, it forecasts broken marriage, divorce. If found in the Expression it tells of loss of material things. If found in the Path of Life, it warns of many losses, of social place, home, business, etc.

The Nineteen:

This signifies the former misuse of power and other unpaid debts. If found in the Soul Urge, it brings exposure of secret thoughts. If found in the Expression, it forecasts loss and hard times as life progresses. If found on the Path of Life, it warns of wasted energy and time, with the end result being loss.

This author can lay out a chart and interpret the numbers. In regards to unpaid debts, known as the "Testing Numbers," he cannot answer the question of when they will be collected, or how many times each will be collected. From the reading of many charts, it seems that the usual time for collection is during the Cycle of Productivity. The only sure thing that can be answered is that collected, they most certainly will be.

I would like to leave this subject with one more quotation, this time from the Lord's Prayer as given to us by Jesus. "Forgive us our sins, as we have forgiven those who have sinned against us." The KEYWORD in the quotation is *AS*. AS we forgive others, so shall we ourselves be forgiven. Perhaps two more quotations would be in order. "Ask and you shall receive," and "Ask in my name, and it shall be given you." There is no power on the face of this earth as strong as prayer. The only possible way I know of to bypass these debts is by living a positive path, by prayer, by asking for forgiveness, by giving forgiveness, understanding, compassion, and love.

Janet has some pretty strong, steep debts to pay for in this life. We can only hope that she can find the positive path through knowledge. I am kind of glad that Janet is fictional, not real. If she were a real person, I would advise her to pick her husband in this life with care, make sure it is for all time, that she will be able to adjust, be willing to give of herself, or she is going to pile Karma upon Karma. I perhaps dwell over-long regarding this subject, but I have seen the heaviest Karma brought upon people in this life for leaving marriages unjustly. It seems to be our most pervasive (omnipresent) source of trouble here on earth. The longer and deeper I dig into the secrets of the numbers, the more I realize the eternity of the Cosmic God-Force.

A change of name or the use of a side-name will bring vibrations to the person using it. The main paths of life arising from the birthdate cannot be affected, the main essence of the name at time of birth will remain, but never-the-less, new vibrations can be attracted, unwanted ones partially discarded. A married woman will pick up the vibrations of her husband's name, especially the last name. The longer that she uses it, the stronger will become the vibrations. There are many considerations to be taken into effect for a name change. No one should change the total aspect of a name without first consulting a professional. A man who is Jimmy to his mother, Jim to his wife, and James to his boss is both giving off and attracting a different set of vibrations for each separate version of his name. A complete chart should be done using each name.

Chapter 25

THE EXPRESSION PLANES

Each letter in the name falls into a plane of expression, and has its own particular place on that plane. The letters are either mental, physical, emotional, or intuitive (spiritual). Further explanation of the letters will be given in the chapter concerning letters.

Each plane is further divided into three categories: creative, vacillating, grounded.

The layout for the chart is as follows:

	Creative	Vacillating	Grounded
Mental	A	H J N P	G L
Physical	E	W	D M
Emotional	I O R Z	B S T X	——
Intuitive	K	F Q U Y	C V

Using the entire span of letters in the name Janet Audrey Hendrich, which has a total of nineteen letters, the following is constructed.

	Creative	Vacillating	Grounded
Mental	2	5	0 = 7
Physical	3	0	2 = 5
Emotional	3	1	= 4
Intuitive	0	2	1 = 3
	8	8	3 = 19

It is found that Janet operates firstly, on the mental plane, secondly, on the physical plane, thirdly, on the emotional plane, and lastly, on the intuitive plane. Her activities are mostly vacillating, a state serving as a bridge between the creative and the grounded. Her tendency, however, would lean very heavily towards the creative, and last of all, towards the grounded.

What this means exactly, is that Janet, with her high mentality, has the ability to originate and create ideas. With her vacillating mental emphasis on the category, a mode which acts as a follow through, she has the necessary ability to follow through to completion what she has started. She is lacking, on the grounded mental level, and would have to draw on the vacillating for help here. This grounded ability is the where-with-all to see things through to completion. The physical aspects are in good proportion, but as she lacks the necessary bridge between the grounded and the creative, her physical plane would either be down in the dumps or riding sky high. The emotions do not play a large part in Janet's life, but what emotions there are will have a strong pull to run high, without grounding. The intuition is very good and should be trusted.

One plane is neither better nor worse than another plane; it is just the plane of expression upon which any given individual would operate. Those on the mental plane will test everything with their mind, all would be referred to the mind. Those on the emotional plane will refer all to their emotions, those on the intuitive plane will process all their experiences through the intuition. Those who operate mainly on the physical plane will handle matters using physical sense based considerations. It is rare to find a chart in which the majority of letters are on the intuitive plane. One to four letters here is usually the norm, and shows excellent intuition.

The creative letters are the self starters. The vacillating letters are the letters that sway back and forth, can't make a steady, firm decision. The grounded letters are firmly set and immovable.

These letters, or any letters that form a name that is currently in use are part of the vibrations that any individual would be attracting and sending out.

Chapter 26
OTHER PERSONALITY TRAITS

Reconstructing Janet's Inclusion chart here will be necessary in order to obtain additional information.

3	1	2
2	5	0
1	2	3

Traits outlining what considerations things presented to the self, will be looked upon as follows:

Idealistic   All odd numbers including the "11"
Grounded   All even numbers including the "22"
Vacillating One, Six, Twenty Two

For this chart, the letter "V" will be counted as a "22" instead of a "Four"; and the letter "K" will be counted as an "11" instead of a "Two." Janet's chart would be as follows:

Idealistic   14
Grounded   5
Vacillating 3

Janet has a total of fourteen letters of odd value, five letters of even value, with three of the total amount of letters acting as vacillating. Janet, therefore, will "test" all new things put before her through her ideals rather than the grounded aspects of construction. All things will be tested in the light if they will affect the inner self, as opposed to how they will affect others. In the world of numerology, this chart is usually referred to as the Great With-In, Great With-Out.

The abundance direction of the inner love experienced through the self's encounters with life may be measured on the following basis: For insight into the amount of love of self, the top row from the inclusion chart should be studied (1-2-3); for love of family, the second row from the inclusion chart (4-5-6) is the arc to go through. The "Seven" acts as a bridge (vacillating) between the love of family and the love of humanity. The love of humanity is the combination of the "Eight" and the "Nine."

Thus for Janet the following is constructed:

Love of Self	6
Love of Family	7
Vacillating	1
Love of Humanity	5

Janet would place her family before herself. The love of humanity is running a very close second. In the professional world this chart is known as The One, The Many, The All.

Chapter 27

THE ELEMENTS
AND ELEMENT FORECASTING

Still utilizing the inclusion chart, there is one additional chart that may be compiled: the Chart of the Elements. The best way to find true elements would be from an astrology chart, but numerology, being the closest science to astrology, is able to come close to astrology on discovering the Elements. This chart may also be used for interpreting.

The elements with their corresponding numbers are as follows:

FIRE	1	3		9
EARTH	4	6	(P)	8
AIR	5	6	(O-X)	11
WATER	2	7		22

The "Six" letters are split between Earth and Air as indicated above.

Janet's chart would be as follows:

FIRE 8, EARTH 4, AIR 5, WATER 2.

In addition, the elements for the following aspects should be found:

PATH OF LIFE	3	FIRE
SOUL URGE	9	FIRE
EXPRESSION	4	EARTH

Using the single digit value for each of the three separate names, the elements for each name may be located.

FIRST NAME   (5)   AIR
SECOND NAME   (2)   WATER
THIRD NAME   (6)   AIR & EARTH

Using the elements as a means of interpretation, the compatibility of a cycle can be matched with that of a pinnacle to see if there is conflict. A soul urge can be matched against an expression. A personal day may be matched with the path of life. The list is endless. Each name may be matched with any other number in the chart to find their relation. The expression and soul urge may be matched with the expression and soul urge of any other person to find the compatibility between the two.

The names may be used as a guide for what is being sent out, and what is being received.

In interpretation, the main number to always watch is the Major Challenge. If it is in conflict with any of the other numbers on the main path of life, there is going to be trouble. If a Cycle or Pinnacle matches the Challenge, special attention must be paid to the Challenge at that point or conflict is going to arise.

The other simple way of interpreting compatibility between numbers is the system of odds and evens. All the odd numbers (1-3-5-7-9-11) are compatible with each other. All the even numbers (2-4-6-8-22) are in harmony with each other. The odd numbers and the even numbers combined run into conflict with each other.

This system of matching odds and evens is simple, but does not hold true in all cases. There are exceptions to this which will be discussed in the second study. One of the dangerous combinations is that of 4-8.

Following is the chart of how the elements mesh with each other:

FIRE WITH: FIRE, Powerful, but mostly turmoil due to excessive power.
AIR, Harmony.
EARTH, Restrictive.
WATER, Explosive, but workable.

AIR WITH: FIRE, (See Above)
AIR, Powerful, but not stable.
EARTH, In conflict.
WATER, Workable.

EARTH WITH: FIRE, (See Above)
AIR, (See Above)
EARTH, Workable, but very hard.
WATER, Harmony.

WATER WITH: FIRE, (See Above)
AIR, (See Above)
EARTH, (See Above)
WATER, Not usually workable as too self-containing.

Following is a chart of what each of the elements is expressing:

FIRE,	1	Originality, creativity.
	3	Self-expression.
	9	Universal love.
AIR,	5	Understanding.
	6	Responsibility.
	11	Universal understanding, faith.
EARTH,	4	Work.
	6	Responsibility to family.
	8	Material aspects.
WATER,	2	Personal emotions.
	7	Universal understanding.
	22	Universal emotions.

Constructed below is a chart for Janet using the main points, which could be considered as points of expression in her life.

THE INCLUSION		1	2	3	4	5	6	7	8	9
		3	1	2	2	5	0	1	2	3

PLANES OF	Creative	8/19	Idealistic	14
EXPRES-	Vacillating	8/19	Vacillating	3
SION	Grounded	3/19	Grounded	5
	Mental	7/19	Self Love	6
	Physical	5/19	Family Love	7
	Emotional	4/19	Vacillating	1
	Intuitive	3/19	Humanity Love	5

THE ELEMENTS: FIRE 8, EARTH 4, AIR 5, WATER 2.

In bringing to a conclusion this basic study concerning Janet, the foregoing chart has presented the correct manner to lay out a name and a birthdate. All the pertinent information applicable to Janet's main life vibrations are easily picked out.

With the exception of the personal yearly vibrations, everything discussed in the study to this point, is contained. It is the author's feeling that no interpretation of this chart is necessary.

There will be a further study pertaining to Janet offered in the Excursion, but this will need its own set of charts, which are entirely different from what has been worked with to this point.

MASTER CHART

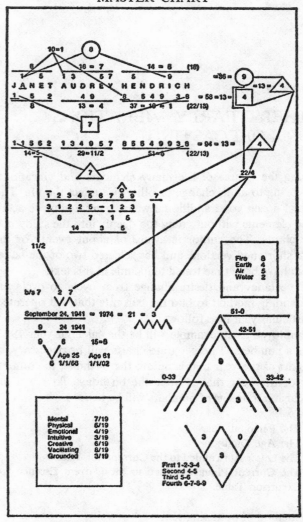

Chapter 28

OTHER YEARLY VIBRATIONS
FOR FORECASTING

During the course of life many elements and vibrations come into being to alter, change or otherwise affect the life. There are several dozen good additional ways to get a glimpse at a few of these elements without going too deeply into the study of particular charts. The author is aware of about twenty or thirty of these shortened versions and has selected two of the better ones which have been time tested to include in this text.

Expectancy and desire change from cycle to cycle and one outstanding method to find the currents that will operate during a particular year is as follows:

Employed as an example will be the calendar year 1973 using Janet's numbers. Two separate charts will be necessary, one for the part of the year that is before the birthday, the other for the part of the year that is after the birthday. To reach the final conclusion four sets of numbers will be needed.

1. The Personal Year
2. The Age Digit
3. The Letter Aura added to the Current Sub-Path
4. The Current Pinnacle added to the Current Essence from the Excursion Table.

The method of obtaining same:

1) The Personal Year factor should be well known to all at this

point. The calendar year 1973 is an "Eight" Personal Year for Janet.

2) The Age Digit was discussed in a previous chapter. However, for use on this chart it will be altered to a slightly different form. In 1973 before her birthday Janet will be age 31 going on age 32. For the digit to employ before the birthday both ages are reduced to single digits and added together (31 = 4, 32 = 5; 4 + 5 = 9). The digit employed before the birthday will be a "Nine." For the remainder of the year after her birthday Janet will be age 32 going on age 33. Both of these ages are reduced to single digits and added together (32 = 5, 33 = 6; 5 + 6 = 11/2). The digit that will apply after the birthdate is 11/2.

3) The Letter Aura is obtained by taking each letter in the first name and applying it against nine years of life. In the name "JANET" there are five letters. The "J" would be in operation from age 0 to age 9. The letter "A" would then follow from age 9 to age 18. The name Janet would span a forty five year period at which time the original "J" would be returned to and the process would start all over again. This process, using the letter interpretation as well as the numerical value of the letter, is in itself, a good way to pick up a minor undercurrent that will operate for each nine year period.

Regarding Janet, the letter that would apply for the ages involved would be the letter "E" for both the period before the birthday and after the birthday during the year 1973. Therefore, the digit that would form the first part of this combination is a "Five."

The Sub-Path or Life Cycle is or should be well known. It is "Six."

The "Five" is added to the "Six" for a total of "Eleven/ Two" and the digits that form the third part of this chart have been found, for both the periods of before and after the birthday.

4) The Life Pinnacle is also well known at this point, if the author does not assume too much, and it is "Six" for both before and after the birthday.

The essence from the Excursion Table or, as it is sometimes referred to, the Immediate Period Table, will not be discussed in this chapter. This is an involved process and will be gone into in great detail in a following chapter. For the time being the author will supply the necessary figures. In both instances, both before and after the birthday, the Essence is "Eight."

The "Six" is added to the "Eight" for a total of "Five" (6 + 8 = 14 = 5).

All the necessary digits have now been found. One last word of caution. In many instances the digits involved will change at the time of the birthday so care must be exercised in the computations.

By adding the Personal Year (1) to the Age Digit (2) the Spiritual aspects of the period will be obtained.

Addition of the Letter Aura/Sub-Path (3) digit to the Pinnacle/Essence (4) digit will give the physical aspects.

Addition of the two above totals together will give the major overtone for the period.

Addition of the Personal Year (1) to the Age Digit (2) in turn added to the Pinnacle/Essence digit (4) will indicate a major factor to be concerned with.

	Before Birthday	After Birthday
EXAMPLE:		
Personal Year (1)	8	8
Age Digit (2)	9	2
SPIRITUAL ASPECTS	17 = 8	10 = 1
Letter Aura/Sub-Path (3)	2	2
Pinnacle/Essence (4)	5	5
PHYSICAL ASPECTS	7	7

Spiritual Aspects	8	1
Physical Aspects	7	7
OVERTONE	15 = 6	8
Personal Year (1)	8	8
Age Digit (2)	9	2
Pinnacle/Essence (4)	5	5
FACTOR	22/4	15 = 6

When the student has reached the point of full understanding of all the numbers, the numbers behind the final digits will play an important role. However, for the time being, concern will only be given the final digits.

The period of January 1st to September 24th in the year 1973 is going to present to Janet the Spiritual aspects of "Eight." This will involve Janet in a Spiritual or inner-self way with finances, position, power, possible Karmic debts. After her birthday and until the end of the year a rebirth will occur, new ideals, new thinking, perhaps an entire new outlook upon her life.

The Physical Aspects are the same both before and after the birthday for the entire span of the year "Seven." Janet will spend much time alone this year, and perhaps feel much loneliness.

The Overtone is going to present Janet with a period of love, romance, responsibility, adjustments, etc. before the birthday. The last three months are going to again present a concern with the "Eight."

The Factor of 22/4 before the birthday is going to present a concern with work (4) and a period of laying foundations or building (22) on a large scale. The Factor after the birthday again matches the Overtone "Six" and will add much strength to the aspects.

In New York City there is an outstanding numerologist by the name of David Clarkson Swarm who has appeared on many radio programs in the East. David has employed this chart in the past few years to thousands of people's charts, and informs

me that it has never erred. I have used this method on countless
charts and found it to be not only informative, but also exact.

The following form can be applied to this chart for easy interpretation:

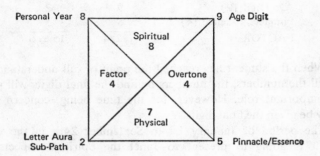

Personal Year 8 ─────────────── 9 Age Digit

Spiritual
8

Factor   Overtone
4   4

7
Physical

Letter Aura 2 ─────────────── 5 Pinnacle/Essence
Sub-Path

The above chart is Janet's before her birthday.

For the second forecast method the Month and Day of birth
reduced to the Single Birth Digit will be added to the Personal
Year. (The addition of the month and day of birth together
is of course the "Achievement" and is known in professional
circles as the Birth Digit.)

Employed again will be Janet's digits.

$$\begin{array}{ll} \text{Birth Digit} & 6 \\ \text{Personal Year} & 8 \\ \hline & 14 = 5 \end{array}$$

Now a new element has entered the scope. The element of
change.

This change may be tied in with the factors involving the
"Six" as the "5" and "6" go well together in love aspects. It
may also indicate change in other factors. The "Sevens" and
"Eights" are very heavy in these charts and, using this final element of "Five," I would interpret this especially with the Spiritual Aspects of "8" before the birthday and "1" after the birthday as being involved in a spiritual rebirth. These rebirths,
which always seem so brutal at the time, are always for the best

after they are over and the transformation is accepted. If this matter was pursued a little further, and the Universal Year of "Two" (1973) were added to the total of "Five," an essence of "Seven" would be obtained truly indicating a Spiritual Change.

Time and time again in order to secure a better understanding many numbers and many factors have to be looked into. The total essence of these factors is sometimes the final key.

All of these factors and tones will, of course, operate within the Personal Year vibrations of "Eight."

A major overtone to the life span may be found by employing an old Chinese numerology chart. The individual digits are used from the entire birthdate. A very brief outline is now presented.

BIRTHDATE: 9-24-1941

Each digit is placed in its respective category as follows:

	3	6	9
EXAMPLE	2	5	8
	1	4	7

			99
COMPLETED	2		
	11	44	

A brief and simple interpretation would be when the diagonal line is complete (1-5-9) things will come easy in the life.

When a vertical line is complete (1-2-3, 4-5-6, 7-8-9) things may be obtained only by constant effort.

A complete horizontal line (3-6-9, 2-5-8, 1-4-7) denotes an easy flow to the life with constant ups and downs.

No completed lines would indicate a life blocked in many areas and tremendous effort would have to be put forward to overcome the barriers.

An abundance in any number would give immense drive pertaining to the attributes of that number.

The number at the base of either the vertical or horizontal lines is the key to the type of struggle which will be encountered.

Chapter 29

THE LETTERS

Each letter in the alphabet has its own special meaning; some are mental, while others are physical, emotional, or intuitive. Many of the letters are just what they appear to be. The letter "O" is closed, self contained. The letter "A" is planted firmly on the ground, well bridged, reaching for the sky. The letters play a large part in forecasting for the past, present and future. A true understanding of the letters would be a separate text unto itself. It is also important to interpret what a grouping of letters together would mean. This takes time, patience, as well as understanding. How the letters are used to forecast will be investigated in the next chapter, concerning the excursion chart. A deeper understanding of the letters will also be offered in the second part of this text. Listed below is a simple breakdown of the letters, some of their basic meanings.

A   Mental, original, independence, leadership, direct, inspired. The basic meanings are change, new activities, travel. Often indicates a change of home.

B   Emotional, self-contained, shy, love seeking. "B" pertains to the emotional health, and is a sign of emotional problems when it appears. It is also a sign of deep emotional love affairs.

C   Intuitive, expressive, balanced, has special meaning for the medium, the psychic.

D   Physical, efficient, practical. The transit of a "D" will usually
    bring lowered physical health. It is also a sign of travel.

E   Physical, inspired, helpful. The sign of physical love affairs or
    marriage. The "E" further pertains to change, new activities,
    could mean a possible move of home. It also pertains to travel.

F   Intuitive, uncertain, hard working. Means responsibility. Be-
    cause it is the sixth letter, the responsibility is usually of the
    domestic type.

G   Mental, expressive, alone. Pertains to secrecy. A good letter to
    see appear because it will bring with it the positive gain of ma-
    terial wealth.

H   Mind, advancement, accumulations. Being the eighth letter it
    pertains to money, but also being vacillating, the money could
    be either gained or lost.

I   Emotional, high strung, repetitive, passionate, vacillating. Op-
    erating from one extreme to the other. The appearance of the
    "I" brings with it a bad case of nerves or high strung emotions.
    Tension. It could cause delays and accidents.

J   Mental, vacillating. Being a "One" letter it is mental, but it
    does not possess the inspiration of the "A." This letter usually
    pertains to responsibility of a mental nature.

K   Intuitive, receptive, the master eleven. Inspiration, revelation.
    Because of the high tension of the "Eleven," the appearance of
    the "K" could bring a set of bad nerves with it.

L   Mental, slow moving, all experience submitted to the mental
    plane for review and consideration. This letter is associated with
    travel.

M   Physical, practical, being a "Four" letter it signifies hard work.
    It could be unfeeling, unexpressing, snarling. "M" being physi-
    cal, hard, pertains to health of a lowered nature. It is also a
    traveling sign. It further indicates love affairs or marriage of a
    physical nature. The "M" is a hard letter. The love affairs could
    well be unhappy ones.

N   Mental, being mental as well as a "Five" letter it would indi-
     cate a move of home, or changes of a mental type. It will bring
     with it new activities, further pertains to sensual matters, namely
     sex, love affairs, marriage. It also is connected with finances and
     money.

O   Emotional, powerful, strong, willful, brooding. The "O" being
     a "Six" letter pertains to responsibility, to love affairs or mar-
     riage. It is also very divorce prone. Under its sign, a consid-
     erable amount of travel might be incurred.

P   Mental, self-sufficient, inexpressive. The "P" is associated with
     secrecy.

Q   Intuitive, unstable, erratic, could mean high mentality or just
     the opposite. The "Q" being an eight letter would pertain to
     finances.

R   Emotional, understanding, high-powered. The "R" produces
     high emotions or could produce bad nerves. It is another of
     these letters that could cause sickness, delays, accidents. It is
     a signifier of loss, especially emotional.

S   Emotional, the most emotional of all the letters. The appearance
     of the "S" is going to bring heavy emotions, usually bad.

T   Emotional, spiritual, high strung, full of self-pity. Change will
     usually happen under its transit. New activities will take place.
     Possible moves, love affairs or perhaps marriage.

U   Intuitive, unwilling, slow, conservative, attracting. "U" is the
     letter that represents financial loss, could bring with it a bad
     case of emotions over the loss.

V   Intuitive, the high master number of "22." The great builder.
     As the "11" it also means inspiration, revelation. This is further
     the sign of the true mystic. The "V" is further related to the
     moon, and would have all the attributes of the "2" Moon sign.
     The transit of the "V" will bring travel with it.

W   Physical, explosive, vacillating, powerful, erratic. The double
     "V." It will bring travel, change, new activities. Possible move
     of home or business. Being a "Five" letter it also pertains to
     love affairs.

X   Emotional, sometimes associated with the black arts. Turmoil,
    self-pity. Being a "Six" number, deals with adjustments, love,
    mostly of the sexual type.

Y   Intuitive, vacillating, perceptive, erratic. The "Y," being the
    seventh letter, pertains to secrecy.

Z   Emotional, understanding, inspired. The "Z" being an "Eight"
    letter would pertain to finances but because of its nature would
    also pertain to secrecy.

It is of importance when interpreting letters to remember
value and octave on which they are found.

Chapter 30

THE EXCURSION

It is not necessary for one to be a fortune teller in order to achieve a fairly good idea of what is in store for him in the future. A correct interpretation of the numbers, and letters combined will give a pretty fair picture.

At the time of birth, via the name, a good portent of things to come was laid out. Who laid it out? The answer is that you, yourself did, before your birth. You planned your life, picked your parents to fit the circumstances of planning, even picked out the name and birthdate.

The last chart in this first study will now be set-up. This chart will be for the past, present, and future.

In 1973 Janet will be thirty two years old, so inserted on the chart will be the ages of thirty to thirty five, as we will concern ourselves with this period. This will show us the high points in her life during this period, what will occur in the immediate future.

Along the side of the chart, running in a row, enter the ages that it will be concerned with.

AGE
30
31
32
33
34
35

Using Janet's first name, the numerical values will again be obtained.

JANET
1 1 5 5 2

If the chart were to start at birth the "J" would be placed next to the first year. The "A" would be placed next to the second year. The "N" having a value of "Five" would be used next to the next five years, as would the "E," with the same value of "Five," be used for a five year period. The "T" with a value of "Two" would then be run for a two year period. The "J" would then be returned to, and the procedure would be run out again. These letters are in operation from birthday to birthday, so on a chart that was started in the beginning, the first age to be entered would be a zero. Thus the first set of letters would be in transit from birth to the first birthday. The second set of letters would be in operation from the first to the second birthdays. We are now searching for the letters that will fall from the thirty first to the thirty sixth positions to lay out on the chart. The letters which correctly fit this position are N–N–N–N–N–E. They will be entered on the chart as follows.

It is important that it is understood fully that the very first letter would not pertain to the first birthday, it pertains to the first year, represented by the "Zero" birthday, representing the age of "Zero" to "One." Age "One" represents the second year.

AGE	TRANSIT
30	N
31	N
32	N
33	N
34	N
35	E

Concerning Janet's second name, the same procedure is followed, the correct letters are placed in their proper places.

AUDREY
1 3 4 9 5 7

```
AGE  TRANSIT
30    N  U
31    N  U
32    N  U
33    N  D
34    N  D
35    E  D
```

Using the exact same procedure, suit will be followed with the third name, in exactly the same manner. The name to be used on all excursion charts must be the exact name (entire) as of time of birth.

```
H E N D R I C H
8 5 5 4 9 9 3 8
```

```
AGE  TRANSIT
30    N  U  R
31    N  U  I
32    N  U  I
33    N  D  I
34    N  D  I
35    E  D  I
```

The three letters on each line must have their numerical value added together, entered alongside the line. This becomes the essence of the year.

EXAMPLE:
```
Age 30  N  U  R
        5  3  9  =  17  =  8
```

The Essence from the thirtieth to the thirty first birthdays is "Eight."

```
AGE  TRANSIT  ESSENCE
30    N  U  R     8
31    N  U  I     8
32    N  U  I     8
33    N  D  I     9
34    N  D  I     9
35    E  D  I     9
```

The correct personal years, and universal years will be entered for each of the ages on the chart. Janet's thirtieth birthday was in 1971, that was a "Six" personal year for Janet, a "Nine" universal year.

AGE	TRANSIT			ESSENCE	P.Y.	U.Y.	DATE
30	N	U	R	8	6	9	1971
31	N	U	I	8	7	1	1972
32	N	U	I	8	8	2	1973
33	N	D	I	9	9	3	1974
34	N	D	I	9	1	4/22	1975
35	E	D	I	9	2	5	1976

The vibrations of the letters and the essence are in operation from birthday to birthday, while the vibrations of the personal and universal years are in force from January 1 to December 31. The final entry can now be made on the chart. This is the duality. A little further explanation may be in order. The vibrations of Janet's thirty first year pertaining to letters, essence, will be in operation from September 24 to September 23 of the following year. The yearly vibrations will be in operation for the calendar year. What this means is that the entire set of vibrations for Janet concerning this given year will be split. From September 24, 1972, until December 31, 1972, she will have the following vibration.

$$(N \quad U \quad I \quad 8 - 7 \quad 1)$$

From January 1 until September 23, 1973, the following will be in effect (N U I 8 − 8 2).

A further example is offered.

AGE 31	9/24/72 to 12/31/72	NUI	8 / 7 1
	1/1/73 to 9/23/73	NUI	8 / 8 2
AGE 32	9/24/73 to 12/31/73	NUI	8 / 8 2
	1/1/74 to 9/23/74	NUI	8 / 9 3

Discourse concerning the duality can now be continued. The single most important element on this chart is the essence. When the essence is the same as the personal year, a negative

effect comes into force, known as the duality. This duality will
be in force in Janet's case, if she is affected, for the periods of
9/24 to 12/31, and/or 1/1 to 9/23, or longer.

The duality will be entered between the essence and the personal year, lines will be drawn to connect them if any duality
appears. With this operation the chart will be complete.

AGE	TRANSIT			ESSENCE	DUALITY	P. Y.	U. Y.	DATE
30	N	U	R	8		6	9	1971
31	N	U	I	8		7	1	1972
32	N	U	I	8	8	2	1973
33	N	D	I	9	9	3	1974
34	N	D	I	9		1	4/22	1975
35	E	D	I	9		2	5	1976

It is discovered from the foregoing chart that the duality of
"Eight" is in operation from January 1, 1973, until December
31, 1973. The duality of "Nine" is in effect from September 24,
1974, until December 31, 1974.

The duality acts as a negative factor, to wit:

1–1   Excessive activity, no results.
2–2   Bad emotions, poverty, disappointment, lowered health.
3–3   Scattering of self, bad nerves.
4–4   Immense work, hardness, limitation.
5–5   Misuse of personal freedom, immoral sexual activities.
6–6   Excessive responsibility, discord at home.
7–7   Withdrawal, limitation.
8–8   Financial loss, lowered health.
9–9   Loss, sacrifice, bad emotions.
11–11   Bad nerves, mental strain.
22–22   Nervous breakdown, possible insanity.

A further explanation of combinations of numbers may be
obtained from the second study in this text.

As the essence is the single most important ingredient in this
chart, offered now is what the essence usually means. But as the
full chart must be taken into consideration, this interpretation
of the essence will not apply in all cases.

1   New beginnings, assertion of self, might mean that the self is alone as opposed to being with others or married. It is usually a period where the self must go it alone, will spend lonely times.

2   Emotions, association, subservience, love affairs, marriage, divorce, strife.

3   Pleasant, social.

4   Work, limitation, hardness.

5   Change, travel.

6   Responsibility, obligations, marriage, divorce, love affairs, sex. A possible move, harmony, strife.

7   Wisdom, knowledge, loneliness, poverty, great gain. Anything can happen in the transit of the "Seven."

8   Lack of cash, concern about finances.

9   Emotions, finish, completion, change, loss.

11 Inspiration, attainment, the aspects of the "Two" could also apply. Tense, nervous.

22 Great undertakings, projects. The aspects of the "Four" could also apply.

The letters in the transit are explained in the chapter concerning letters, a further explanation is offered in the second study. The letters in transit during any given year will attract to the self the vibrations which they represent, but the essence is the over-all important feature of the year. A letter pertaining to love affairs means that the opportunity will present itself to the self. This does not mean that it will be done. Each individual has free will. The absence of a letter pertaining to love affairs does not mean that one cannot take place during the year. These letters are just the most important aspects of each given year. The personal years and universal years play an important role. By referring to the chapters pertaining to them, understanding will be made clear. It is important to note where one set of letters ends, and another set begins. This will bring new features into the life. First vowels should be taken into consideration, especially if the first vowel is "A." This will be a big change, usually a move of home. Other factors should also be taken into consideration such as the Pinnacles, Challenges, Cycles, Path of Life, Expression, Soul Urge. Each letter should be carefully inspected. An "S" will bring emotions, upsets, etc. If emotional letters appear on the chart it is possible to trace them back to their intersection with another letter, thus gaining knowledge of the cause of the emotions; *although* this last procedure does not hold true in all cases.

A travel letter must be studied on the planes of expression to see if the travel is emotional, physical, mental, etc.

Referring to Janet, starting in 1971 at age 30, it is found that the first letter is "N," meaning change, activities, possible move, love affairs, marriage, of a mental nature. We will assume for a point of information that Janet was married prior to 1971. The line of "Ns" running down the chart is her marriage line. The dropping of a marriage line at any point does not mean divorce, unless the other signs call for same. It is found that every single year Janet will be making a change of activities, possible moves of home might be undertaken. The "N" also pertains to finances; Janet is in some way concerned with this aspect. We find in the second row the letter "U," which means financial loss. Under this letter she is suffering from a bad case of emotions due to the loss. The essence of these three years are all eight which is in keeping with the "U," and shows a great concern over material aspects. The duality at age 31 which continues until age 32 shows big financial loss, a lowering of the health. At age 33 the financial loss gives way to the "D" indicating physical health of a lowered nature. Janet, because of the financial loss and negative emotions it generates, has brought on a lowered vitality or health problem. The "D" also means travel, so it may be assumed that Janet's health is not too badly affected, she no doubt will be taking a few vacations or trips to get back some of her strength. It is discovered with the "R" that Janet has just ended a bad case of emotional nerves that have been affecting her for the past several years. In looking at the "I" that follows it is noted that the emotions have not gone after all, but just changed in texture. Looking across 1971 it is seen that Janet's marriage is remaining firm, but she is changing activities. She is losing money, as well as suffering from a bad case of nerves. Janet's personal vibrations

here have called for adjustment in her domestic life; the outside
vibrations have called for loss, emotions, sacrifice, finish, completion. The same set of circumstances prevail in 1972, 1973.
There seems to be little change in Janet's affairs. Her personal
year in 1972 is the "Seven" which is a bad year for finances. In
1974 the financial loss seems to stop, the essence of the year,
and the ones that follow become finish. The duality is going to
bring a big loss, sacrifice to Janet, along with a bad case of
emotions. In 1975 under the "N" sign of change of activities,
the "One" vibration of the personal year, Janet will change
jobs, the outside vibrations being those of work. 1976 will be
bringing a change for Janet, hopefully for the better.

Nothing but the high points have been touched in this brief
rendering of a short period in the life of Janet.

In ending this study concerning Janet, it is unfortunate that
she could not have had a better send-off, but that is the way the
numbers read. A cheerful note is that things are not as bad as
they appear as Janet's main path of life is the pleasant, expressive "Three."

A knowledge of the numbers will help all in planning their
lives; the knowledge of what is to come or what is expected will
aid all in adjusting themselves, and making plans. To take advantage of good vibrations, sit tight during bad vibrations.
Above all, every single individual has freedom of choice, free
will.

To return to the Excursion Chart which is sometimes called
the Immediate Period Table, the apex of letters must be
watched. Using the name JAMES as an example there would be
a rotation of the letters "S-J-A" in a three year period. This is
very informative. This is a transition period of emotional death
and rebirth, a new form of life. The trinity of the "Ones."

The duality of the Essence and Personal Year has been gone
into in detail. There also exists a duality of letters. When two
identical letters appear in the same year additional problems
will occur. The most critical of these years will be when one set
of letters is ending and a new set beginning. The letter duality
will present the following aspects.

A—A   The same as the 1—1 Duality, over-activity, little results of a concrete nature.

B—B   Very bad emotional years.

C—C   The individual involved would be very accident prone.

D—D   Indicates serious illness.

E—E   Bad nerves, female sex organs could be adversely affected.

F—F   Possible heart attack.

G—G   Serious illness, treachery on the part of others.

H—H   Critical in matters of health. Could result in death but to correctly interpret this duality the essence must be taken into consideration.

I—I   A period of sacrifice. Immense emotional pulls.

J—J   Over-burdened with responsibility. Tense, some of the attributes of the A—A would apply.

K—K   Nerves would be on edge of break-down.

L—L   Accident prone.

M—M   Similar to D—D, indicates serious illness but recovery will be quicker than D—D.

N—N   Possible quick death by accidents due to purposeless over-activity.

O—O   Prone to heart attack or other serious disorders pertaining to the heart.

P—P   Indicates long term illness.

Q—Q   Would indicate break-down under pressure. In some respects worse than the H—H but again essence must be taken into consideration.

R—R   Accident prone. Scale of living, if accidents could be avoided, would be on international scale.

S—S   Possible emotional break-down.

T—T   Possible death, possible deception from others.

U—U   Over-indulgence in sensual matters. For females, possible hospital care for female organs.

V—V   Possible illness that could result in loss of vital organs or limbs.

W—W   The aspects of the "Five" letters as well as the aspects of the double "V."

X—X   Extreme misery, possible insanity.

Y—Y   Extreme loneliness.

Z—Z   The aspects of the H—H and Q—Q. (Note—this author has never seen a chart with the double "Z." He feels that the results of this combination would be disaster.)

Almost all duality is negative. Again the warning is put forth that for correct and proper interpretation the entire span of letters and numbers as well as essence must be taken into consideration. Forecasting cannot be done with one single element alone. The essence in the Excursion Table is a forecast unto itself. "Nine" not only means finish, completion, it also means long distance travel if coupled with the appropriate letter. Coupled with other letters it could bring romance, usually with a foreigner. The letters must be watched to see what planes of expression they operate upon. They must further be watched for which level of the expression plane they form upon. This author could fill a large volume with nothing but the Excursion Table and still not scratch the surface. The only way to learn to forecast from this table correctly is to become a student of the numbers. This table is a most valuable and informative aid in forecasting and no correct forecast can be made without employing it.

A brief interpretation can be used with the letter "A": If coupled with a "9" essence or personal year, the result will be long range travel. If paired with a "7" essence or personal year it will bring travel upon, over, or near water, usually eastbound.

Accepting the theory of reincarnation, there are very few persons living this life who do not have lessons to learn. Until these lessons are met, overcome, understood, accepted in the heart, there will exist tension, discord, problems, negative aspects in any life. The main life challenges, the achievement, the inclusion and the birthdate challenge must be given prime consideration. All life is to be judged in the positive until proven negative. Pertaining to problem or Karmic numbers in the life, all paths are to be judged negative in this aspect until proven otherwise.

It is now possible to attack the interpretations of this chart in a different, most informative manner.

Using each of the three names that comprise the original birth name, the formula would be as follows: First name represents the physical aspects of life, second name representing the emotional elements, with the final name representing the spiritual aspects. It is of importance to keep in mind that the same letter will react in different manners depending upon which realm it may fall into.

Some of the key trigger letters such as "A" will represent take-off points for a new mode of life as indicated by following letters. This also would mean that the old mode of life would die in order for the rebirth to be possible.

It is also necessary to understand that each letter has a numerical assigned value in the alphabet and thus the division before or after that position would represent different ages of the life (i.e. youth as opposed to adult).

Following is the interpretation using this system of interpretation, which in no way subtracts from the interpretations already given in this chapter, but does add to the knowledge obtainable from any given chart.

PHYSICAL

A—Represents changes in residence, health, financial aspects. Before age 10, it is the indicator of activity and move of home. After age 10, it will bring sudden and abrupt changes and sometimes upheavals. It could create problems in the domestic life. It will bring with it either financial gain or loss depending upon the letters that will follow it. If followed by a G it will bring financial gain, by a U financial loss. Followed by an I, it will bring nervous disorders, by an R a serious upcoming illness.

B—Before age 11, it is an indicator of nervous problems and adverse conditions in the home. After age 11 it is the sign of poor health due to nervous problems and illness. Finances and material aspects suffer during this transit.

C—This letter at any age will offset bad financial letters in the other two realms. Before age 12 it denotes an intelligent, creative child. After age 12 during its transit there will be much creativity, travel and interest in art. This three year period will bring increased interest in social affairs and will seek beauty in all things and people.

D—Before age 13 this letter will bring poor health and physical strain. It is further an indicator of many unsettled home conditions entailing many changes of residence. After age 13 it denotes travel and trips of long duration. Followed by the letter U it will indicate a trip of an unpleasant nature due to injury or death of a loved one.

E—Before age 14, insecurity and constant change in the life. After 14 it will bring good health, probable moves of home and/or business. Many things started under this vibration are not of a long lasting duration. During its transit much upset will be experienced. It will bring a change in material aspects either for better or worse depending upon the letters in the adjoining spheres.

F—This is the indicator of unhappy home life before the age of 15. It will bring too much responsibility to the child, many times caused by divorce or death of a parent. After age 15, it will bring a tremendous amount of domestic responsibility. This letter denotes trouble in the home oft times caused by death or illness of loved ones. Its bad influence is particularly felt during the height of its potency in the middle two years of the six year cycle.

G—The child under this influence until the age of 16 will be secretive and withdrawn. It will bring a home life that is basically free of financial problems. After age 16 it will bring positive financial gain.

H—This letter by its very nature, vacillating, will bring many ups and downs into the life before the age of 17. After 17, it deals with financial aspects that will be as well up and down and in a short period of time go from one extreme to the other.

I—This is not a good letter in transit. Its effects are usually strongest felt during the peak or middle of its transit, namely the fifth year of the nine year cycle. At any age it will bring delays, accidents, divorce, misfortune, nervous upset, problems of all sorts and even bad health depending on the adjoining letters.

J—Before age 10 the child will be intelligent and active, quick to learn and accept responsibility. After age 10 the appearance of this letter during its one year transit will bring increased responsibility of a good nature such as a promotion at work or new business contacts that will be beneficial.

K—At any age this letter will bring increased nervous tension but have little effect on any other aspects.

L—One of the nicer signs. The child under its influence will be intelligent, healthy and creative. After age 12, it will bring success and happiness. It is also the sign of travel (extensive).

M—A bad sign for health matters at any age. This is not a good letter to have appear. It will bring moves and travel of an unpleasant nature. Before age 13, the child will be prone to lowered resistance in health matters. After age 13, this letter also deals with financial matters and will have a bad effect upon same.

N—Before age 14, this transit will bring many sudden changes of many natures into the life. Some for good, some not. After 14, this vibration deals primarily with finances and travel and will bring many swift changes in the material realm as well as changes in the love life of the person affected. This letter being by its very substance a letter of change is one of the key trigger letters that is an indicator of things to come. What many times transpires during its transit is determined by the letters that follow it. Followed by the I or R it is an indicator of loss. On the other hand if it itself follows the I or R it is a sign that the changes will be good and matters will improve for the better.

O—The letter of protection, protection in the life, good health, stable home life. After the age of 15 it will bring travel, material gain, new responsibilities of a good nature.

P—Before age 16, it denotes a highly moody, withdrawn child, somewhat on the secretive side. After 16, it is a difficult period especially for love affairs and usually denotes affairs of a secretive nature.

Q—At any age this letter which deals primarily with financial matters is going to bring power, authority and financial gain. It denotes moves in many directions of a good nature and probably a move to a larger more imposing home. It is further a good health sign.

R—A very bad letter in the physical position. It will bring loss, sacrifice, delays, accidents, lowered health. It carries a warning to be careful of accidents especially caused by travel during the fifth year of its nine year transit.

S—It will bring at any age a move of residence for the better. It will also bring nervous upsets caused by changes but all changes will prove to be beneficial in the long run.

T—This is a good vibration and will bring travel, possible moves of home and interest in romance at any age.

U—Perhaps the worst letter in transit. The sign of loss. Before age 14, loss in the home. If coupled with an emotional R or followed by a physical R it is the sign of death to a close relative. After age 14 it will bring loss and trouble in all financial and material aspects.

V—The sign of good health and solid construction in the life with friendships and relations. After 22, the vibration changes little and will bring success.

W—Another springboard letter of change. Change of home, relationships. After age 14 it is a bad sign for finances and romance and life will be up one day and down the next.

X—An unfortunate letter for health before age 15. After 15, it will bring position, authority, secrecy but also lowered resistance to health problems. It sometimes reverts to infamy instead of fame.

Y—The crossroads, finances could go either way. It does not deal with health. It brings with it at any age many decisions that will alter or change the life particularly during the fourth and fifth year of its seven year transit.

Z—A nervous vibration that will lead to an aggressive child before the age of 17. After 17, its vibration will bring success and financial gain in all material matters.

EMOTIONAL

A—Before age 10 will bring many emotional changes and unsettled home life. After age 10 will end old relationships and bring new ones.

B—Before age 11 brings unhappiness in home life and disputes with parents. After age 11 is self-destructive and leads to many broken alliances. This letter in the emotional realm will lead to much self-pity and inner suffering because of acts it itself has created. During its transit it is usual for the individual affected to separate from the one loved most.

C—A period of emotional happiness at any age.

D—In this emotional position will have little effect upon the early life. After age 13 could bring large troubles of an emotional nature into the life. Many persons transiting this sign have difficulties with the law enforcement agencies. This is not a good sign to commence a love affair-marriage under.

E—Before age 14 will bring an intense desire for personal freedom leading to trouble at home. After age 14 brings many successful love affairs but does not usually lead to a long term marriage.

F—At any age will bring large domestic problems and responsibility.

G—The early years like the physical realm will bring secrets, moodiness and changing emotions. After age 16, in the emotional area the G denotes a period of difficult relationships.

H—At any age it will bring ups and downs into the emotional life.

I—At any age will bring self-destruction and emotional conflict. It is the sign of divorce, broken affairs especially during the fifth year of its nine year transit. The entire nine years will be a period of inner self emotional suffering.

J—Before age 10 brings upsets in the home life and increased responsibility. After age 10 it denotes broken relationships and leads to many misunderstandings.

K—Before age 11 will bring many emotional changes. After age 11 brings a confusion into the emotional life.

L—At any age of life, one of the very best periods. A time of happiness, joy, beauty. Very good sign for long lasting relationships and a carefree life.

M—In this position the M brings a good solid home life for the child. After age 13 will usually lead to marriage in its second or third years. If the individual is already married it many times brings outside affairs which leads to a bad emotional period.

N—The emotional life of the youngster will suffer many ups and downs. After age 14, it deals mainly with love of a sexual or physical nature, will bring many transit affairs but few permanent relationships.

O—The letter of the protection of Venus in this position brings the child the protection of a happy secure home life with all the emotional protection that goes with it. After age 15 it is a six year period of emotional happiness, protected home life. It will lead to marriage for those unmarried during the middle of its transit, namely the third and fourth years.

P—Before age 16 the emotions run wild. There is much interest in early sex. After age 16, it brings many secret love affairs but little happiness with same.

Q—This is not a good sign on the emotional line. Being a financial letter it adds little to the emotional life, but by the same token distracts little.

R—Before maturity is reached this is the letter of loss and emotional suffering in the home. In later years it brings broken relationships especially during the fifth year of its nine year transit. Marriages entered under this letter usually end in separation or divorce. It is unfortunate for all emotional involvements.

S—On the emotional plane this letter will bring many turmoils into the life during its one year reign. Matters usually are straightened out after its disappearance however.

T—This letter will have very little effect upon the child but after age 14 will bring marriage usually in its second year. This is somewhat of a tricky letter in the emotional position and must be judged by the letters following, preceding it, or adjoining it. Followed by an O it will bring a long-term happy marriage. By a P, the beginning of a long-term secret love affair often with a married person. If an O precedes this transit it could well bring a termination to the marriage at least on a temporary basis. If preceded by a P, it will bring a termination to a secret love affair. If the letter O appears on the same line it is going to bring a long-term happy marriage. If the letter P appears in one of the other realms at the same time it will bring exposure of a secret love affair that will cause emotional damage to all affected.

U—The worst aspect again. At any age will bring emotional loss. A period of intense emotional upsets.

V—At any age a period of happy emotional relationships.

W—A time of emotional change at any age. During the middle or third year of its transit it will bring an end or a beginning to an important affair. This will be a restless period emotionally with the keyword being change.

X—A bad time for any type of emotional relationship due to nervous tension.

Y—Will bring a time of decision. A period of secrecy. A time when ill-advised emotional involvements are commenced. There will be a tendency to over-drink or engage in experiments with drugs and/or sex. This is not a good period for the emotions and relationships started under this sign will usually wash out before the end of the transit.

Z—This letter dealing mostly with finances will have little effect upon the emotional life with the exception that the person under this sign will usually be very hard to live with and will usually develop somewhat of an ego-maniac personality.

SPIRITUALLY

A—A period of new spiritual beginnings of a good nature.

B—Has little importance in the spiritual realm being concerned with other matters.

C—Will bring many new aspects into the life in a spiritual way. A very fortunate letter.

D—A nervous, tense period in this realm.

E—Will bring many changes, many new spiritual experiences. Not a bad letter at all in this position.

F—Will bring peace and harmony into the life. Will bring increased awareness.

G—A period when the spiritual life will be in abeyance.

H—Like the G, this letter will have little concern with the spiritual realm being mostly concerned with finances.

I—The best of all positions to find the I, at any age, a period of introspection, soul-searching, bringing changes for the better.

J—Does not pertain to spiritual activities.

K—A period of inspiration and revelation. A time of important spiritual change in the life.

L—A period of immense forward strides in the spiritual realm.

M—Leads to mix-up in the inner self. Will bring unhappiness with the inner self but offers little in the way of change.

N—A time of change. Sometimes forward, often backward, but at all times change.

O—A time of spiritual understanding, a time of much learning, a happy period, content.

P—Leads to much spiritual wisdom. A period of progress in this realm.

Q—This letter will bring backward sliding in this position.

R—There are those who maintain that in this position the R is favorable. I disagree. It will bring new spiritual knowledge but at the cost of emotional suffering.

S—A period of inner turmoil which will lead to new concepts and understanding.

T—The T will have little effect one way or the other in this position.

U—A period of frustration. A time when if not guarded against hurt may be caused unjustly to others especially loved ones.

V—A strong constructive period of attainment regarding the spiritual realm.

W—Will bring a change of thinking spiritually or perhaps even a change of religion.

X—Not a good letter in this position as it often leads to the black arts.

Y—In this position the Y will bring a crossroads in the inner self with good results.

Z—Will have little effect upon the spiritual self but could lead to unhappy times if handled in a negative manner.

The key to the foregoing is not to confuse the realms or vibrations of any given letter. It must also be pointed out that these are the aspects that are present in any given life at any given time and the negative aspects are there to be overcome. In the words of the wonderful Florence Campbell—"We are given the numbers, we choose the aspects."

A new insight has now been gained into the Excursion Chart. It once again denotes that all life is a learning process repeating itself. A person with the middle name of Jean for the sake of illustration would every twelve years complete an emotional cycle and reenter the same cycle once again. Thus any given individual deals with the same aspects in any realm over and over again in life.

The interpretation for marriages or love life which so many are interested in must be found on the middle or emotional line. The spiritual line deals with the inner self while the first or physical line deals with finances, movement and other aspects primarily.

Bearing the foregoing segment of the three planes of expression regarding this chart, one may now take a deeper look into the essence of any given year with new insight. An 11–2 essence with good spiritual letters is going to bring a year of many new insights into the spiritual realm. It is possible to tell if an eight essence is going to bring financial loss or gain depending upon the letters in the transit.

The essences should be handled as compound numbers, as opposed to fadic digits for those understanding the meaning of the compounds.

Chapter 31

ADDRESSES AND TELEPHONE NUMBERS

All numbers that go to make up part of life will have an effect upon that life. There is a strong undercurrent of belief within the circles of professional numerology that people are attracted to a certain set of numbers for a period of time because they have lessons to learn from these particular numbers. The numbers do give off, attract vibrations, so we will delve into a few of the important ones to be found in daily living.

THE POSTAL ZONE NUMBER

This number outlines the expression, lessons, of people living in this zone area. Used as an example will be the number 22091. For those that are interested, this is the postal zone number currently in use in a part of northern Virginia.

The Expression is found by reducing all the numbers to a single digit. Example:

$$2 + 2 + 0 + 9 + 1 = 14 = 5 \text{ EXPRESSION}$$

The Expression will be exactly the same as that offered in the chapter concerning the expression.

The residents of this area of Reston, Virginia which is located just outside Washington, D.C., are mostly military officers. More than any other group of people, the military indicates change, travel, personal freedom for the officers. Very few of these officers in the area live here for more than a three year tour of duty.

The challenge for this area would be found by using the pyramid.

EXAMPLE:

```
2    2    0    9    1
  0    2    9    8
    2    7    1
      5    6
        1
```

The major challenge "One," is exactly the same as the challenges in the chapter pertaining to challenges.

To find the minor challenges, the ten numbers that went into the making of the pyramid are employed. Discount the actual number itself—22091.

Ones	2
Twos	2
Fives	1
Sixes	1
Sevens	1
Eights	1
Nines	1

The "Zero" is not counted. The minor challenges would be the numbers with the greatest total. In this case there are two minor challenges, the "One" and the "Two."

The Karma or lesson to be learned would be found by referring back to the original number, 22091. The digit that appears most often is the Karma.

EXAMPLE:

Twos	2
Nines	1
Ones	1

The Karma is the "Two." Readers may refer back to the chapter regarding the Inclusion to find its full meaning.

THE STREET ADDRESS

This is very indicative of the people who live in this house.
Used as an example will be the number 12384.

```
1  2  3  8  4  =  18  =  9  EXPRESSION
  1  1  5  4
  0  4  1
  4  3
  6————MAJOR  CHALLENGE
```

The minor challenge would be "Four."
The Karma would be large and contain many lessons. The
Karma would be the numbers 1, 2, 3, 4, 8.

The exact same process was used for the street address as for
the postal zone number. The street address is of course more
personal as it concerns just the people living in a particular
house, while the zone number is concerned with an entire area.
Everybody in the zone area is affected, it is the first and primary
vibration.

THE APARTMENT NUMBER

This will show the expression or personality of the people living in this particular apartment. It many times also indicates
what their greatest need is. Used as an example will be the
number "Eight."

The Expression is an "Eight," showing a concern for and
with money.

Using a single digit there is no challenge.

The Karma would be the number "Eight."

THE AREA CODE NUMBER

This, like the zone number, takes in an entire general area.
Used as an example will be the area code "703" (Virginia).

7　0　3　=　10　=　1　EXPRESSION
　7　3
　　4————MAJOR CHALLENGE

The minor challenges would be "7," "3."
The Karma would be "7," "3."

THE TELEPHONE NUMBER

This is personalized like the house number. The first three
digits represent the exchange, and again take in an entire area
served by that exchange. The last four digits are the very personal ones. The only difference in procedure regarding the telephone number is concerned with the major challenge, as there
will be two of them. All other factors are found in the same
way.

Employed as an example will be the number 123-4567.

1　2　3　4　5　6　7　=　28　=　10　=　1　　EXPRESSION
　1　1　　　1　1　1
　　0　　　　0　0
　　　　0
　MAJOR
CHALLENGE
　　MAJOR
　CHALLENGE

The major challenge may be considered by those who calcu-
late they have no lessons to learn, as no challenge. Otherwise it
would run the entire span of the challenges.

The minor challenge would be "One."
The Karma would be "One."

Any individual will usually have one expression on the telephone, another for personal visitors to his home. The foregoing will be an aid when dealing with people either at their home, on the telephone, as it is an excellent indication of exactly what to expect.

PLACES

Cities and States attract, and give off vibrations. If considering a move in which there is freedom of choice, it would be wise to see if the expressions and other factors of a given place fit in with personal ones, to see how an individual would fare in that given locality.

EXAMPLE:

$$N \ E \ V \ A \ D \ A = 20 = 2$$
$$5 \ 5 \ 4 \ 1 \ 4 \ 1$$
$$\overline{22}$$

What better description of Nevada than the "Two." Marriage, divorce, sex, association, subservience, cooperation, inertia.

Looking at the full spectrum of numbers, it is found that two "Fives" are present, representing personal freedom, constant change, the immoral sex that Nevada is noted for, with its legalized prostitution. The two "Fours," pertain to work, and Nevada is a state of work. The hidden "Twenty Two" represents the intense building programs which are always underway in Nevada. The two "Ones" show the assertion of the individual. What better place than Nevada?

Looking into the letters, the "D" representing health is also true. Many people go to Nevada for health reasons. The inspired mentality of "A" is very evident there, as is the sex connected with the "E," and "N."

Perhaps it would be well to end this chapter with a current expression now in vogue in Clark County, Nevada, taken from a movie of the same name. "Viva Las Vegas." In reality Las Vegas is the home of some of the best informed people in this country concerning the mystic sciences.

Chapter 32

THE NUMBERS REVIEWED

In preparing this text, the effort has been made to keep it as simple and informative as possible.

Before closing the first study, the numbers will be reviewed from "One" to "Nine" plus "Eleven" and "Twenty Two." This author has seen the numbers bring success, greatness, fame, material rewards to many. Also, he has witnessed misery, defeat, divorce, strife, unhappiness. It is the free will of each person to choose the positive or negative aspects of his or her own destiny. A "Nine" Destiny will bring attainment, greatness, riches, etc. It will also bring misery, suffering, loss, bloodshed, sacrifice, etc. The Destiny cannot be escaped from, but the positive or negative aspects are by choice. Presented will be what must be overcome with any given number, what to expect if this is done, what to expect if it is not done. Those who live the nine year cycle of man in a positive way will reap the rewards. Those who live it in a negative manner will find themselves at the end of the nine year period no further ahead than the previous nine years, in many cases stripped of everything. Worse, they may carry old lessons into the new cycle. Readers by now should be familiar with the numbers that concern their own individual lives. A true interpretation of these numbers is going to be put straight on the line, no rosy pictures will be painted. Numerology is not fortune telling, it is instead, a way to understanding through knowledge of numbers.

The One:

Lesson   Self must not be imposed upon others. Self must
              stand on own two feet.
Negative   Failure, ruin.
Positive   The world, money, success, fame, attainment.

The Two:

Lesson   Must learn to cooperate. Must learn subservience,
              to take a back seat. Must not lean upon others.
Negative   Divorce, bad emotions, nerves, unhappiness, un-
              employment.
Positive   Prosperous business or profession. Happy mar-
              riage, good friends.

The Three:

Lesson   Must achieve self-expression in all forms.
Negative   Loneliness, strife.
Positive   Outstanding creativity in all forms of Expression.
              Happiness, beauty, love.

The Four:

Lessons   Must apply self to work.
Negative   Misery, hard times, lack of cash.
Positive   Security, comfort, stability, gain.

The Five:

Lessons   Must learn and accept law of change. Must not
              mis-use personal freedom especially in sexual mat-
              ters.
Negative   Unhappiness of the worst sort, misery, suffering,
              loss.
Positive   Personal freedom, a life most people can only
              dream about. Travel, romance, love, sex, attain-
              ment.

The Six:

Lessons	Must accept responsibility, learn to adjust to all situations. The warning is strong against divorce.
Negative	Strife, divorce, failure, unwanted obligations.
Positive	Huge authority, happy home, outstanding marriage, security, attainment.

The Seven:

Lessons	Above all faith. Faith in yourself, faith in others. Understanding must be secured. Knowledge must be sought. Faith in whatever your own personal belief of God is, this is a must.
Negative	Poverty, loneliness, misery, unhappiness.
Positive	Wisdom, knowledge.

The Eight:

Lessons	Must learn the correct use of power and material objects. Must not become overly concerned with material affairs, while at same time paying sufficient attention to them, especially in regard to detail.
Negative	Ruin, destruction, failure, catastrophe.
Positive	Money, power, position, prestige.

The Nine:

Lessons	Must learn universal love, understanding, compassion.
Negative	Ruin, finish, loss, sacrifice, loneliness, unhappiness, bad nerves, failure.
Positive	Greatness, success in all matters. The "One" got the world, the "Nine" gets the universe.

The Eleven:

Lessons	Must give revelation in return for the inspiration received. Must not be self-seeking, or engage in commercial enterprises.

| Negative | Failure, misery, unhappiness, loss, complete down-fall, bad emotions, run away nerves. |
| Positive | Fame, fortune, success, love. |

The Twenty Two:

Lessons	Must build for the world and humanity, be it on a large or small scale. Must not engage in the black arts, the penalty for this is insanity.
Negative	Complete and utter ruin in all areas, limitation.
Positive	Immortality, greatness, achievement in all matters, huge fortune.

The Second Study

Chapter 33

THE SAGA OF THE NUMBERS

The numbers have always been with us. Throughout the centuries there have been many methods used by numerologists for forecasting, divination, prophesy. *The Sacred Book of Magic of the Hebrew Kabbala* used pentagrams of numbers and letters to bring about magical ends. Pythagoras, the father of numbers, made use of several quaballahs that he himself devised. In venturing into an advanced study of numbers and letters, in which it is necessary to assign a certain numerical value to any given letter, so that the true meaning of the letter may be revealed, it will be important to take into consideration the full meaning of the letter. In looking over old charts devised by Greeks, Romans, Egyptians, Hebrews, Arabs, it is found that the numerical sequence of a letter in the alphabet is not as important as the sound of the letter. There is not going to be a big problem with the English alphabet, but help can be obtained by referring to the other alphabets. Before progression with the letters moves forward, it is necessary to compile at least a minimum amount of information concerning each particular number. It would be impossible to compile a complete list and explanation in just one volume as the numbers take on a different meaning every time the sphere or realm of their activity changes.

It is important that the true meaning of the numbers be understood fully. There is duality in all the numbers; but their functions will become clearer now. Each number will be fully described in its relation to man. In obtaining the true meaning of each number, the knowledge and wisdom from Tarotic, Hebraic, and other cultures, have been taken into consideration. The immense knowledge obtained from Astrology over the eras have in many cases given the final meaning to the number. The meanings will be both positive and negative. Two elements will decide which they will be. A number in conjunction with another number which, in turn, is in conflict with the first number, will bring strife. If the life is positive, the strife will be made easy; if the life is negative, the strife will be disaster, destruction, ruin. Each individual must be his own judge as to the positive or negative aspects of his own life. Man is on this earth to learn, to achieve, to grow. He is here for completion, for mastery. He is here to live the Cycle of Man and each person in his own life is dealing with a different set of numbers. Life can be enjoyable, happy, pleasant, but in order to achieve this man must live the universal law of the numbers of life. He must live the law of the God-Force. Man has all the time necessary in order to achieve the understanding of the numbers. He is free to repeat the same cycle over and over again: the numbers will teach him the same lesson each time. The numbers do not give; they, themselves, must be adjusted to. They cannot or will not be twisted to suit individual needs or wants. The positive is the kingdom of the earth and the heavens; the negative is Hell, misery on this earth now, and in succeeding lives.

The first study in this text was concerned with "THE NUMBERS OF LIFE," presented now in the Saga of the Numbers are THE NUMBERS OF DESTINY.

The Zero:

THE ZERO IS INFINITY. It has no beginning, no end. It may be joined but never allows penetration. All life has come from the Zero, will rejoin the Zero. It is love, understanding, mercy, compassion, forgiveness, knowledge, wisdom. The Zero is the sum total of life and death. The Zero is the God-Force.

The One:

THE ONE IS THE ASPIRATION OF MAN. The number One means exactly what it implies: it is God in the heavens, the Devil in the lower regions, Man on the Earth. It is the Sun in the solar system. It is the Heart in the body. It is the beginning; it is masculine, it is alone, it is positive. It is the first card of the Tarot. The Magician or Juggler. It is unity, it is universal. It has solar vibrations: its element is fire. It is ambition, intention, passion, activity, mentality. It is the center of all, the assertion over all. The One is comprised of a single stroke running up and down. The One is attainment, drive, success. In the beginning there was Adam in the Garden of Eden, he was number One. As Adam ruled the garden, so the One rules the entire span of numbers. As the solar system revolves around the Sun, so does the spectrum of numbers revolve around the One.

The Two:

THE TWO IS THE DUALITY OF MAN. The Two is the dual, the ancient Greeks called it the Duad. It is feminine, negative. It is the woman and mother. As the Moon reflects the Sun, so does woman reflect man, as the mother associates with the father, so does the Two associate with the One. As the Two works in conjunction with the One, so does woman work in conjunction with man. It is marriage. The Two is togetherness. It is the second card of the Tarot. The High Priestess. Its element is water. The One and the Two work well together. The Two, true to its feminine traits, is full of uncertainty, change, emotions, vacillation. It therefore represents divorce. It is agreement, but it is also separation. It is relationship with emotion and doubt. It is passive, consummation. It is isolation. It is profit and loss. It is war and peace. It is agreement, but it is disagreement as well. It is gain and it is loss. It can bring trouble, misery, strife, unhappiness, ruin, death, destruction, depending upon its relationship to other numbers. The Two possessing the wisdom of woman, is both love and hate. It further means togetherness, association, marriage, sex, and in regard to other matters, subservience.

The Three:

THE THREE IS THE EXPRESSION OF MAN. The sign of the trinity and triangle. The Three is the birth. It is the expression of the One and the Two joined together. It is the destiny of the One (man) and the Two (woman). It is their faith, their soul. It is the sum total of their creation, birth. The Three associated with the horn of plenty, the bountiful harvest, good luck, fruitfulness. The creation of joining fire (1) with water (2) creates a powerful steam force. The correct element of the Three is Air, with vibrations of fire, water, also earth. It is the third card of the Tarot. The Empress, meaning fertility, holding in her hand the orb of the world. The Three is marriage, versatility, expansion, riches, success, attainment. The Three will bring good fortune, acquisition, increase. The Three works well with the Six and Nine, as well as with the One, and the Two. The Three will react with mental creations when joined with the Nine, Four, and Five. With the Six, it tends towards expression in the arts.

The Four:

THE FOUR IS THE LIMITATION OF MAN. The man (1) has joined with the woman (2); their expression (3) was the birth. The Four, whose element is water, in itself represents all the four elements, fire, earth, air, water. It is also the embodiment of the spirit, mind, soul, body of man. Now must the triangle face the four square. Now begins the struggle for existence. The grim battle for manifestation, order, completion, growth, endurance, accomplishment, discovery, understanding, order. Now must the triangle and man learn to get along, to build. Now must man realize that there are boundaries, limitations, that he will have to use his strength, power, wisdom, to form a solid creation of building to create what is needed. Now must man sacrifice himself through work and hardship, in order to grow, to achieve, to understand. The fourth card of the Tarot, the Emperor, represents the authority of man in his grim struggle. The number Four is growth, completion of man's spirit, his mind, body, soul, pitted against the four elements via the hard task of work, endurance. Man is to build, achieve, plant; this he must do by the sweat of his brow. The Four will often get along with the numbers Two through Seven. The Four will bring prosperity and position, if man will apply himself to work. Escape from the work means drudgery, limitation; and those who try to evade the four square will bear the cross upon their shoulders. The Four is of the Planet Earth, and thus earthbound and limited.

The Five:

THE FIVE IS THE EXPANSION OF MAN. In the number Four, man has built his life, his home. Now with the Five, he starts to look around, to employ his fifth sense. The Five is the expansion of man, the growth, breadth, aspiration. With the Five, man is seeking the universal life, he needs his freedom, and independence to find it. At the end of the path, man will find understanding of justice and faith, but during his travels along the path he will find adventure, pleasure, happiness, union. The Five is associated with the sensual aspects of man. The fifth card of the Tarot, The Pope or Hierophant, is the one who beckons man away from the worldly concerns. The Five is further associated with alliance or marriage. The element of the Five is of course air; associated with the Planet Mars signifies freedom, change. The Five could bring misfortune, possible evil, especially in the sensual. In order for man to enjoy the freedom of the Five, it is necessary that he be free of financial problems, so the Five could bring an upswing in finances. The Five means activity, change, expansion, freedom, independence; it pertains to love associations, marriage, sensuality. The Five is reason, travel, commerce. As sure as the rewards are, so the punishments for backsliding are just as swift, for man must learn to use his new freedom correctly or the only changes he will find will be unpleasant. The transit of the Five will bring with it anxiety, worry, restlessness. The Five gets along best with other Fives, better than with any other number.

The Six:

THE SIX IS THE HARMONY OF MAN. Man, in traveling his path of freedom, discovers loneliness. In his loneliness he seeks love, affection, marriage; but in this marriage, he must learn to accept the responsibility and make the adjustments, or he will find trouble, divorce. The element is both earth and air. The Planet is Venus. The sixth card of the Tarot tells the very informative story of The Lovers. The symbol is expressed by a young man standing between two women, one representing vice, the other virtue; One the happy home, the secure marriage, the other the negative Five path of sensuality. There is a conflict here, caused by passion. The card means union or re-union as well as antagonism. Above the lovers floats the Spirit of Justice. Justice is ready to shoot the vice, and man, if necessary, to put man on the correct path of beauty, universal love. The Six is the number of entanglement, it means marriage, divorce, responsibility, adjustments, obligations. It means peace, solutions, pleasure. It gets along well with the Three and Nine, sometimes with the numbers One to Four. It does not get along with the Five, and especially not with the Eight. The Six means harmony, discord. It means cooperation, attainment, sex.

The Seven:

THE SEVEN IS THE PERFECTION OF MAN. The cosmic number, the number of God, the day of rest. Man on his journey finds that he needed to rest, and to meditate in order to attain perfection. In caring for his body, he found that his mind also needed caring for in matters of religion; he became concerned with his spirit, and therefore, necessarily, the spirit of God. The seventh card of the Tarot is the Chariot, representing the divinity in the human, winging his way to heaven in control and triumph. The Seven has long been associated with royalty, honor, fame, as well as rest and happiness. It can bring success, greatness, and triumph, if not actively sought after. The Seven is powerful for public dealings. It brings with it change, uncertainty, vacillation. It works well with the Two. It will get along with the One to Four. It is disaster pitted against the Eight. The transit of a Seven can bring harmony, wisdom, perfection, completion, balance, immortality. It can bring agreement, treaties, peace. It can also bring discord, death, immortality, loss, loneliness, misery, poverty. The positive is for those with faith who seek nothing whatsoever for themselves, the negative is for the others.

The Eight:

THE EIGHT IS THE MANIFESTATION OF MAN. After his rest, man must return to the struggle. The Eight, in one respect, has long been associated with power, rulership, material aspects. The Eight, however, by the very substance of its being is a split number with two zeros, placed one on top of each other. This power or money could well go the other way. As much as it promises, it is destructive. The eighth card of the Tarot is Justice. The Planet is Saturn, the planet of fate and Karma. Here will man be held responsible for his actions. In the hands of Justice are the scales of balance, proportion. The Eight is concerned with material aspects, power. It is the path of the growth of man. Its element is the earth. The ancient Greeks held that all things end with the Eight, that Eight signifies the completion. The number has long been considered unfortunate. No disagreement is offered. Many people consider that because the Eight represents monetary attraction, it is good. The number Eight in the path of man is for growth, accumulation of knowledge, understanding. The understanding of material aspects is needed, as is the understanding of power. This is the correct aspect of the path of the Eight. The Eight being a split number, when divided, results in two hard fours. The leftover Karma from past lives consisting of the 13, 14, 16, 19, are usually collected during the transit of the Eight. This is the time the bills are paid. The bills may be of the spirit rather than of matter. The Eight is reaction, revolution, fracture, rupture, segregation, anarchism, death, decay, loss. The philosophic Eight brings with it delay, disappointment, fatality, privation, loneliness, stagnation, evil, deception, trickery. In all

things not pertaining to finances it will bring loss. With finances
or the acquisition of power, it will bring either loss or gain. The
most difficult number to be paired with the Eight is a Four.

The Nine:

THE NINE IS THE COMPLETION OF MAN. Many scholars
interested in the numbers hold to the ancient Greek theory that
all things end at Eight. The cycle of man is Nine. The ninth
card of the Tarot, The Hermit, represents the withdrawal of
man for the purpose of meditation upon life, in order to gain
wisdom and to teach. The Hermit, aloof, alone, is the embodiment of all knowledge. The Nine with the element of fire is
the knowledge of human or universal love. Man has traveled on
his path of life from the beginning (1), through association (2),
to the expression (3), suffered the toils of work (4), enjoyed,
learned through the expansion, freedom (5), accepted, loved
(6), meditated, enriched his spirit (7), directed, led, achieved
(8), and now, in the Nine, has the all encompassing knowledge
of the cycle of man. This is the time for the great love without
boundaries. The seed man has planted in the beginning, toiled
over, cultivated (1), will now in the Nine be harvested. The
Nine has been associated with imperfection, grief, but only with
suffering can man achieve the great love. It has further been associated with prosperity. It is a number that can be either fortunate or unfortunate, for what was planted, must be the fruits of
the harvest. The transit of the Nine brings emotional change,
loss, strife, violence, privation, enterprise, anger, dreaming,
traveling, going forth, energy, penetration, regeneration, intensity of purpose, freedom, zeal. The Nine is the end. It is impulsive, it is successful, it is failure.

The Ten:

THE TEN IS THE UNITY OF MAN. Man has now returned
to the unity of the One, only this time with all the knowledge of
the cycle behind him. The Ten, which is the number One with a
Zero behind it, is again the beginning, only this time with the
knowledge of the cycle of man behind it. The Tenth card of the

Tarot, The Wheel of Fortune, symbolizes the change, the ups and downs, of man. It is the rise and fall. The Ten brings success, happiness, faith, self-confidence. The Ten in truth is a One, but it is a One with a high octave being represented by the Zero behind the One. It is going to react as the One, but will have connected with it its own particular attributes. It does not contain the lessons of the One because the Ten has achieved understanding, unless, of course, there is backsliding. The Ten is the rebirth, and brings with it happiness, success, with that success will go the responsibility of success, the adjustments to rebirth. The Ten is well experienced, moves quickly on to success and happiness, but can suffer the ups and downs if the responsibility and adjustments are not met.

The Eleven:

THE ELEVEN IS THE REVELATION OF MAN. One plus One = Eleven = freedom from the negative path of the Two. The element of the Eleven is air, the element of the Two is water. The freedom of air over the confinement of water. Man in this cycle has become the messenger of the gods. He will be given inspiration, his pursuit to follow its revelation. Under the Eleven, man can attain the heights, be master of all. The Eleven is spiritual, humanitarian. The number is considered bad for material aspects, but in all other matters is fortunate. The eleventh card of the Tarot is Strength. Its message is courage, spiritual power. The fall from the Eleven to the Two would be a long, hard one. The Eleven will bring success, fame. The negative path is the negative path of the Two with poverty and discord added.

The Twelve:

THE TWELVE IS THE SADNESS OF MAN. One plus Two = Three. Again man in his travels is reaching for self-expression; three being the number of birth, man is searching for rebirth of his expression. Expression and rebirth of the spirit. The 12th card of the Tarot, The Hanged Man, one must die in the social order to continue growth. Again man is faced with a choice. The Twelve which consists of the One (positive), the Two (negative), is aiming for expression, for birth (3). The birth of the spirit of God. With the birth man himself will realize that he is a part of God. The Three is self-expression or birth, but (when derived from the "Twelve") of a spiritual nature. Discounting the 1-2 combination pertaining to the number "Twelve," it foretells of trouble, danger, unhappiness. The positive path is knowledge, charity, wisdom.

The Thirteen:

THE THIRTEEN IS THE TRANSMUTATION OF MAN. One plus Three = Four. Man (1) plus spiritual expression (3) equals uprighteousness (4). The Thirteen, being a higher octave Four, is still concerned with work, but work of a much higher octave or nature. Man (1) on the negative path, plus too much self expression of the negative type (3), equals unrighteousness (4). The thirteenth card of the Tarot, Death, resulting in rebirth to the spirit, brings great change. The number Thirteen has been associated with bad luck. This is not valid. It is just another number for man to cope with in his path of growth. The warning of the Thirteen is clear, man must apply himself to work, and responsibility or material death will follow. The Thirteen as it pertains to love affairs is very fortunate.

The Fourteen:

THE FOURTEEN IS THE FORGETFULNESS OF MAN. One plus Four = Five. The Fourteen is a higher octave Five, but on the negative Five path represents sexuality. Fourteen tied into Karma, reincarnation, is represented by the fourteenth card of the Tarot, Temperance. Man's spirit is descending downward, forgetting past experiences, is backsliding toward matter. The number Fourteen is unfortunate. Once again will man have to sacrifice, adapt himself to get back to the correct path. Trial, sexuality, motion, energy, indecision, are some of the trademarks of the Fourteen standing in its own light.

The Fifteen:

THE FIFTEEN IS THE MYSTERY OF MAN. One plus Five = Six. Adjustments, but now adjustments of a spiritual nature. The fifteenth card of the Tarot, The Devil, indicating man's lack of humanity, destructive force, black magic. The Fifteen is not only unfortunate: it is evil.

The Sixteen:

THE SIXTEEN IS THE CATASTROPHE OF MAN. The sixteenth card of the Tarot, The Tower, struck by lightning. The material fall of man, so that the spirit can be rebuilt. The One (man) plus Six (love/marriage/sex) = Seven (Spirit). Man has fallen into the trap of vice, sensuality. The luxury and style of life must be destroyed in order that the spirit may grow. The Sixteen is ruin, destruction, of every nature. It is a very unfortunate number. Numbers derived directly from the Sixteen foretell of accidents, danger, defeat.

The Seventeen:

THE SEVENTEEN IS THE REALIZATION OF MAN. One (man) plus Seven (spirit) = Eight (hope). Now the Eight takes on a new meaning. The seventeenth card of the Tarot, The Star, representing the reward, hope, inspiration. This number is considered fortunate.

The Eighteen:

THE EIGHTEEN IS THE TREACHERY OF MAN. One plus Eight = Nine. The One (man) plus the Eight (material aspects) equals the Nine (spirit of humanity). The eighteenth card of the Tarot, The Moon, tells the entire story of the Eighteen. This is the worst element in man brought to bear upon his fellows, bloodshed (the power of the Eight) caused by the One (man). Trickery, deceit, treason, rape, murder, war.

The Nineteen:

THE NINETEEN IS THE REBIRTH OF MAN. The One (man) plus the Nine (spirit-cosmic love) = Ten, equals

One (a new creation). Man once again is reborn. The nineteenth card of the Tarot, The Sun, representing a new birth of a
high octave. Material success, happy marriage. Man has left the
material world. He has been liberated, achieved contentment,
attainment. Man must be reborn with a clean slate. The Nineteen is also Karmic. Man must pay his old debts in order to
achieve rebirth of a new order.

The Twenty:

THE TWENTY IS THE AWAKENING OF MAN. The twentieth card of the Tarot, Judgment, bringing to man the
awareness, knowledge of the universal. Known as the number
of life, Twenty is considered fortunate. A negative path will
bring obstacles, a positive path exaltation. This number represents the true freedom, liberty of man from all earthbound aspects. It is a high octave Two.

The Twenty One:

THE TWENTY ONE IS THE ELEVATION OF MAN. Two
plus One = Three. The ultimate expression. The twenty
first card of the Tarot, The World, bringing with it the full expression of truth, and honor. The completion of cosmic consciousness.

The Twenty Two:

THE TWENTY TWO IS THE MASTERY OF MAN. The ul-
timate expression of love, wisdom, mastery. This is the path of
the master number. The number of the mystic. But Two plus
Two = Four, in this case, a high octave Four. To fall from
the Twenty Two would be to bring on the most unfortunate circumstances. It foretells of accidents, restraints. Its symbol
would be the final card of the Tarot, The Fool, who is falling
over a cliff. The fool is the positive inner force which influences
gratification of the flesh.

The Twenty Three:

THE TWENTY THREE IS THE ROYAL STAR OF THE
LION. Two plus Three = Five. The associations of man (2)

plus the expressions (3) of man equal freedom (5). The vibrations of this number are good, and will bring success, fame, honor.

The Twenty Four:

THE TWENTY FOUR IS THE NUMBER OF CAIN. Two plus Four = Six. A very bad combination. The worst of all the Sixes. The greatest sacrifices will be needed.

The Twenty Five:

THE TWENTY FIVE IS THE NUMBER OF TRIALS. Two plus Five = Seven. It foretells of a struggle.

The Twenty Six:

THE TWENTY SIX IS THE NUMBER OF JEHOVAH. Two plus Six = Eight. It foretells of suffering, greed, disaster.

The Saga of the Numbers could continue into infinity. The number Twenty Five hidden behind a Seven Soul Urge would foretell of a struggle within self in order to find the spirit. A Nine Expression that was reduced from an Eighteen carries a very bad warning with it.

ALL THE NUMBERS BEHIND EVERY SINGLE FINAL DIGIT MUST BE TAKEN INTO CONSIDERATION IN ORDER TO OBTAIN A COMPLETE, INFORMATIVE INSIGHT.

Chapter 34

THE LETTERS ANALYZED

The letters in an individual name are the sum total of the Soul Urge, Expression, Quiet Self, Planes of Expression. The letters in transit are vibrations that are being drawn in and given out. Disregarding any numerical value a particular letter might be associated with, it is necessary to have knowledge of exactly what each letter in itself pertains to.

The correct interpretation of letters is not in their numerical sequence in the alphabet; it is the sound of the letters. Many times this interpretation is not based upon a single letter, but the combined sound that two or more letters would make together. In the combination of the letters "O," "H," pronounced "Oh," the sound is of the single "O." As with the foregoing illustration, it will be found many times that certain letters are silent when in combination with other letters. In many cases the same letter will give off different sounds, thus taking on added meaning with the sound change. A good example of this would be the letter "G." The "G" can be soft, quiet. It can also be hard, guttural. The correct interpretation of any given name to reach the over-riding influence or vibrations must be obtained by breaking the name down into sound syllables.

Where a combination of letters result in one sound, the main vibration or attraction would be the sound itself. The quiet letters would play only a secondary influence. Throughout time, various alphabets have used different sets of letters in various combinations to comprise that alphabet. The actions or attributes of that letter were always based on the sound. We understand the full meaning of the numbers one to nine. The correct interpretation of letters is to assign the correct numerical value to that letter. Each language must be interpreted by its sounds, not by its letters. I have no wish or desire to change the numerical values of the letters in the English language as given in this book and accepted in the world of numerology. I do, however, wish to enlarge upon the given meaning of the particular letters. Presented in the first study in this text was a chapter on the meanings and vibrations of each letter. This will now be enlarged. The basis for this enlargement is founded upon a study of the ancient languages, and the vibrations or numerical values assigned to that particular sound by scholars.

The effort is being made in this text to find the true meanings of the letters in the English language without going too deeply into their particular sounds, which is a study unto itself.

Each individual letter for correct interpretation must be aligned with the number or numbers that represent it. To correctly coordinate the full meaning and potential of an individual number, it must be aligned with the planet that it represents. The movement of the numbers is exactly the same as the movement of the planets when in aspect with each other. I am not going to dwell long on this subject. For some time there has existed between professionals a difference of opinion as to exactly which planet the numbers are assigned. Notwithstanding, the full interpretations of the numbers are understood. I am not going to try to correlate astrology and numerology in this text. It is not important for our study to know whether Mars is number Five or number Nine. We fully understand the meaning of the number Five and Nine. The foundation of numbers is built on the One, Two, combination. Without exception, all are in agreement that: the "One" is the Sun; the "Two" is the Moon. The "One" is the center, attainment of all; the "Two" is the subservient. The day, the night.

With this brief background, the actual values of the letters can now be examined.

LETTER "A"

This letter is assigned the value of "One." There is no other interpretation possible for this letter. "A," in the English language is the foundation, the Sun. It has all the attributes of the number "One." It is inspired mentality, movement, progress, activity, creation. The "A" in the Soul Urge creates an active, highly mental, fast moving person, especially if it is the first vowel. The "A" in the Expression is creation, attainment. The "A" in transit will bring increased activity, changes, movement, travel.

LETTER "B"

The "B," when found in the name in proportion to the total number of letters in the name (all letters and numbers must be taken in proportion to the complete spectrum), will, in regards to drive or personality in the same proportion, create a shy, retiring, withdrawn personality. The "B" is deep, loving and love seeking. It is subservient. The "B" in transit pertains to love affairs, marriage, emotional problems. All letters that are enclosed such as the "B," "D," "O," "P," etc., are self contained, and indicate in correct proportion that part of self that is withdrawn and contained. The correct interpretation for the letter "B" is the number "Two." The "B" is either fortunate or unfortunate depending upon its correlation with other letters.

LETTER "C"

The "C" is open, flowing, expressive. The correct interpretation for "C" is the number "Three."

LETTER "D"

Enclosed, withdrawn, physical, pertaining to health. Limited, pertaining to the number "Four." The "D" will bring growth, potential.

LETTER "E"

Being a vowel, it is inspired, active. The "E" is physical. It will bring change, activity, travel. In the Arabic, the twenty sixth letter of their alphabet, "Ha" which is equivalent to our letter "H" is assigned the value of "Five." There is something of value to be learned here as the Arabs were very well advanced into the sciences such as astrology. Our "H" mainly represents finances. The Arabic interpretation does fit into the five category, for to enjoy the freedom of the "Five," it is necessary to be free of financial concern. Therefore in addition to the "Five" value which fits the "E" perfectly, must be added some of the elements of the "Eight." The "E" in transit will bring an upswing in finances. The "E" pertains to love affairs of a physical nature as opposed to an emotional nature because of its "Five" value.

LETTER "F"

This letter has a true value of "Six." There is little doubt as to its meaning. It is responsibility, domestic adjustments, marriage, divorce.

LETTER "G"

It represents religion, other matters of the soul. It warns against self-seeking, but does promise financial gain. It will bring happiness, success, greatness, triumph, if not actively sought after. It will also bring loneliness, meditation. The "G" has a correct value of "Seven" but is not a complete "Seven" as the number "Seven" pertains to so much more.

LETTER "H"

The "H" with its value of "Eight" pertains to finances, either going out or coming in. The Arabic "Ha," the sixth letter of their alphabet is assigned the value of "Eight." The "Ha" corresponds to our letter "H." The Greeks assigned their seventh letter, "Eta," the value of "Eight," as did the Hebrews their eighth letter, "Cheth." The twenty sixth letter of the Arabic is also identical to the sixth letter, both being "Ha." To the second "Ha," was given the value of "Five." The question now arises as to what degree do the activities of the "Five," freedom, change, enter into the association with the "H"? Certainly material wealth is freedom of a sort, but the "Five" differs greatly from the "Eight." Never-the-less, falling back on the Arabs, some of the attributes of the "Five" must be given to the "H." The study of old charts reveals a very close association between the "Eight" and "Five." The "H" is very closely associated with child bearing as well.

LETTER "I"

The explanation of the "I" in the chapter pertaining to letters is very explicit. The "I" has a true value of "Nine." On the positive side, it is completion, the attainment of all, success in all. The negative is loss, finish, emotional upsets, loneliness. The "I" will have a direct influence upon given lives when it is the first vowel. The "I" is intense, repeating, sad, emotional, giving, striving.

LETTER "J"

The "J" being the tenth letter of our alphabet is assigned the value of "Ten." (A higher octave "One.") The ninth Greek letter, "Iota," the tenth Hebrew letter, "Yod," were both assigned the value of "Ten." In one chart attributed to Pythagoras, the "J" is given the value of "600," being the number "Six" with two zeros attached to it. The twenty eighth letter of the Arabic, "Ya," which relates to our letter "T," is given the value of "Ten." The Arabic letter "Jean," which relates to our letter "J," was given a value of "Three," which fits in very nicely here. In dealing with the "J" we are dealing with an experienced letter, a letter of rebirth. If we adapt the keyword "pleasant," the birth associated with the "Three" fits in, as is not the "Ten" the rebirth of man. The "J" brings with it happiness, success, rebirth; with that success goes the responsibility of birth, of the "600." The "J" while it has the attributes of the "A," is still somewhat unlike the "A." The "A" is the creator, the originator. The "J" is well experienced, moves quickly on to success, happiness, but one can suffer the ups and downs caused by the very substance of its being, vacillation.

LETTER "K"

The eleventh letter of the Hebrew "Kaph," is given a value of "Twenty." The tenth letter of the Greek, "Kappa," is also given the value of "Twenty." In Arabic both the twenty first and twenty second letters are identical ("Kaf"), they are associated with our letter "K," and are given the values of "100" and "20" respectively. Pythagoras is attributed to having assigned the value of "Ten" to the letter "K." In the English alphabet the letter "K," given the value of "Eleven," stands as a master number, but can in essence be reduced to a "Two" of a high octave, namely to "20." It does possess the association, cooperation of the "Two" in a higher octave. The Arabic value of "100" would also be appropriate as this would signify the tremendous creativity and inner push, of the two number "Ones" that comprise the "Eleven." Thus the "Ten," attributed to Pythagoras, would also fit. The promise of the "K" or "Eleven" on the positive side is fame. The high octave number "Ones" comprising the "Eleven" would surely be the placement of self (1) over and above all else, as in fame.

LETTER "L"

The "L," being the twelfth letter of our language, is assigned a value of "Three." This is correct, but it is a very high octave "Three." The Hebrew "Lamed," the Greek "Lambda," the

Arabic "Lam," all of which correspond to our "L" are given the value of "Thirty" which is the correct value for our "L."

LETTER "M"

The letter "M," being the thirteenth letter will be a high value of the "Four." The "M" is unmoving, thus limited. It is firmly set, firmly planted. The explanation in the chapter concerning letters explains the "M" in sufficient detail.

LETTER "N"

The letter "N" being the fourteenth letter is assigned the value of "Five," the "Five" of a high octave. The reaction of the "Five" or "Fifty" will be sacrifice, adaptation, sexuality, energy, motion, forgetfulness. It will bring a concern with finances either positive or negative. The main key to the letter "N" will be found in the Planes of the Expression Chart, as will keys for all the other letters. The "N" is mental, vacillating.

LETTER "O"

The chapter concerning letters outlines the "O" in great detail. The influence of the "O" must be very carefully watched if it is the first vowel. In addition it foretells of fatality, trouble, temptations, black magic. All the temptations of the "Six" must be overcome as well.

LETTER "P"

The letter "P" will have the high octave value of the "Seven," the "Seventy." The Hebrew "Pe," is valued at "Eighty." The Greek "Pi," is valued at "Eighty." Pythagoras is said to have valued the "P" at "Sixty." Using the "Eighty" value of the Hebrews and Greeks, finances can be brought into the picture. The "Sixty" value, attributed by Pythagoras, will bring a high octave "Six" in as well. This foretells of the loss of power as told of in the Tarot card. The "Sixty" is adjustments to be made of a high octave. The "Seventy" is a negative backslide of the "Seven." It needs to be returned to the positive path. It foretells of accidents, catastrophe, defeat, danger, weakness, upheaval, until the spirit is restored to the "Seven," "P" being the sixteenth letter, associated with the sixteenth card of the Tarot, The Falling Tower. Again we are presented with some more insight into the "Seven," which this letter is valued at. It is possible for anything to transpire during the transit of a "Seven."

LETTER "Q"

Very much like the "O," only with something added. Pythagoras is reputed to have valued the letter "Q" at "Seventy." This would tie in as the "Seventy" is the high octave of the "Seven" (Spirit). There is new hope after the lightning struck tower of the sixteen. Hope in material aspects, hope in spiritual aspects. The seventeenth letter "Q" reducing to its "Eight" value would forecast that the material aspects of the "Eight" will take a turn for the better.

LETTER "R"

The letter "R" should be valued at "Ninety," a high octave of the "Nine." The spirit (9) is being sought after to get away from the power, bloodshed (8). The "Ninety" relates to military aspects, hardness. The Arabic letter "Ra," which corresponds to our letter "R" values the letter at "200." The Hebrew "Resh" also corresponding to our "R," values it at "200" also. The Greek letter "Rho," which is related to our "R" sets the value at "100." Pythagoras is reputed to have valued the "R" at "Eighty." The "R" is the eighteenth letter of our alphabet. The combination of the "One" and the "Eight." Our value is set at "Nine." With the "R" all the numbers must be taken into consideration. The explanation of the number "Eighteen" in the saga of the numbers must be considered. This letter pertains to money, power; it is also the assertion of the self or man over that money and power. The explanation in the chapter regarding letters is precise. This is not a good letter in transit.

LETTER "S"

The correct value of the letter "S" is "100." An even higher octave of the "One." All the attributes of the "One" are still present, but now man is operating in the light of the Universal God. The spirit has been reborn, man is aware of the God Universe. Man in his worldly concern and ignorance will try to reject this if possible. The transit of the "S" will bring the worst emotional upheavals and upsets that the self can experience. The Arabic alphabet has two letters equivalent to our "S"; the letter "Sad," valued at "Ninety," a high octave of the spirit of "Nine," and the letter "Sa," valued at "500," the highest octave of the "Five." A large change has taken place and man is finally free. The "S" will bring change, the change will be for the better after it has transpired, but during that change, agony and misery will be suffered. Pythagoras valued the "S" also at "Ninety" in one of his many charts. The Hebrew letter "Sin" is valued at "300" which is the high octave of expression, the expression of the new man, rebirth. The vibrations, discounting the emotional upheaval, are excellent. The "S" represents the highest ideals of the "One."

LETTER "T"

The letter "T" is spiritually evolved, tense, eager for knowledge, self-sacrificing, carries burdens, strained with the inner self. The 20th card of the Tarot, which fits this, our 20th letter, is bringing to man awareness of the universal. The letter "T" will be valued at "200." It will have the attributes of the "Two" and "Twenty," but will bring with it original, determined action, as well as trouble and hindrances. It will also bring rewards.

LETTER "U"

This letter is going to present a problem. With its position in our alphabet it should have a value of "300." This would not be correct, however. The "300" brings success, achievement. The "U" reacts more as a "Nine" than it does as a "Three." For Expressions or Soul Urge, the value of "Three" is in order. For forecasting, the "U" must be given the attributes of a high octave "Nine" or "Four."

LETTER "V"

The letter "V" will have a value of "400." The positive is that of the "Twenty Two": it will stand alone and above. The negative will be the highest octave of the "Four." It must also be given many of the elements of the "Two."

LETTER "W"

The double "V." The explanation in the chapter pertaining to letters fits the "W" correctly.

LETTER "X"

I consider this a very nasty letter. This carries the cross more than any other letter. It can bring emotional destruction. It has long been associated with the black arts. There is no difference between White, Gray, or Black Magic. It is all metaphysics. The difference is with the person who engages in it. The penalty for those who would interfere with the free will of others is utter destruction. This is a letter to be careful of, heed its warnings. The transit of the "X" is going to bring a crisis.

LETTER "Y"

Spiritual uplift. The explanation in the chapter about letters is sufficient to describe this letter.

LETTER "Z"

See the chapter pertaining to letters. This letter is not in over-abundant use in our alphabet. Its main concern is with finances.

To obtain a correct interpretation of any letter, its numerical value, its numerical sequence in the alphabet, the numbers that comprise this sequence, its sound and the letter itself, all must be taken into consideration. Each letter has its own attributes. Our method of assigning certain values (numerical) to these letters is correct. With the possible exception of the "U," the interpretation of the letters is in agreement with the numerical values, one to nine, that are assigned.

We all come from somewhere, we all are going someplace. The numbers and letters are the sum total or essence of our past lives, what we have to work with. They are the plan for this life; they represent what will have to be encountered and overcome. The "Numbers of Life" are neither hard nor easy. They are what each individual makes of them. Those who will stop fighting their numbers will find that life will change almost overnight from the negative to the positive. The knowledge of life is revealed in numerology. It is the revelation. It is the WHAT, WHERE, HOW, WHY.

Chapter 35

THE RELATIONSHIP OF NUMBERS

There should be little doubt left in the minds of anyone of what the numbers "One" to "Nine" mean. The question now is how does the transit of one number affect a corresponding number. The effort will be made to present a simple outline. The Path of Life number is stationary. For the entire life the number will be the prime number, immovable. It is the main aspect that will be encountered in life. The Cycles (Sub-Paths) are next. The Pinnacles will present the high points or periods for special lessons to be learned. The Main Life Challenge numbers are going to operate against all three of these paths. The Soul Urge, inner drive, motivation of the self will come up against these paths also, the Soul Urge is a part of self that cannot be changed, but it can be made to adapt. The Expression is going to likewise come up against these fixed paths. The Expression also can be made to adapt or change.

The foregoing pertains to the Main Indicator of Life. This can be adapted to a chart for the yearly vibrations or otherwise.

Presented now is the aspect of one number in relation to another number.

The results of "One" being encountered by any other number will result in the following:

The "One" is the Sun, the attainment, the success.

WITH ONE	Over activity, strain on self, producing no results.
WITH TWO	The "One" will prevail. The "Two" will be subservient. A conflict of interests may be presented, causing emotional strain.
WITH THREE	Complete accord, harmony, success.
WITH FOUR	The "One" will prevail, but discord could be caused by the limitation of the "Four."
WITH FIVE	Complete accord. If the "One" is crossing the "Five" it will bring attainment. If the "Five" is crossing the "One" it will bring change (i.e. a sub-path would cross the main path of life).
WITH SIX	Accord if the "Six" crosses the "One," it will then bring responsibility, love affairs, promotion. Discord if the "One" crosses the "Six." The self will seek to get out from under the obligations.
WITH SEVEN	If the "One" crosses the "Seven" it will bring change, uplift. If the "Seven" crosses the "One," it will cause conflict by slowing down the life.
WITH EIGHT	If the "One" crosses the "Eight," it will bring success in material matters. If the "Eight" crosses the "One" it can result in Karmic debts being collected.
WITH NINE	Mostly in accord. Can bring on emotional strain. Can also bring greatness.
WITH ELEVEN	Harmony, providing the self-interests of "One" do not interfere with the God-Force interests of "Eleven."
WITH TWENTY TWO	Complete accord.

The "Two" is the Moon, the subservient.

WITH ONE	SEE ONE
WITH TWO	Emotional upset, lowered health, poverty, loneliness.
WITH THREE	Disharmony (slight). Harmony in love matters.
WITH FOUR	Once in a while, accord. In many cases, emotional limitation. In material matters it works well if the individual is not self-seeking.

WITH FIVE	Conflict, mistakes. It will also bring on excessive sex.
WITH SIX	Harmony in love affairs, domestic life. In other aspects complete destruction.
WITH SEVEN	The aspects of the "Seven" will prevail, peace, mediation. Will be in accord, but could bring on emotional upsets.
WITH EIGHT	Accord.
WITH NINE	Discord, emotional upsets.
WITH ELEVEN	Accord, providing the "Eleven" is being lived as an "Eleven." Otherwise the 2-2 would prevail.
WITH TWENTY TWO	Both accord (usually) and discord (once in a while).

The "Three" is the birth, creation.

WITH ONE	SEE ONE
WITH TWO	SEE TWO
WITH THREE	Scattering of self, bad nerves, upsets.
WITH FOUR	Conflict, the expression of "Three" does not like the limitation of "Four." The confinement of "Four" resents the expression of "Three."
WITH FIVE	Complete accord.
WITH SIX	Accord.
WITH SEVEN	Both accord and discord. The "Seven" will tone down the "Three." The "Three" will uplift the "Seven."
WITH EIGHT	Both accord and discord.
WITH NINE	Accord.
WITH ELEVEN	Accord.
WITH TWENTY TWO	Accord.

The "Four" is the Earth, limitation, hardness.

WITH ONE	SEE ONE
WITH TWO	SEE TWO
WITH THREE	SEE THREE
WITH FOUR	Hardness, limitation, work overload.
WITH FIVE	Conflict, more so than the 3-4.
WITH SIX	Accord.

WITH SEVEN   Accord.

WITH EIGHT   Loss, privation, Karmic. It is true that the 4-8 come from the same family of numbers but together on the main chart of life, they will bring ruin.

WITH NINE   Both accord and discord. If the "Nine" crosses the "Four," accord. If the "Four" crosses the "Nine," discord.

WITH ELEVEN   Discord.

WITH TWENTY TWO   Accord if the "Twenty Two" is being lived up to. Otherwise the 4-4 will prevail.

The "Five" is the freedom.

WITH ONE   SEE ONE

WITH TWO   SEE TWO

WITH THREE   SEE THREE

WITH FOUR   SEE FOUR

WITH FIVE   The 5-5 is in complete agreement, but will usually bring on the mis-use of personal freedom.

WITH SIX   Complete discord.

WITH SEVEN   Accord if the "Five" is being lived correctly. Complete discord otherwise.

WITH EIGHT   Accord if the "Five" crosses the "Eight." Discord if the "Eight" crosses the "Five."

WITH NINE   Harmony (usually).

WITH ELEVEN   Accord, discord.

WITH TWENTY TWO   Accord, discord.

The "Six" is Venus. It is love, sex, marriage, responsibility.

WITH ONE   SEE ONE

WITH TWO   SEE TWO

WITH THREE   SEE THREE

WITH FOUR   SEE FOUR

WITH FIVE   SEE FIVE

WITH SIX   Usually too much responsibility. Problems in domestic life.

WITH SEVEN   Accord, discord.

WITH EIGHT	Usually accord, but can bring a problem into a marriage.
WITH NINE	Complete accord.
WITH ELEVEN	Accord.
WITH TWENTY TWO	Accord.

The "Seven" is the spirit, it is the God-Force.

WITH ONE	SEE ONE
WITH TWO	SEE TWO
WITH THREE	SEE THREE
WITH FOUR	SEE FOUR
WITH FIVE	SEE FIVE
WITH SIX	SEE SIX
WITH SEVEN	Too withdrawn, limitation, tenseness.
WITH EIGHT	Complete utter conflict, financial loss, emotional upsets.
WITH NINE	Accord if the "Nine" crosses the "Seven." Discord if the "Seven" crosses the "Nine."
WITH ELEVEN	Usually accord, once in a while discord.
WITH TWENTY TWO	Usually discord, sometimes accord.

The "Eight" is the planet Saturn. It is Karma. It is material aspects.

WITH ONE	SEE ONE
WITH TWO	SEE TWO
WITH THREE	SEE THREE
WITH FOUR	SEE FOUR
WITH FIVE	SEE FIVE
WITH SIX	SEE SIX
WITH SEVEN	SEE SEVEN
WITH EIGHT	Complete financial loss, bad health. The best to be hoped for is limited income and physical strain.
WITH NINE	Sometimes accord, usually discord. The Karma and the finish together.
WITH ELEVEN	Complete accord.
WITH TWENTY TWO	Accord.

The "Nine" is the completion, the greatness, the finish.

WITH ONE	SEE ONE
WITH TWO	SEE TWO
WITH THREE	SEE THREE
WITH FOUR	SEE FOUR
WITH FIVE	SEE FIVE
WITH SIX	SEE SIX
WITH SEVEN	SEE SEVEN
WITH EIGHT	SEE EIGHT
WITH NINE	Emotional upheaval of the worst sort. Considerable loss in all aspects.
WITH ELEVEN	Greatness.
WITH TWENTY TWO	Accord.

The "Eleven" is the inspiration.

WITH NUMBERS ONE TO NINE, SEE RESPECTIVE GROUPS
WITH ELEVEN   Highly charged, tense, nervous.
WITH TWENTY TWO   Accord.

The "Twenty Two" is the ultimate.

WITH NUMBERS ONE TO ELEVEN, SEE RESPECTIVE
                GROUPS
WITH TWENTY TWO   Possible insanity, possible greatness, immortality.

Chapter 36

ANCIENT NUMEROLOGY

Presented in this chapter will be a few of the many ways used to forecast via numerology in the past. This author neither confirms nor denies the performance of these charts. Some of them have been used by the author with amazing results.

The first method is based upon the year of birth alone. This is one of the charts from which the author has obtained excellent results. The year of birth is added together, but not reduced to a single digit. The total of this is added to the reduced year of birth. The sum of these numbers, corresponding to the age of the individual, will foretell major happenings in his life at that point. The total of that year will be added again to find the next important points in the life.

EXAMPLE:

$$\begin{array}{r} 1933 \\ 16 \\ \hline 1949 \end{array} \quad = \quad 16 \quad (1+9+3+3=16)$$

Age 16

$$\begin{array}{r} 1949 \\ 23 \\ \hline 1972 \end{array} \quad = \quad 23 \quad (1+9+4+9=23)$$

Age 39

$$\begin{array}{r} 1972 \\ 19 \\ \hline 1991 \end{array} \quad = \quad 19 \quad (1+9+7+2=19)$$

Age 58

The exact origins of this device are unknown. To this technique may be added Tarotic influences. The "Sixteen" being the sixteenth card of the Tarot, is depicted by The Falling Tower. Using this Tarotic influence it would be assumed ruin of some sort at age sixteen. Since there are only twenty two major Tarot cards, the twenty three would be reduced to a "Five." The Hierophant, the one who leads one away, is the corresponding card, and could imply that at age thirty nine, either the self, or someone close to the self will depart from the usual life. It could pertain to divorce. The "Nineteen" would apply to the nineteenth card of the Tarot, The Sun, indicating material success, happy marriage, the world, attainment.

Disregarding the Tarotic influences, the lives and important happenings with exact dates of many famous persons in history will prove out.

The second method is that of Tarotic influence. The current year and the current age are added together and reduced to a number from one to twenty two. The result is read like the Tarot, and would pertain to that specific period.

EXAMPLE:

$$\begin{array}{r} 1973 \\ \text{Age} \quad \underline{40} \\ \overline{2013} \ = \ 6 \end{array}$$

The card that would apply is The Lovers, meaning a happy love affair will exist or come into being during this period.

The third is also fairly simple. Again, the origins are unknown. The day of birth is added to the month of birth, which is added to the year of birth, subtracting from the year of birth the first two digits as they pertain to an era. What is being sought is the final digit plus the secondary number.

EXAMPLE:

Birthdate: September 24, 1941
September is a 9. The 24th stands as is.
The 19 is eliminated with the 41 being
added to the sum total.

$$9 + 2 + 4 + 4 + 1 \ = \ 20 \ = \ 2$$

This is a type of personality forecast. The secondary number of twenty is broken up into its two components. "Two" and "Zero." The "Zero" has no meaning outside of a high octave of the "Two." The secondary influence of the personality is "Two" or subservient. The controlling factor is the final digit which in this case is also the "Two."

The fourth and final presentation will be an old Hebraic Quaballah with interpretations of the letters as opposed to numerical value. The phonetic values of the letters have already been taken into consideration. This chart may be fine for the Hebrew language, but this author holds little stock in it as far as the English speaking world is concerned. On the other hand, some outstanding results have been witnessed from the use of this chart. In the chapter regarding letters, many of the points of this chart were discussed. As far as letters are concerned, the chart is fairly correct, but will prove to be incorrect when applied to our language for purposes of Soul Urge, etc.

This is only one of many charts originating with the Hebrews and Greeks. Many of their charts only use the numbers one to eight.

Number One	A	E	Y	I (long)		
Number Two	B	K	R	Pp	G (hard)	Q
	O (short)		X			
Number Three	J	G (soft)		Sh	L	
Number Four	D	T	M			
Number Five	N					
Number Six	U	Oo	V	W	S	
Number Seven	Z	O (only if initial)				
Number Eight	P	Ph	F	H (quiet)	Ch (hard)	
Number Nine	Th	Tz				

Somewhere in the past this chart reached its present above state in an effort to adapt it to the English language. This chart was presented here for the readers' interest. This author has no further comments regarding this chart, and does not care to run an example pertaining to its operation. The subject will be left with the comment that for every time this author has seen a good result obtained from this chart, there have been several with negative results.

Chapter 37
A NEW QUABALLAH

No idea on this earth is new. No man has had a thought or a feeling that some other person has not had before him. Presented in this chapter will be a new Quaballah which this author has devised, and which has been used with great success by the author. The idea or the method is not new, as both have been used in many Quaballahs for thousands of years. Pythagoras himself used similar charts. What has been done with this new Quaballah is to give a correct interpretation of numerical valuations of letters to be used in conjunction with our present English speaking society.

The letters will be valued as follows:

A	1	J	10	S	100
B	2	K	20	T	200
C	3	L	30	U	400
D	4	M	40	V	400
E	5	N	50	W	500
F	6	O	60	X	600
G	7	P	70	Y	700
H	8	Q	80	Z	800
I	9	R	90		

Special attention will be paid to the fact that the "U" is valued at "400."

Using the information already learned in the second study

pertaining to the essence of the letters and numbers, there can now be assembled the following chart to be used for interpretation.

1   New changes for the better. Usually indicates move of home. Travel might be expected. New beginnings. The assertion of self.

2   Upset emotions, new alliances. Possible love affairs, marriage, divorce. Possible ruin of plans, tragedy.

3   Birth of new ideas. Happiness, joy, possible birth of child.

4   Lowered health, travel, business reverses, mental strength.

5   Love affairs, possible marriage or divorce. Travel, move of home, changes in life style, change in finances.

6   Marriage, divorce, domestic adjustments, responsibility.

7   Triumph, success in all matters, financial gain.

8   Change of finances, either gain or loss. Change in personal power going either up or down.

9   Bad emotions, nerves, upsets, delays, grief, loss.

10   Success, happiness, new responsibility. Possible birth of child.

11   Success, attainment, inspiration, strength, new associations, self assertion, high tension, nerves, love affairs, marriage, divorce.

12   Travel, trouble, unhappiness, downfall, loss.

13   Health, love affairs, marriage, travel, material loss with new change to follow.

14   Sacrifice, change of activities, move of home (possible), change in finances, marriage, divorce, failure, downfall.

15   Tragedy, divorce, adjustments, responsibility, travel, love affairs, marriage, divorce.

16   Destruction, ruin, loss of every type, adjustments, catastrophe, accidents, defeat, betrayal, sensuality.

17   Upswing of finances, new hope.

18   Deception, divorce, loneliness, delays, accidents, bad nerves and emotions.

19   Possible loss but a new rebirth, change, happiness, good fortune, success, marriage, love affairs.

20   Hindrances, decisions, marriage, divorce, love affairs, change.

21   Success, wisdom, new creations.

22   Travel, restraint, accidents, hard fall, always present is inspiration.

23   Change for the better, new activity, travel.
24   Great sacrifices, travel.
25   Great struggle, possible birth of a child.
26   Great disaster, suffering, disappointed love.
30   Travel, success.
40   Bad health, possible divorce, losses.
50   Change in activity, finances.
60   Divorce, responsibility.
70   Great success after struggle.
80   Large financial success, full health, self assertion in all matters.
90   Grief, sickness.
100   The mastery of all.
200   Great delays, disappointment in love.
300   Huge attainment.
400   Total ruin.
500   Tremendous change in all aspects.
600   A great new responsibility.
700   The mastery and attainment of all, power.
800   Large accumulation of power, prestige, influence, conquest.
900   Huge struggle, disruption.
1000   The perfection of self, great forward strides.
2000   A new partnership, betrayal in love matters.
3000   The zenith of self-expression, self-assertion.

Reviving Janet Audrey Hendrich, the following is laid out:

J	10	A	1	H	8
A	1	U	400	E	5
N	50	D	4	N	50
E	5	R	9	D	4
T	200	E	5	R	9
		Y	700	I	9
				C	3
				H	8
	266		1119		96

                              1481

The final total (1481) would be Janet's main path of life. This would indicate the major happenings to occur during the life. Since there is no number 1481 on the chart, the 1000 would stand alone. There is no 481 on the chart, so the 400 would also stand alone. There is no 81 on the chart so 80 also would stand alone. The final number would be a one. The first influence would be that of the "1000." The second influence that of the "400." The minor influences would be "80," and "1."

The "1000" would be the perfection of self, great forward strides. This indicates Janet's main course of life would be achievement, attainment. The "400" would mean total ruin. Some aspect of Janet's life is always going to be in a turmoil. The "80" indicates a minor period of grief, sickness. The "1" shows a life of constant change, many moves, new activities. This of course will be a minor vibration in the overall life.

Taking the secondary set of numbers (266-1119-96). Each in turn would apply to one of the three cycles or sub-paths.

During the first cycle, Janet would come under the aspects of the numbers 200-60-6.

During the second cycle, Janet would come under the aspects of the numbers 1000-100-19.

During the third cycle, Janet would be under the influence of the numbers 90-6.

As the cycles are secondary to the main path of life, so would the above cycle numbers be secondary to the total 1481.

The first name applies to the first cycle, the second name to the second cycle, the third name to the third cycle.

There are five letters in Janet's first name so the total amount of time in the first cycle would be divided into five equal parts. The letters in turn (their numerical digit) each would come into operation one following the other during this period.

The second cycle would be divided into six parts as there are six letters in the second name. The last cycle would be divided into eight equal parts as there are eight letters in the last name. We all know when we were born, none of us really know when we are going to die, thus, the last cycle will be assumed to be of a twenty seven year period.

The following chart may be constructed. It all fits fairly closely with what has been discovered to be expected during the course of Janet's life. The author has found this Quaballah to be very informative for exact periods of certain happenings.

There is nothing like old time tested methods. It is known what the studies in the first half of this text can do, they work well, forecast to perfection. This new chart which has been devised by the author has only been in existence for the last couple of years. It is of unknown quality.

This chart has been tested upon the lives of over two hundred people currently alive. It has been tested as much as possible against the lives of persons in the history books within the past few hundred years.

This author does not in any way suggest that this chart be used in place of the time tested methods. It is presented here as an additional study into numerology, as adapted to our modern lives. The application of this chart by the author against the lives of a few hundred people is hardly sufficient evidence, but the indications are there. The new Quaballah has been over ninety percent accurate.

The following chart is laid out with the corresponding numbers. No interpretation will be necessary as the interpretation of the numbers is in itself contained in this chapter.

The application of these numbers against the name does not change any of the major points in life such as the Soul Urge or Expression, with the possible exception of the "Us" re-evaluation at "400," rather than "300." For Soul Urge, etc. reduce the "U" to "300."

The use of higher octave numbers present a much clearer picture of the personality as found within the name. The ages and/or dates may be added if wished. The correct duration of each period is found by dividing the number of letters into the time of the cycle. As with other charts in numerology, all data must be kept relative.

QUABALLAH

PATH OF LIFE	CYCLES	PERIODS
		10
		1
	200 60 6	50
		5
		200
		1
		400
1000 400 80 1	1000 100 19	4
		9
		5
		700
		8
		5
		50
	90 6	4
		9
		9
		3
		8

Chapter 38

THE COMPLETE KNOWLEDGE OF LIFE AND DEATH

Now we will deal with the ultimate knowledge existing in numerology. The information in this chapter can be traced back over ten thousand years. It is a knowledge that even many professional numerologists do not possess. Without the knowledge of the material presented in this chapter the understanding of numerology is incomplete. The understanding of this chapter will be a study that will take many a lifetime to absorb completely. Those who can master this chapter will have at their disposal the knowledge of all life, past, present and future. The knowledge of the destinies of empires, corporations, individuals. To any who have not mastered the second study in this text this chapter will be worthless. A full complete knowledge and understanding of the numbers and letters must have been gained.

A warning goes with this knowledge. Do not use it for self-seeking. Do not misuse it. Those who are fortunate to gain an understanding will have the obligation to use this knowledge to aid others. Possession of this knowledge is the possession of ultimate wisdom. The knowledge of all life. The knowledge of life and death.

This chapter will deal with one of the forms of Kabalism. There are several good Kabalas currently in use, all originating in ancient eras. This particular Kabala was recently presented in a text by another numerologist and I would like to enlarge upon its interpretations. I offer as a suggestion the advice that more attention be paid to the numbers and less to the forms. The same identical form can mean two entirely different things, depending upon the numbers from which they are derived. I came upon this Kabala some twenty years ago and have had moderate success with it.

For the purpose of study in this chapter, the following fictional names, James Arthmas, will be employed. Birthdate is relatively unimportant.

As we will only be concerned with the first nine letters in the name it is immaterial what the balance of the letters in the name are. No forecast of death will be made as this author will never forecast death on any chart.

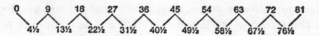

The first step is to set up a span that will represent the complete cycle of man, nine times nine, equaling eighty-one. The span therefore represents eighty-one years.

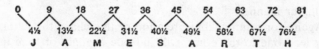

Before progression is made further, the above should be studied and fully understood. The total span represents eighty-one years. Each triangle covers a nine year period. The top of each triangle is exactly nine years apart running in sequences of nine. Each complete nine years represents one of the Major Life Pinnacle Cycles. The uphill climb goes from the midway point of each nine year cycle to the end of the cycle. The downhill drop runs from the start of the cycle to the midway point. Each midway point is exactly nine years from the next midway point. Each twenty-seven year period of which there are three (0–27/27–54/54–81) represents one of the sub-paths or Major Life Cycles.

The entire span must be judged and interpreted in the spirit

of the Path of Life. Each twenty-seven year period must likewise be interpreted in the spirit of the sub-paths of life. The life
path and sub-paths, while they will set the tone to the life, may
be played down in this Kabala, as the Kabala deals with specific
occurrences that will happen in the life and not the course or
path of the life. Likewise, the Soul Urge or Motivation can be
taken into consideration for an additional tone but again it can
be played down. No further concern will be paid in this text to
the birthdate, outside of the knowledge that its aspects must
temper the interpretation. The letters may be added to the
chart. Concern is only made with the first nine letters. These
letters must be, of course, the first nine letters in any name as of
the time of birth. Each of the letters is entered in the chart
under the half-way points. The letters that we will employ for
this chart are J-A-M-E-S-A-R-T-H. Each letter covers a nine
year period of the life. (I.e. Expanded Name Aura.)

Concentration should now be applied toward understanding
exactly what age periods each letter covers. The letter "J" represents birth to age nine. The letter "A" which follows covers the
period from age nine to age eighteen. The other letters follow
in similar manner.

Again, for a minor interpretation of this chart, the letters, as
they lead one to the other, will indicate changes of tone in the
life. The basic meanings of the letters will apply. "A" means
start, self, alone, etc. "A" is mentally inspired, while "S" is
emotional, vacillating. Each period will be covered by the
meanings of the letters themselves as well as the numerical
value of the letter. The entire numerical value must be taken
into consideration. The "S" must be dealt with as a "19," not
as a "1." The aspects of the "J" running into the "A" and then
the "A" running into the "M" must be taken into consideration,
but, again, they only set tones or moods when what is being
sought is specific incidents in the employment of this chart, not
general tones. The basics of numerology will supply general
tones in sufficient quantity. A tone for the period of 4½ to
13½ may be set by adding the "J" to the "A" for a total of
"20" (19 + 1 = 20). This would reduce to 2–0 over 2 and in-

dicate a merger, marriage, or partnership affecting the person involved, but again, it is only a tone setter.

The major triangle now can be completed. The single digit forms of each letter is entered below the letter. By ADDITION each digit will be added one to the other and reduced to a single digit to form the complete triangle.

Within the triangle are 45 numbers each interrelated with the other to form the whole. The intensity of any single number will again set a tone to the life. Also within the triangle are 36 minor triangles, again interrelated, each in turn can be removed

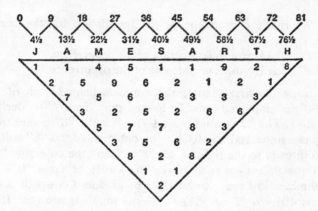

and looked into for aspects that will occur during the span of the life; but looking at the minor triangles without looking at the numbers they derive from is of little value. The final digit in the major triangle will set an additional tone to the life especially from age 36 to age 45.

Again, the Personal Years should be taken into consideration with the interpretations, but they also will have little impact upon the specific occurrences that are spelled out in the span.

Concern will be paid to age 36 to 40½.

There are two aspects to use for interpretation, the first one being the triangles (minor) for that age span. They will be found directly under the age of 40½ running from top to bottom. They are as follows:

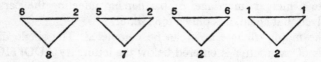

Taking the first triangle

The "6" is the cornerstone or the foundation for the occurrence.

The "2" is the key or the operation of the occurrence.

The "8" is the capstone or outcome of the occurrence.

Also using the first triangle the numbers behind each of the three digits employed must be looked into. The "6" is derived from 5–1. The "2" comes from 1–1 while the "8" comes from the cornerstone and key itself. The outcome of the "8" will be found directly to the right of the "8" namely the adjoining "3."

On downhill spans such as age 36 to 40½ or age 45 to 49½ the numbers are read to the right hand side. On uphill spans such as 40½ to 45 or 58½ to 63 the numbers are read from the left hand side.

There should not be any reason for an explanation of the numbers at this stage of the study but the general meanings as applied to the Kabala are offered below.

One   Self, Alone
Two   Partnership (Either business or marriage)
Three   Family, Travel
Four   Hardness, Limitation, Death
         (This chart would also apply to many people)
Five   Change, Travel
Six   Home, Marriage
Seven   Spirit, Travel (The travel would have water involved as the element of "7" is water)

Eight　　Discord, Rupture, Delays, Money, Movement
Nine　　Completion, Foreign, Emotions, Loss, Gain, Travel, Humanity (Many People)

Beyond the number "Nine" if the total aspect is wished to be looked into and instead of dealing with a 1–2 as 1–2 it can be dealt with as a "12" so the meanings of the numbers ten upwards can be applied.

In the minor triangle no number is to exceed sixty-four if it can be reversed and reduced. 9　　5 must be reversed and
　　　　　　　　　　　5
treated as 5　　9. The tricky part is that the numbers leading
　　　　　5
to the minor triangle numbers are not reversed and the aspect has to be watched carefully not to misplace the numbers in wrong positions.

The second aspect for each age period is the number line. Once again on downhill spans the numbers are pulled out to the right, on uphill spans to the left. The following examples are offered.

> Age 22½ to age 27 (Number Line) 4 5 7
> Age 58½ to age 63 (Number Line) 9 1 3 2 7 5 8
> Age 9 to age 13½ (Number Line) 1 5 5 2 7 5 2 1
> Age 63 to age 67½ (Number Line) 2 1

As with the minor triangles, the numbers leading to these line numbers must be looked into. They will be taken from the left or right depending upon the age span.

Regarding when these occurrences are to happen, the Number Lines are the lead up points to the minor triangles. The number line will transmit the occurrences in life during the first 3½ year period of the 4½ year span leading up to the minor triangles which will occur during the last year of the 4½ year span. Obtained from the major triangle will be all the aspects affecting the life from age 36 to age 40½. Age 36 to age 39½ (Number Line) 1 2 3 6 3

"1" Derived from 19/10 (S) leading to "1"
"2" Derived from 1—1 leading to "1"
"3" Derived from 2—1 leading to "3"
"6" Derived from 7—8 leading to "3"
"3" Derived from 6—6 no lead

Age 39½ to Age 40½ (Minor Triangles)

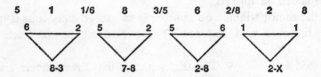

One final word on reversals, in some cases a reversal is not possible such as 8—8.

In this Kabala the "1" is an important aspect as it represents the self, and the position of the "1," especially in the Number Line, is of importance.

The interpretation will now proceed. I will start with the specific incidents that happened or are to happen between age 39½ to age 40½ (November 25, 1972, to November 25, 1973).

The "S" is setting a strong tone; it indicates emotional upheaval, rebirth, and leads directly to the below "1," which indicates self alone. With this tone in mind each triangle will be taken on a separate basis.

First Triangle   6   2
                            8

The cornerstone is "6" Home, Marriage. Leading to the "6" is the 5—1. The five means change. The one means self. The "One" is behind the "Five" indicating that the change will not be to the liking of the self.

The key is "2" Partnership, Marriage. The "2" is derived from the 1—1 which is a bad combination indicating that the self will be abused or misused in the marriage or partnership.

The capstone is "8." Coming off from a cornerstone in which a change is being forced upon self in regards to the family, home, and marriage; and a key where the self is being abused in a partnership/marriage, this "Eight" can be summed up in one Keyword, "Divorce."

Because of this rupture/divorce the "Eight" leads to travel (3) and/or results that will affect the family.

Second Triangle   5   2
                          7

The cornerstone is "5," Change, Travel. This is derived from the "8" used in the first triangle (Divorce) and the home, marriage (6). The base of operations thus is that the self will travel because of the rupture/divorce that affected the family, home. The key is "2," marriage/partnership. The "2" is derived from 3—5 meaning travel, change, family, with heavy emphasis on sex.

The capstone is "7" Spirit, Travel toward or over water.

The interpretation gradually evolves to this situation; because of the divorce the self will travel toward water, and along the way will form a liaison or marriage with another person. Because of the spiritual aspects of the "7," the self will also do much deep inner thinking.

The "7" leads to an "8" which indicates that this arrangement is doomed to rupture.

Third Triangle   5   6
                        2

The cornerstone is "5" derived from 5—6 indicating that a change will be made in the family, home, leading to travel.

The key is "6" derived from 6—2 meaning that a new liaison or partnership will be formed.

The capstone is "2" derived from the cornerstone and key which indeed indicates a new partnership/marriage/love-affair. There can be no other interpretation offered than that the self will separate from the first arrangement and form another. There will, of course, be travel involved.

This new arrangement (2) leads to another "8" which again shows that the liaison is destined to still another failure.

Fourth Triangle   1   1
                           2

The cornerstone of "1," self, is derived from a rupture (8) partnership (2).

The key is derived from the same combination only reversed 2–8.

The capstone will be still another merger/partnership/marriage/love-affair. Leading off are the two "Ones," which indicates that the self will be misused in the arrangement.

There is no follow through for this last two.

The foregoing was not a very happy tale. It is, however, the correct interpretation.

Only in a Kabala can a story be produced like this one, so full of the very details of the life of an individual.

Now to deal with the Number Line leading up to the final year of the span. 1–2–3–6–3.

The self is in front of the marriage, family, home, family. It will be noted that the family is interrupted by the six (marriage/divorce). Thus indication that the family will be reunited. The final "Three" is derived from 6–6 indicating responsibility, obligations, adjustments, overburdened with domestic affairs, such as only a reconciliation could create. The Number Line, while it pertains mostly to the first 3½ years of the span, will lead right up to the final point, especially with the last numbers such as the three. At this point any reader who has progressed this far should be able to interpret the numbers for himself and no further interpretations should be necessary.

Death can be picked out of the triangles and lines. This does not mean the death of the person involved but could be the death of a person close to the subject. Sex can be determined of people involved, and ages as well. There is no major occurrence that will happen in any life that is not shown on a Kabala.

As with the Excursion Chart this author can show how it is done but each reader in turn will have to become a student of the numbers in order to obtain correct and useful information. Each reader in turn who may be interested will have to teach himself how to forecast. There is no set rule, there is no formula such as is offered every now and then for a combination of numbers. All lead off numbers have to be taken into consideration and the elements involved could be a complete reversal of any preset code.

Chapter 39

CYCLES

Now the question is, why do some individuals have a better "1" year than others? Why is one "9" year more or less good than another "9" year in an individual life?

The Personal Years are the main vibration and control the overtone of the life. However, there are additional cycles which influence the Personal Year and spell out specific emphases.

This chapter is going to deal with five of these cycles. If the study lays out the Personal Years with the Magi Cycle and the Astrological Cycle, a very keen insight will be provided into any Personal Year. Both the Magi Cycle and the Astrological Cycle operate from birthday to birthday, the same as the Excursion; therefore these two cycles will operate within the overtone of two different Personal Years. However, it must be pointed out that the aspects suggested by the Magi and Astrological Cycles usually come into being directly following the birthday.

THE MAGI CYCLE

The Magi Cycle operates in a series of nine years and repeats itself although the octave of the Magi may often increase. This Magi Octave Cycle of nine years will repeat with the same Personal Years every cycle.

To locate the Magi Overtone, the year of birth is employed

and reduced to a compound number. The following examples are offered.

$$1960 \quad 1 + 9 + 6 + 0 = 16$$
$$1961 \quad 1 + 9 + 6 + 1 = 17$$

To locate the Magi Overtone for any given year the compound number of the year of birth is added to the current calendar year. Example: if an individual was born March 1, 1933, the "16" of the year 1933 would be added to the calendar year 1975 to locate the vibration for the period of 3/1/75 to 3/1/76.

$$1975$$
$$16$$
$$\overline{1991}$$

The total of 1991 would then be reduced to a compound digit of "20" by adding $1 + 9 + 9 + 1 = 20$. With the Magi Cycle only compound numbers are worked with, never fadic digits. To be more exact, no number under the total of "13" is ever employed. Often, especially in this point of time, a total digit such as 2023 or 2024 might be derived. The 2023 would add to a fadic "7" and the 2024 would add to a fadic "8." If this occurs in your calculations, these numbers must be handled in a different manner. The "20" of 2023 or 2024 would stand alone. The "23" of 2023 would be added together for a total of "5" and in turn added to the "20" of 2023 for a total compound number of "25." The same method would be employed with 2024. Example:

$$\frac{2\ 0}{20} \quad \frac{2\ 3}{5} = 25$$

$$\frac{2\ 0}{20} \quad \frac{2\ 4}{6} = 26$$

Utilizing the birthdate of Janet Audrey Hendrich, which is September 24, 1941, a chart will be constructed on the first 43 years of her life. The student will notice that every nine years the cycle repeats itself. Often, however, the octave increases; an "18" may be replaced with a "27," or if the chart has progressed far enough a "19" could be replaced with a "28." Nonetheless the same basis numbers appear every nine years and coincide exactly with the rotation of the Personal Years. This begins to give an insight into why different Personal Years react differently for different people.

Magi Cycle		JANET'S AGES		
18			24 to 25	
19		7 to 8	16 to 17	25 to 26	34 to 35
20		8 to 9	17 to 18	26 to 27	35 to 36
21	0 to 1	9 to 10	18 to 19	27 to 28	36 to 37
22	1 to 2	10 to 11	19 to 20	28 to 29	37 to 38
23	2 to 3	11 to 12	20 to 21	29 to 30	38 to 39
24	3 to 4	12 to 13	21 to 22	30 to 31	39 to 40
25	4 to 5	13 to 14	22 to 23	31 to 32	40 to 41
26	5 to 6	14 to 15	23 to 24	32 to 33	41 to 42
27	6 to 7	15 to 16		33 to 34	42 to 43

Individuals who cycle a Positive Magi with a Positive Personal Year have very good years indeed, but, in turn, must of necessity cycle the Negative Magi with the Negative Personal Years and have extremely difficult times. Individuals who have a coordination of Positive Magi with Negative Personal Years do not experience the vast highs and lows of the first category.

Interpretation of the Magi Cycle:

13 Often brings drastic moves of a physical nature. Often indicates death but must be held in relativity to the other aspects on the chart. Is a difficult vibration.

14 Brings domestic responsibility. Good financial vibration, but indicates danger from speculation. Very often brings a divorce/ separation of an unwise nature.

15 Favorable financial vibration. Brings both great joy and/or great sorrow. Emphasis is upon love affairs, births, and in certain instances deaths, of those close.

16 Unfavorable vibration. Accident-proneness. Brings unforeseen problems in negative personal years, but can also bring unexpected opportunity in positive personal years. A negative travel vibration. Deception can be expected in business matters.

17 Fortunate vibration. Good for dealing with financial matters of personal situations.

18 Brings deception, trickery, deceit, lies, treason, and betrayal in both personal and business matters. Be careful of enemies. Not a good period to travel. A bad vibration in which to commence new things.

19 A strong love vibration. Brings romance, success, and honor relevant to the life.

20 Brings good changes and opportunities into the life. New contacts, new interests, and a pleasant period.

21 The strongest of the success vibrations. Almost anything that is wished can be accomplished under its influence. Look to the personal year for deeper insight.

22 Indicates that personal affairs will be very pivotal and changeable within a short period of time. No major decisions should be made under this vibration, the outcome will be negative.

23 Usually brings legal proceeding of one type or another. Indicates extensive travel. Brings many changes of a positive and/or negative aspect. Look to the personal year for guidance.

24 A strong family love vibration, but sometimes brings illness to a close family member. Individuals under this influence will always find themselves in strong family ties.

25 Brings minor petty annoyances in all matters. Not a good health vibration; attention must be paid to this aspect.

26 Excellent financial vibration for income, but all investments and speculations are predoomed to failure. Both things can be equally true. Income will be good from older holdings, but new involvements can show loss. Do not become involved in matters of a financial nature in which partnerships are concerned.

27 Identical to 18 in every respect, only more intense.

28 Brings loss through confidence in others. Brings competition in all that you are involved with.

29 Brings deception and trickery in both business and personal affairs, but not as serious as the 18 or 27.

30 Very conducive to mental activities. A good period for writing.
31 Negative financial vibration. Often indicates loneliness.
32 A favorable vibration for personal matters, but be careful of all decisions made.
33 Another family vibration. Bring matters of a personal and/or family nature to the foreground.

It must be called to the attention of the student that all these interpretations must be held in relation to the individual life, and must be tempered by the other main vibrations in life.

There are six other minor Magi Undertones that are also operating with the main Magi Cycle, but space does not permit their inclusion in this volume.

THE ASTROLOGICAL CYCLE

This cycle operates in a set of twelve years and is the only cycle in numerology that does so. The Astrological Cycle is a brief introduction into astro-numerology and will set a vital emphasis upon any Personal Year in which it falls. This cycle also operates from birthday to birthday. The Astrological Cycle operating in a wave of twelve years operates against the Personal Years, which operate in a wave of nine years. The number thirty-six, being the common denominator of both twelve and nine, informs students that it is possible in a lifetime to have only a specific astrological house operate within a set of four different Personal Years.

With this cycle the student will have sufficient information to correctly compile the emphasis of any individual's Personal Year. The main chart to put together is a combination of four cycles: Personal Years, Magi Cycle, Astrological Cycle, and the Excursion.

Locating the Astrological Cycle for any individual is a simple matter, as all individuals operate in the identical cycle, as follows:

Astrological Cycles		Ages		
1	0 to 1	12 to 13	24 to 25	36 to 37
12	1 to 2	13 to 14	25 to 26	37 to 38
11	2 to 3	14 to 15	26 to 27	38 to 39
10	3 to 4	15 to 16	27 to 28	39 to 40
9	4 to 5	16 to 17	28 to 29	40 to 41
8	5 to 6	17 to 18	29 to 30	41 to 42
7	6 to 7	18 to 19	30 to 31	42 to 43
6	7 to 8	19 to 20	31 to 32	43 to 44
5	8 to 9	20 to 21	32 to 33	44 to 45
4	9 to 10	21 to 22	33 to 34	45 to 46
3	10 to 11	22 to 23	34 to 35	46 to 47
2	11 to 12	23 to 24	35 to 36	47 to 48

Using the above formula, this chart can be progressed to any age that is desired. Please note the fact that all individuals begin life in cycle "1" and then progress backwards through "12," "11," "10," etc.

Interpretation of the Astrological Cycles:

1 This year brings an emphasis upon personal assets such as appearance, and the influence made upon others. It is a good time in which to seek and obtain publicity. Will bring new associations that will be helpful to personal ambitions.

12 Causes ungrounded subconscious fears to arise. Physical health and tensions come to the foreground. Usually brings matters of a secretive nature and often brings involvement in a love relationship of a secretive nature. There is a lot of emphasis upon dealings with public institutions such as hospitals, etc. Health must be guarded closely. In a "7" Personal Year bad health is indicated. In a "5" or a "3" Personal Year love affairs are indicated.

11 Help can be expected from outside sources. Will bring opportunity for advancement especially in the "1" and "5" Personal Years. The main emphasis is upon material growth.

10 The overtone here deals with career, credit, reputation, and

personal status. In order to correctly judge whether or not it indicates growth or decline it must be judged relatively to the personal years. Often brings involvement with bureaucrats. In a "9" year, could bring trouble such as an IRS audit. For law-breakers in a "9" year this cycle will usually bring prose-cution. Conversely, in a "1" Personal Year or an "8" Personal Year, might bring to a businessman beneficial government con-tracts. Additionally, often brings concern with parents.

9   The overtone here is one of long-distance and/or foreign travel. Often brings problems or concern with in-laws. Causes one to become introspective. Litigation often arises and must be judged in conjunction with the Personal Year. Brings a lot of dealings with people far removed and in foreign parts. A very strong love vibration, especially involvement with a foreigner. (A for-eigner is someone who comes from someplace the subject does not, so the involvement could be with someone from another state as well as from a foreign country.)

8   Emphasis is upon any financial holding owned jointly. Also upon inheritance. Brings unexpected income. Sex problems often arise under this force. This vibration, further, rules death. If in a "2" Personal Year, someone close might pass away. If in an "8" Personal Year, will usually bring inheritance of some sort.

7   The emphasis here is upon marriage and/or close personal in-volvement. If in a "6" year, it brings marriage. If in a "5" year, it brings romance. If in a "9" year, it often brings the end of marriage/romance. At any rate, the overtone is upon marriage, and in any year will bring this to the foreground. If already married, it will at the least bring all the problems under the surface in the relationship very much to the foreground.

6   A concern and/or an involvement with a small pet usually arises. Brings stress on relationships with the people who are worked with. Above all, brings a year of hard, intensive, gruel-ing work, which is in no sense negative. An excellent year in which to put the physical body into shape. A good time to diet, visit a doctor or dentist.

5   Indicates love affairs, especially linked with young children and/or pregnancy. A lot of emphasis is upon entertaining and being entertained, and going out to amusement.

4   Usually indicates domestic problems arising. Very often brings the termination, in one manner or another, of a long-term close emotional involvement. The Personal Year must be checked in this aspect. Dealings in real estate will come to the foreground. Can bring problems with or because of parents. Often ends many long-term relationships.

3   More than any other year, emphasis is upon communications and news being delivered to the subject. Also indicates a lot of short trips. Relationships with brothers and sisters will be in the foreground in one manner or another.

2   The emphasis is upon money, finances, and income. The Personal Year must be checked to see if it is positive or negative.

MONTH CYCLES–DAY CYCLES–DAY RAYS

Before progressing into any of these cycles it must be pointed out once again that interpretations must be relative to the individual life and age group. Further, it must also be pointed out that these cycles operate within the major year cycles and are subject to various interpretations based upon these year interpretations. A negative month cycle will have little effect in the over-all pattern of a positive year, but will, in turn, create even more difficulty in a negative year. At any rate, all things will be equally true, but must be held in relation to the individual life.

In order to create a month-cycle chart or a day-cycle chart it is necessary to determine positive/fair/negative numbers for any individual. These aspects will be determined in a manner used only for these two particular charts. However, it can be noted with interest that the negative numbers are usually the missing numbers in the inclusion chart or presented in the inclusion chart as an overabundance.

The nine basic fadic digits will be dealt with. A return will be made to the study of Janet Audrey Hendrich.

Positive numbers are found in five ways. The first positive number is the Soul Urge/Motivation. The second positive number is the Quiescent/Quiet Self. The third positive number is the Expression/Personality. The fourth positive number is the Life Path/Destiny. The fifth positive number is the number coordinate of the planetary ruler of the astrological house of birth.

Janet's Soul Urge is "9," so nine is her first positive number. Her Quiet Self is "4," so her second positive number is four. Her Expression is also "4" and numbers are not repeated, so this is negated. Janet is on a "3" Life Path, so the number three is also positive. Janet was born on September 24 and thus is Libra. Libra is ruled by Venus, which vibrates to the number "6," so six becomes a positive number for Janet. However, being born on September 24, she is also on the cusp of Virgo, which is ruled by Mercury and vibrates to the number "5," so the five also becomes positive.

People born on the cusp of any sign must be credited with the numbers of both signs. The chart for these birthdates and signs is offered below.

Capricorn	December 22 to January 19
	Cusp—December 21, 22, 23
	Ruler—Saturn
	Number vibration—8
Aquarius	January 20 to February 18
	Cusp—January 19, 20, 21, 22
	Ruler—both Uranus and Saturn
	Number vibration—both 6 and 8
Pisces	February 19 to March 20
	Cusp—February 18, 19, 20, 21, 22
	Ruler—both Neptune and Jupiter
	Number vibration—both 5 and 3
Aries	March 21 to April 19
	Cusp—March 20, 21, 22
	Ruler—both Mars and Pluto
	Number vibration—both 9 and (22) 4

Taurus	April 20 to May 20
	Cusp—April 19, 20, 21, 22
	Ruler—Venus
	Number vibration—6

Gemini	May 21 to June 21
	Cusp—May 20, 21, 22
	Ruler—Mercury
	Number vibration—5

Cancer	June 22 to July 22
	Cusp—June 21, 22, 23
	Ruler—Moon
	Number vibration—both 2 and 7 (the Moon vibrates to both numbers)

Leo	July 23 to August 23
	Cusp—July 22, 23, 24
	Ruler—Sun
	Number vibration—both 1 and 4 (the Sun vibrates to both numbers)

Virgo	August 24 to September 23
	Cusp—August 22, 23, 24
	Ruler—Mercury
	Number vibration—5

Libra	September 24 to October 23
	Cusp—September 22, 23, 24
	Ruler—Venus
	Number vibration—6

Scorpio	October 24 to November 22
	Cusp—October 22, 23, 24
	Ruler—Mars
	Number vibration—9

Sagittarius	November 23 to December 21
	Cusp—November 22, 23, 24
	Ruler—Jupiter
	Number vibration—3

Note that people born on the cusp have two or more positive numbers. Further, both the Sun and the Moon vibrate to two different numbers. Thus, it is possible for a subject to acquire as many as four positive numbers from the sign of birth.

Progressing with Janet's chart, we can construct the following:

POSITIVE NUMBERS

9   from the Soul Urge
4   from the Quiet Self
3   from the Life Path
6   from the Astrological House of Birth
5   from the Cusp of the Astrological House of Birth.

> Her "4" of the Expression offers no assistance, as
> it was already covered by the "4" of the Quiet Self.

The next set of numbers to be dealt with is the Fair Numbers. These are derived from two sources, the fadic digit of the day of birth and the Life Power Number.

Janet was born on the twenty-fourth of the month, and the fadic digit of "24" is "6." However, she already has the number "6" as a positive number, so this is now negated. Her Life Power Number is a "7," so this becomes her only Fair Number. The chart is now progressed:

POSITIVE	FAIR
3	7
4	
5	
6	
9	

Finally, to find the negative numbers, all the numbers which do not appear in either the positive or the fair column become negative. Thus Janet's chart is now completed in this first aspect.

POSITIVE	FAIR	NEGATIVE
3	7	1
4		2
5		8
6		
9		

Once these numbers are found, they will remain consistent throughout the subject's life.

Progressing with Janet's month cycles we must construct a second chart to find the cycle vibratory beat connected with her name. Beginning with the total name as given at birth, the first letter, "J," is counted as one, with each succeeding letter being counted until the thirteenth letter is reached, under which is placed the number "1." The thirteenth letter is the "E" in Hendrich.

JANET AUDREY HENDRICH
1

Beginning with the letter "E" in Hendrich, or the number "1," count forward thirteen letters, using as the number-one count the letter "E." This leaves a space of twelve letters between succeeding counts. Beginning with the letter "E" in Hendrich as number one, the "N" in Hendrich becomes number two, and so on. At the end of the name Hendrich the count continues again with the name Janet. The second thirteen occurs at the letter "A" in Audrey, under which the number "2" is placed. Beginning with this "A," again count thirteen to the letter "C" in Hendrich, which becomes "3."

JANET AUDREY HENDRICH
2   1   3

The same method is followed until the original position of "1" under the first count is reached. In Janet's case this becomes a count of "20," as follows:

JANET   AUDREY   HENDRICH
19 8 16 5 13   2 10 18 7 15 4   12 1 9 17 6 14 3 11
                                             20

In Janet's case the entire name was used to find the vibratory beat, which is 20. This is not the case with all names. A name may vibrate to two, or any other number. A new example is offered, utilizing a name that does not use all the letters. In short, when the original position is reached the count will stop.

MARY HELEN SMITH
 7   6   5   4   3   2   1
                        8

The vibratory beat on the above name, Mary Helen Smith, which has fourteen letters, is "8."

It must now be found out which of these vibratory beats Janet is operating in during any given calendar year. We will use for example the calendar year 1975. In 1975 Janet will reach her thirty-fourth birthday. From the age of thirty-four is subtracted the total vibratory beat of "20" as many times as possible, leaving fourteen. Janet in 1975 is in the fourteenth beat of her 20-cycle vibratory name.

For further illustration let it be assumed that another person in 1975 will reach the age of fifty. Let it be further assumed that this person has a total vibratory beat of "8" to the name. Eight can be subtracted from age fifty six times ($6 \times 8 = 48$), leaving "2." This person would be in the "2" beat for the year 1975.

In the calendar year 1976 Janet will reach age thirty-five. Her "20" would then be subtracted from age thirty-five to give "15" and she would be under the "15" function for 1976.

Janet's birthday is in September. In 1975 her month cycles would begin in September with the number "14," or the "I" in Hendrich. In 1976 her month cycles would begin in September with the number "15," or the "E" in Audrey.

Years operate birthday to birthday, and months operate from

birth anniversary to birth anniversary. Thus, Janet's months operate from the twenty-fourth to the twenty-fourth. A person born on the eighth of the month would have his months operate from the eighth to the eighth.

Janet was born in September, so her month cycles commence in September. A person born in March would have his month cycles begin in March.

During the calendar year 1975, because of the count of "14" associated with this year, Janet will begin her month cycles with the letter "I" in Hendrich. This letter "I" will be in effect from 9/24/75 to 10/24/75. The letter in effect for the period of 10/24/75 to 11/24/75 would be the following letter, or the "C" in Hendrich. The letter in effect for the period of 11/24/75 to 12/24/75 would be the letter "H" in Hendrich. The letter in effect for the period of 12/24/75 to 1/24/76 would be the "J" in Janet. There the progression must stop, as only one year can be dealt with at a time. The calendar year 1975 for Janet begins on 1/24/75 and ends on 1/24/76. To find the months before September, the count is made backward. The letter "R" in Hendrich would be in effect from 8/24/75 to 9/24/75, and so on. The count cannot progress backward past 1/24/75. The following chart is offered for further clarification.

```
J     12/24/75 to 1/24/76
A
N
E
T

A
U
D
R     1/24/75 to 2/24/75
E     2/24/75 to 3/24/75
Y     3/24/75 to 4/24/75
```

        H   4/24/75 to 5/24/75
        E   5/24/75 to 6/24/75
        N   6/24/75 to 7/24/75
        D   7/24/75 to 8/24/75
        R   8/24/75 to 9/24/75
        I   9/24/75 to 10/24/75—(1975 Vibratory Beat)
        C   10/24/75 to 11/24/75
        H   11/24/75 to 12/24/75

The last step is to determine if any given month will be positive or negative in aspect for Janet. The month of September 1975 vibrates to an "I," which has a value of "9." This "9" means little in itself. This change is taking place on the twenty-fourth of the month. Look at which day the twenty-fourth falls upon. Then refer to the day-ruler chart offered further in this chapter. If for example, this day was a Friday which vibrates to "6" the positive-fair-negative interpretation would be made depending upon the subject's position with the number "6." Fair numbers are a mixture of both the positive and negative aspects.

Meanings of the letters in the Month Cycle Chart:

A   Positive   Indicates a firmness in life and association with intellectual people.
    Negative   Indicates the individual is prone to become impulsive to his own detriment.
B   Positive   A time of constructive building on all planes.
    Negative   Indicates lack of building.
C   Positive   Indicates a period of creativity. Also indicative of the birth of a female child.
    Negative   Indicates inner emotion for which there is no outlet.
D   Positive   New opportunities will be presented.
    Negative   The opportunities will be unable to be attained.
E   Positive   Brings positive change and growth. Can also mean the birth of a male child.
    Negative   A scattering of energies in too many diverse directions.

F	Positive	Means positive, smooth conditions.
	Negative	Indicates adverse conditions.
G	Positive	Indicates responsibilities of a positive nature.
	Negative	Indicates responsibilities of a negative nature.
H	Positive	Indicates good financial income.
	Negative	Indicates poor financial income.
I	Positive	Good financial return for inspirational ideas.
	Negative	Poor financial return for inspirational ideas.
J	Positive	Positive adjustment and justice.
	Negative	Injustice.
K	Positive	Indicates kindness.
	Negative	Indicates lack of kindness.
L	Positive	A smooth month which often brings love affairs.
	Negative	The subject will be driven along by adverse circumstances.
M	Positive	Indicates completion of older affairs. Often brings hidden love affairs.
	Negative	Indicates hard conditions and that many things can topple because of the lack of a firm foundation.
N	Positive	Brings an awareness of the needs of humanity.
	Negative	Brings lack of increase and negative emotions.
O	Positive	Indicates money coming in. Change for better in domestic situations. Possible water trips.
	Negative	Indicates loss of money. Problems in the home. Negative emotional experiences.
P	Positive	Brings recognition relevant to the individual life.
	Negative	Brings loss of prestige.
Q	Positive	Brings a general uplift in life.
	Negative	Can cause very weird situations.
R	Positive	Good conditions for finances, travel, and personal relationships.
	Negative	The reverse of the above.
S	Positive	Brings unexpected things of a positive nature.
	Negative	Brings unexpected things of a negative nature.
T	Positive	Brings opportunity to become engaged in new pursuits.
	Negative	Causes confusion and hard, intense conditions.

U Positive   Indicates love affairs.
   Negative   Indicates negative love experiences.
V Positive   Brings inner revelation.
   Negative   Indicates no cooperation from others and danger in-
              volving large bodies of water.
   Either positive or negative can bring conditions involving
   large corporations and/or the government.
W Positive   Indicates success in business ventures.
   Negative   Indicates failure in business ventures caused by
              others.
X Positive   Indicates many daring achievements will be under-
              taken.
   Negative   Brings a need of inner courage to face negative as-
              pects.
Y Positive   Indicates an overtone of positive conditions for the
              next several months and that the seeds will be planted
              this month.
   Negative   Indicates the reverse of the positive.
Z Positive   Indicates general increase.
   Negative   Indicates lack of increase.

Moving forward into day cycles, there are two of these in operation every nine days, a major and a minor. Unfortunately
space does not permit the presentation of the Minor Cycle, so
concentration will be made upon the Major Cycle only.

Within these day cycles lies the key to exact forecasting. If a
specific event is going to happen during the course of a given
year, it can be zeroed in on with the personal months and
month cycles, then further reduced to day cycles. The trigger
day will be the personal day that relates to the day-cycle vibrations.

A new chart now has to be constructed. Using the calendar
year 1976, the calendar month of January is a 24/6 universal
month. $(1976 = 1 + 9 + 7 + 6 = 23.$ January $= 1.$ $23 + 1 =$
24, reduced to "6.")

Jan. Feb. Mar. Apr. May June July Aug. Sept. Oct. Nov. Dec.
24/6 25/7 26/8 27/9 28/1 29/2 30/3 31/4 32/5 33/6 34/7 35/8

Students should note that while both January and October are "Six" universal months, because of the compound differences they will vary. This will have no importance in working with this chart but is offered as a point of interest.

For all individuals, the calendar month of January 1976 is a "Six" universal vibration. To locate the correct day-cycle vibrations for the year 1976, the Life Path number has to be brought up to the universal vibration. In the case of Janet, who is on a "3" Path of Life, the sum of "3" has to be added to bring her personal vibration up to the universal vibration. For an individual on a "1" Path of Life the sum of five would have to be added. For a person on a "7" Path of Life, which exceeds the "6" universal vibration, the sum of eight would have to be added to bring the vibration up to "6" $(7 + 8 = 15 = 6)$. It is this added sum only that the interest is in. Because of the difference between Janet's Life Path of "3" and the universal vibration of "6" it was necessary to add three. This three becomes the day-cycle vibration for the month of January. This same process is used for every month in the year; however, once the first month is found things will run in rotation. The completed chart looks as follows:

Universal Vibration	24/6	25/7	26/8	27/9
Calendar Month (1976)	January	February	March	April
Janet's Day Cycle	3	4	5	6

The progression on the chart could be made for the entire year running up to the vibration of "9" and then resuming with "1" the following month.

In the month of January Janet's vibrations for the day cycles commence with three. Thus her first cycle will be in effect from January 3 until January 11—a nine-day period. Her second cycle begins the day after, which is the twelfth (also a multiple of three) and operates for another nine-day period, until the twentieth. The third cycle begins on January 21 and operates until January 29, for an additional nine-day period. The final cycle will not be in effect for a full nine days. It begins on January 30 and remains in force until the February cycles start to come in, on February 4. As Janet is in a "4" cycle for the month of February her cycle changes will take place on the fourth, thirteenth, and twenty-second (nine-day periods beginning on the fourth).

It is now necessary for the reader to become familiar with the following information:

> Monday is ruled by the Moon with a 2/7 vibration.
> Tuesday is ruled by Mars with a 9 vibration.
> Wednesday is ruled by Mercury with a 5 vibration.
> Thursday is ruled by Jupiter with a 3 vibration.
> Friday is ruled by Venus with a 6 vibration.
> Saturday is ruled by Saturn with an 8 vibration.
> Sunday is ruled by the Sun with a 1/4 vibration.

To find out if any particular day cycle is positive or negative the above chart must be consulted. In January Janet's cycle changes occur on the third, twelfth, twenty-first, and thirtieth. It makes no difference if the number 3 or any of its compounds are positive or negative for Janet. It only makes a difference if the days on which the cycle changes take place are positive or negative for her.

January 3, 1976, fell on a Saturday. Saturday vibrates to Saturn, or the number "8." Janet is negative on the number "8," so she would receive a negative interpretation of the number "3" for her first cycle. January 12 fell on a Monday. Monday is ruled by the Moon and vibrates to both the "2" and the "7." Janet is negative with the number "2" and fair with the number "7." Therefore she gets a negative interpretation of the number "12." The fair "7" will negate part of the negativity, but her Monday combination is mostly negative. January 21 fell on a Wednesday, which is ruled by Mercury and vibrates to "5." Janet is positive with the number "5" and thus would receive a positive interpretation of the number "21." January 30 fell on a Friday, which is ruled by Venus and vibrates to "6." Janet is also positive with the number "6" and thus would receive a positive interpretation of the number "30."

The interpretations for the days of the month are as follows:

1   Positive   Places the individual in a situation in which he is working alone in a positive way. Often brings new conditions. This cycle will be strongly influenced by males.

       Negative   Carries a warning to avoid forcefulness or the subject will be forced to work without the help of others.

10   Positive   May indicate legal matters in a positive manner.

      Negative   The reverse of the positive.

19   Positive   Brings unexpected happenings of a positive nature.

      Negative   Brings unexpected happenings of a negative nature.

28   Positive   Brings balance and harmony into the life.

      Negative   Brings the reverse of the positive, indicating lack of success.

2   Positive   A period of routine work. Good time for making agreements.

      Negative   Carries a warning to be careful in all dealings, as deceit on the part of others is indicated.

11   Positive   Good time to make agreements. Finished products will be in the foreground. Good time to buy/sell/trade/travel by car.

      Negative   Indicates loss, especially caused by fire.

20   Positive   Brings balanced conditions. A good time to collect debts. Things will move slowly and the keyword is patience.

      Negative   Indicates loss of time, difficult decisions, emotional upsets, and possible health problems, especially for women.

29   Positive   Identical in all aspects to the number "11."

      Negative   Identical in all aspects to the number "11."

3   Positive   Emphasis is upon love of a personal nature.

      Negative   Indicates upsets caused by personal love.

12 Positive   Indicates the subject will be surrounded by many positive people and friends.

    Negative   Indicates association with negative people, who will try to take advantage of the subject. Often brings secret love affairs.

21 Positive   An easy period filled with friendship.

    Negative   Indicates lack of friends and a feeling of being unloved.

30 Positive   A smooth period that brings expansion.

    Negative   A time of a general scattering of forces.

4   Positive   A smooth period that brings harmonious conditions in all areas of involvement.

    Negative   Very little will work out as planned. Brings a period of discord and grinding work.

13 Positive   Another smooth period. A good time to pay debts.

    Negative   Like the negative "4" but more intense.

22 Positive   Indicates dealings with large corporations and/or the government. Can also mean trips to, on, over, or near large bodies of water. All dealings will be of a positive nature.

    Negative   Brings danger from large bodies of water. Avoid all dealings with large corporations and/or the government, or they will turn out negatively.

5   Positive   Brings good change. A fast-moving period. Will bring dealings with younger people. Indicates short-trip travel. Good time to put the physical body in shape.

    Negative   Brings negative change, accidents, and emotional discord caused by problems in personal relationships.

14 Positive   Identical to the positive "5" and in addition brings a lot of social activity.

    Negative   Identical to the negative "5" and also brings an argument-prone situation.

23 Positive   Identical to the positive "5" but indicates trips in various directions.

    Negative   Identical to the negative "5." Be careful of breaking physical/material objects.

6	Positive	Sometimes brings travel. Indicates new conditions in the home. Excellent time to advertise and/or promote. Slow-moving.
	Negative	Indicates emotional upsets mostly caused by the inner self. Mechanical apparatus is prone to go out of service.
15	Positive	Indicates money coming in. Good for personal relationships. A good period in which to make agreements.
	Negative	A bad period in which to make agreements as the indication is for deceit on the part of others.
24	Positive	Gifts and money can be expected during this period.
	Negative	Indicates money going out and an emotionally upsetting period.
7	Positive	Brings good change. Good time to make agreements. Excellent for airplane travel.
	Negative	The reverse of the positive "7." Brings deceit and treachery from others. Be careful of theft.
16	Positive	Identical to the positive "7" and in addition brings an increase in financial holdings.
	Negative	Identical to the negative "7" and brings a loss of personal prestige.
25	Positive	Brings dealings with younger people. A time of important change. Also has all of the attributes of the positive "7."
	Negative	Indicates deceit and betrayal from others. Indicates negative change.
8	Positive	A good business period. The indication is that older business will bear more fruit than newer business.
	Negative	Poor business conditions in all aspects.
17	Positive	Gifts may be expected. Another business period of success. Again, a good time to deal with older aspects.
	Negative	Past mistakes will rise up and have to be accounted for.
26	Positive	Brings good change in both business and home life.
	Negative	Old relationships will rise to the surface in a negative manner.

9	Positive	Excellent period for personal relationships, travel, and money. A good time in which to deal with legal matters.
	Negative	Negative period for personal relationships, travel, and money. Can bring adverse legal proceedings.
18	Positive	Identical to the positive "9."
	Negative	Identical to the negative "9." Trips planned in this period will never materialize.
27	Positive	Identical to the positive "9."
	Negative	Identical to the negative "9."

The last cycle to be presented will provide additional insight into the day cycles. For every day in the year there is a yearly cycle that changes daily. These day emphases are in the forefront only on the exact day that the day cycle changes, and will cast an overtone on the nine-day period of the day cycles.

These day impacts operate with the astrological signs and are constant every year. If a day-cycle change occurs on a cusp day, then both these day impacts will apply.

Capricorn	Monday	Love upsets
	Tuesday	Bad judgment
	Wednesday	Argument-prone
	Thursday	Mental ambition
	Friday	Materialism
	Saturday	Skepticism
	Sunday	High mentality

Aquarius	Monday	Intelligence
	Tuesday	Skepticism
	Wednesday	Disappointment
	Thursday	High intelligence
	Friday	Gentleness
	Saturday	Virtue
	Sunday	Ambition

Pisces	Monday	Ambition
	Tuesday	Courage
	Wednesday	Restlessness
	Thursday	Fickleness
	Friday	Impossible yearning
	Saturday	Mysticism
	Sunday	Morality
Aries	Monday	Haughtiness
	Tuesday	Contempt
	Wednesday	Generosity
	Thursday	Diplomacy
	Friday	Versatility
	Saturday	Intellectuality
	Sunday	Pleasure
Taurus	Monday	Intelligence
	Tuesday	Disappointment
	Wednesday	Generosity
	Thursday	Independence
	Friday	Longevity
	Saturday	Credulity
	Sunday	Lack of self-control
Gemini	Monday	Restlessness
	Tuesday	Versatility
	Wednesday	Either neglect or attention
	Thursday	Inconstancy
	Friday	Honesty and success
	Saturday	Thoughtfulness
	Sunday	Anxiety
Cancer	Monday	Moodiness
	Tuesday	Sensitivity
	Wednesday	Impulsiveness
	Thursday	Responsibility
	Friday	Drama and music
	Saturday	Congeniality
	Sunday	Love of the beautiful

Leo	Monday	Violent disposition
	Tuesday	Phlegmatic conditions
	Wednesday	Self-confidence
	Thursday	Plastic arts
	Friday	Conceit
	Saturday	Persistence
	Sunday	Success
Virgo	Monday	Persistence
	Tuesday	Egotism
	Wednesday	Justice
	Thursday	Longevity
	Friday	Analytical
	Saturday	Mechanical arts
	Sunday	Economy
Libra	Monday	Independence
	Tuesday	Justice
	Wednesday	Impulsiveness
	Thursday	Ambition
	Friday	Restlessness
	Saturday	Good relations with opposite sex
	Sunday	Boldness
Scorpio	Monday	Gossip
	Tuesday	Kindness
	Wednesday	Speech
	Thursday	Pride
	Friday	Intelligence
	Saturday	Overpowering feelings
	Sunday	Luxury
Sagittarius	Monday	Mechanics
	Tuesday	Humorousness
	Wednesday	Art
	Thursday	Poetry and music
	Friday	Independence
	Saturday	Gloominess
	Sunday	Religion

It is well to keep in mind with all charts and cycles that in a spiritual sense nothing is presented that is negative, as it brings growth and evolvement. However, in the mental, physical, emotional sense many happenings can be negative.

All serious students of numerology would do well to enter a study of the spiritual meanings of numbers; there are several good publications available concerning this aspect. While this does not deal directly with numerology it gives a very deep insight into the meaning of numbers.

The key to understanding all charts is in the Inclusion table. Advanced students should undertake a study of the Inclusion stress lines. This subject is a study for an entire new book, but a brief insight will be presented here.

Utilizing the Inclusion table for Janet Audrey Hendrich, the following is found:

3	1	2
2	5	—
1	2	3

There are eight possible stress lines in each Inclusion table, as follows: The 1-2-3 line, the 4-5-6 line, the 7-8-9 line, the 1-4-7 line, the 2-5-8 line, the 3-6-9 line, the 7-5-3 line, and the 1-5-9 line. Whichever line adds up to the greatest total becomes the stress line. If two or more lines total the same, then there would be more than one stress line.

Janet's stress lines are as follows:

1-2-3	line	Total	6
4-5-6	line	Total	7
7-8-9	line	Total	6
1-4-7	line	Total	6
2-5-8	line	Total	8

3-6-9 line   Total   5
7-5-3 line   Total   8
1-5-9 line   Total 11

Her main stress line is the 1-5-9 combination, denoting a general elevation in life far removed from the position of birth. Students who will take the time to study and analyze the relationship of numbers will soon come to an understanding of what each stress line denotes. However, these lines will be influenced by the surrounding numbers as well.

Chapter 40

THE COMPLETE INTERPRETATION

To gain complete interpretation on any individual chart the following must be done.

The Soul Urge must be taken into consideration as this is one of the prime motivations in life. The Expression must be taken under advisement as this describes the vibrations that any given life is attracting to itself. The cornerstone must be considered as this is what the life is built upon. The Key must likewise be considered; this is the way the life is lived.

The planes of expression and first vowel, must be looked into as this best describes the individual actions.

The fixed paths such as life path, cycle, pinnacle, and pinnacle cycle, must be measured, one against the other, for a long term forecast. Above all the Life Challenge must be given prime consideration in this matter.

For an immediate forecast, the chart of the excursion should be used, taking into consideration the above facts.

For a short range forecast, the personal and universal vibrations are to be used. All of the foregoing must be taken into consideration as well. In the short range forecast, the letters pertaining to that period from the excursion should be used. The Personal Year, Universal Year, Year Pinnacles, Year Challenge, Periodicity, Monthly Cycles, Personal Month, Universal Month, Month, Pinnacles, Month Challenges, must all be considered. If the forecast is to be tightened up even further the day vibrations must be studied.

Each aspect, each number, must be carefully weighed, one against the other.

The very best indicator to be used with all the charts is the Inclusion; as it is the inclusion that informs what we have, what is lacking, and what will have to be made up.

When this information has grown within you in this manner, you will then begin to see how very fascinating and useful a subject numerology can be.

In this text I have presented a very deep study into numerology. I cannot teach any individual how to forecast. Each must teach himself. This takes time, work, and serious application. The main aim of this study has not been to teach forecasting. It has been rather a modest attempt to describe certain cosmic laws, and thereby inducing in the reader a clearer understanding of life.

I do not expect most of my readers to become professional numerologists. I do hope however, I have helped give a greater understanding and interest in the subject. For those who would like to continue the study of numerology, I would suggest that you obtain as much information as possible from as many sources as possible. Apply this information, test it out, learn to discriminate, to separate the wheat from the chaff. When you have gotten what you feel is a solid basic foundation of knowledge, you can then synthesize it into a workable system.

Lastly, for a more complete understanding, the numbers behind the final digit must be taken into account. A "One" derived from a "Ten" must be treated like a "Ten," not like a "One." For interpreting letters, the higher octaves must be employed. Both "A" and "J" are "Ones," however the "J" must be treated as a "Ten." Both in the charts used for forecasting, and in the charts employed for interpretation of traits, the number behind the final digit must be analyzed. A "Nine" derived from an "Eighteen" has quite a story to tell, in any type of chart. The other related numbers have to be taken in conjunction with the "Eighteen" in order to find out precisely what the "18" means, if it means misery to the self, or the self is destined to inflict hurt upon others, if the spirit of the "Nine" has not been reached.

I have found the essence of the Excursion very correct and informative. The essence and duality, if any, on an Excursion chart will answer many questions.

The number "Nine" has to be carefully judged for correct interpretation. The "Nine" can bring an end to good things, it can also bring an end to bad things; sometimes within a short period it makes a complete reversal.

A further outline of how the "Nine" operates in this respect is diagrammed in the following, which are actual charts taken from real life, with real people affected by these numbers.

Personal Year	9	(1964)
Personal Month	9	(September)
Personal Day	9	(9th)
Essence	9	

The month pinnacles were "Nine" for the entire month. The day pinnacles were "Nine" for the entire day. The year pinnacles were "Seven," which were Karmic. The Periodicity was "Three," and was in conflict with the major challenge of the year. The month cycle was "Six."

Every single element on this chart called for finish, destruction, ruin. The key to what type of ruin was the unaffected "Six" (Marriage/Divorce/Responsibility/Obligation).

On this date in a "Nine" Personal Hour, the man who was the owner of the above set of calculations had his wife leave him.

On September 27, 1964, which in every respect was identical to the above chart, the wife returned to the marriage. She returned in a "One" Personal Hour.

The first set of numbers brought a finish to the marriage. The second set of identical numbers brought a finish to the divorce or separation.

The same set of numbers also appeared on the 18th. On this date, the person affected, despondent over the loss of his wife, sold his home and business at great sacrifice. The hidden numbers (9—18—27) give a good indication.

I don't wish to get into too much detail with this story, but will expound upon it a little further.

Both the man and wife operate in the same yearly cycle. All vibrations for both, with the exception of Periodicity, and month cycles, are identical. The months, days, and other elements are in complete agreement. This usually leads to a very happy domestic life.

Every nine years they seem to run into a problem together. The marriage is always happy and secure except for the ninth year. This current year (1973) is also a "Nine" year for both parties involved. Even armed with the knowledge of what to expect, they are having a hard time keeping peace in their home this year. Each succeeding nine years the trouble seems to get more intense. The new "One" year always brings happiness, security.

The key to this trouble is in the Inclusion. The man has an intensity of "One." The wife has a Karma of "Six." He must learn to overcome, subdue the intensity. She must learn the lessons of the "Six."

Each "Nine" year is bringing these people large financial loss because of the neglect of business due to personal problems.

The gentleman involved is my client and understands the problems. The lady does not place much stock in numerology, but nevertheless, in spite of her disbelief, has great trouble with the "Six." The trouble can be overcome if they will both work together.

As it stands now, in the years "One" to "Eight," the wife calls this man "Sweetheart." In the "Nine" year she has another name for him, not so endearing.

For those of you who have via the study of this text become interested in numerology and wish to continue the study you will find rich rewards waiting.

Twenty four years ago at age sixteen because of a "chance" meeting with an astro-numerologist, I became interested in the numbers. Over the years I can say with modesty that I have become a master, but the more I learn the more I realize that I am nothing but a student. There is no end to the knowledge that can be obtained. This text itself has only scratched the very surface. The secret and mastery of numerology is Kabalism. It is unfortunate that there is not more printed material available regarding this aspect of numerology. It is also unfortunate that I could not have presented a text dealing with nothing but this ultimate aspect but it is impossible to begin a study in mid-air without first laying the correct foundations. At any rate a Kabalistic study would avail the average reader who did not possess a deep understanding of the numbers very little useful material. Over the years I have worked on about two dozen different Kabalas and have managed to more or less conquer about fifteen of them. The balance I am still working on, searching for the key that will unlock the knowledge locked within these Kabalas. Due to the lack of published material regarding this subject many of the interpretations were lost centuries ago. I have dedicated my life via numerology to discovering the destiny of man. There is no great secret to this destiny. It is revealed in Astrology, Numerology, the Palm of the Hand, the Tarot Deck, the Subconscious mind, which holds all the truths of the universe, all the knowledge of life, past, present and future. I present to you that there is truth and sincerity in the numbers. Over the years I personally have worked on over ten thousand charts of living people and say to you in all honesty that the numbers have never been deceptive or misleading. In all cases the lives of the individuals whose charts I worked upon went exactly as plotted by the numbers. I, of course, from time to time, have made misinterpretations, but that is only natural. Always I have been able to back-track and find where I have erred.

For those who would like to try an interesting experiment in Kabalism obtain the essence from the excursion chart for an eighty one year period (birth to age 80). Sub-divide this into nine equal segments and construct nine different charts each covering a period of nine years. Using the method explained in the foregoing chapter information may be obtained for each year of the nine year periods.

Any who are interested in expanding upon Universal Vibrations can obtain additional tone effects with the Universal Tone Cycles. Operating within any particular Universal Year will be nine segments that will pertain to the universal aspects much like the Periodicity pertains to the Personal Year. They are as follows:

Cycle 1   January 1, to February 9
      2   February 10, to March 21
      3   March 22, to April 30
      4   May 1, to June 10
      5   June 11, to July 21
      6   July 22, to August 31
      7   September 1, to October 10
      8   October 11, to November 20
      9   November 21, to December 31

Advanced students in the letters will find added results by giving the following letter combinations in the name these values. This does not change the structure of the letter values as explained in this book, this simply enlarges upon them and adds additional knowledge.

PH   Instead of assigning a separate value of "7" to the "P" and "8" to the "H" for a total of 15/6 when the "P" is followed in the name by an "H" assign the values of "6" to the combination and treat this joining as one letter.

WH   This will constitute a change. The dual of the two should be considered as a single "5."

CH   As we are dealing with silent sounds this combination should also change and the dual should be locked together with a single aspect of a "3" value.

The Pythagoreans maintained that all numbers multiplied by nine reduce to nine which is of course the correct foundation and that one unit added to nine becomes "Ten" or the rebirth.

The Four Square was converted to triangle form with ten units to symbolize this effect. The triangle represents birth.

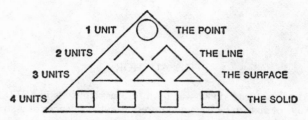

10 Units (Rebirth), the "1" and "3" being without limit, the "2" and "4" being limited, but the combination of the entire four numbers are unlimited in a high octave "1."

There is unity in the harmony of numbers. The discord of numbers creates a rupture.

Occurrences in life seem to happen as if by a natural sequence of events. One often wonders if something in the past had been done a little different, what the outcome would have been. Some prefer to call it chance, I call it destiny.

May the blessings of the eternal God-Force be with you.

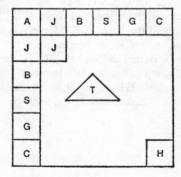

THE AUTHOR:

DR. KEVIN QUINN AVERY was born in Massachusetts in 1933. At the age of sixteen he became interested in the sciences of Astrology and Numerology. At the age of twenty, he became exposed to the ancient science of Huna Metaphysics.

Dr. Avery is a professional numerologist, astro-numerologist and numerical Kabalist. He is considered to be one of the foremost authorities in the world on these subjects, and is one of the leading experts in the Western world on the deep mystical science of Huna Metaphysics.

Traveling widely, he gives lectures on the sciences of Numerology, Numbers, and Metaphysics. He writes columns regarding Numerology and Numbers which appear in many international publications and newspapers. His books have been translated into several languages.

Dr. Avery makes his home in New York City. He is associated with many psychic institutions and is a member of the Board of Directors of the New York Metaphysical Foundation. Additionally, Dr. Avery is connected with the Theosophical Assembly and the Aetherius Society. He is also an ordained minister of the Church of Cosmic Wisdom of Honolulu (Huna).

In conjunction with GIBA 'S.A.R.L. (Élysses Presses Promotions) of Paris, France, Dr. Avery has computerized numerology.